MAXON CINEMA 4D R20 Studio Workbook

Sham Tickoo
Professor
Purdue University Northwest
Hammond, Indiana, USA

Contributing Authors
Arti Deshpande
Tickoo Institute of Emerging Technologies(TIET)

Tickoo Institute of Emerging Technologies (TIET)
Gurugram, India

CADCIM Technologies
Indiana, USA

ISBN: 978-93-89423-08-2
(For distribution in Saarc countries only)

Limits of Liability and Disclaimer of Warranty

Distributors

COMPUTER BOOK CENTRE
12, Shrungar Shopping Centre
M.G. Road
BENGALURU–560001
Ph: 25587923/25584641

BPB BOOK CENTRE
376 Old Lajpat Rai Market
DELHI-110006
Ph: 23861747

DECCAN AGENCIES
4-3-329, Bank Street
HYDERABAD-500195
Ph: 24756967/24756400

INFOTECH
G-2, Sidhartha Building, 96 Nehru Place
NEW DELHI-110019
Ph: 26438245

MICRO MEDIA
Shop No. 5, Mahendra Chambers
150 DN Rd. Next to Capital Cinema
V.T (C.S.T.) Station
MUMBAI-400001

BPB PUBLICATIONS
20, Ansari Road, Darya Ganj
New Delhi-110002
Ph: 23254990/23254991

Published by Manish Jain for BPB Publications, 20 Ansari Road, Darya Ganj
New Delhi-110002 and Printed by Repro India Pvt. Ltd., Mumbai

DEDICATION

*To teachers, who make it possible to disseminate knowledge
to enlighten the young and curious minds
of our future generations*

*To students, who are dedicated to learning new technologies
and making the world a better place to live in*

THANKS

*To employees of CADCIM Technologies and
Tickoo Institute of Emerging Technologies (TIET)
for their valuable help*

Online Training Program Offered by CADCIM Technologies

CADCIM Technologies provides effective and affordable virtual online training on various software packages including Computer Aided Design, Manufacturing and Engineering (CAD/CAM/CAE), computer programming languages, animation, architecture, and GIS. The training is delivered 'live' via Internet at any time, any place, and at any pace to individuals as well as the students of colleges, universities, and CAD/CAM/CAE training centers. The main features of this program are:

Training for Students and Companies in a Classroom Setting

Highly experienced instructors and qualified engineers at CADCIM Technologies conduct the classes under the guidance of Prof. Sham Tickoo of Purdue University Northwest, USA. This team has authored several textbooks that are rated "one of the best" in their categories and are used in various colleges, universities, and training centers in North America, Europe, and in other parts of the world.

Training for Individuals

CADCIM Technologies with its cost effective and time saving initiative strives to deliver the training in the comfort of your home or work place, thereby relieving you from the hassles of traveling to training centers.

Training Offered on Software Packages

CADCIM provides basic and advanced training on the following software packages:

***CAD/CAM/CAE**: CATIA, Pro/ENGINEER Wildfire, Creo Parametric, Creo Direct, SOLIDWORKS, Autodesk Inventor, Solid Edge, NX, AutoCAD, AutoCAD LT, AutoCAD Plant 3D, Customizing AutoCAD, EdgeCAM, and ANSYS*

***Architecture and GIS**: Autodesk Revit (Architecture, Structure, MEP), AutoCAD Civil 3D, AutoCAD Map 3D, Navisworks, Oracle Primavera, and Bentley STAAD Pro*

***Animation and Styling**: Autodesk 3ds Max, Autodesk Maya, Autodesk Alias, Foundry NukeX, and MAXON CINEMA 4D*

***Computer Programming**: C++, VB.NET, Oracle, AJAX, and Java*

For more information, please visit the following link: ***https://www.cadcim.com***

Table of Contents

Preface

MAXON CINEMA 4D R20 Studio

MAXON CINEMA 4D R20 Studio is a 3D software application developed by MAXON Computer. This application is mainly used by professional 3D artists to create impressive 3D scenes, VFX, and broadcast artwork. CINEMA 4D comes in four versions: Prime, Visualize, Broadcast, and Studio. CINEMA 4D Prime is used to create stunning 3D graphics. CINEMA 4D Visualize provides fast and easy solution to architects, designers, and photographers to create realistic animations and is used for product visualization. It also has the ability to import models from all major 2D and 3D file formats. CINEMA 4D Broadcast is a perfect solution for creating high quality broadcast graphics. CINEMA 4D Studio contains all features of CINEMA 4D Prime, CINEMA 4D Visualize, and CINEMA 4D Broadcast. Moreover, it includes character animation tools that makes it easier to create rigs and character animations. It is a user-friendly application which includes features such as sculpting, advance particle system, hair system, and MoGraph.

MAXON CINEMA 4D R20 Studio Workbook is a tutorial-based book and aims at harnessing the power of MAXON CINEMA 4D R20 Studio for modelers, animators, and designers. The book caters to the needs of both the novice and the advance users of MAXON CINEMA 4D R20 Studio. Keeping in view the varied requirements of users, the book first introduces the basic features of CINEMA 4D R20 Studio and then progresses to cover the advanced techniques.

This book will help you unleash your creativity and transform your imagination into reality with ease.

The main features of this book are as follows:

- **Tutorial Approach**

  The author has adopted the tutorial point-of-view and the learn-by-doing theme throughout the book.

- **Tips and Notes**

  Additional information related to various topics is provided to the users in the form of tips and notes.

Conventions Used in this Book

Tip

Special information and techniques are provided in the form of tips that help in increasing the efficiency of the users.

Note

The author has provided additional information to the users about the topic being discussed in the form of notes.

Formatting Conventions Used in the Book

Refer to the following list for the formatting conventions used in this book.

- Names of tools, buttons, options, and menus are written in boldface.

  Example: The **Move** tool, **Basic** button, **Multiply** option, **Create** menu, and so on.

- Names of dialog boxes, drop-down lists, windows, text boxes, spinners, areas, and check boxes are written in boldface.

  Example: The **Save** dialog box, the **Mode** drop-down list, the **Timeline** window, the **Object** text box, the **Size . X** spinner, the **Object Properties** area, the **Fillet** check box, and so on.

- Values entered in spinners are written in boldface.

  Example: Enter **0.2** in the **Size . X** spinner.

- The path for choosing a tool from the main menu.

  Example: Choose **Create > Object > Cube** from the main menu.

- Names of the files are italicized

  Example: *c05_tut2_start.c4d*

Naming Conventions Used in the Book

The naming conventions used in this book are as follows:

Tool

If on clicking an item in the Command Palette or Modes Palette, a command is invoked to create/edit an object or perform some action, then that item is termed as **Tool**. For example: **Live Selection** tool, **Move** tool, **Edit Render Settings** tool, **Freehand** tool, **Points** tool, and **Polygons** tool.

Flyout

If on choosing a tool, a menu containing tools having similar type of function is displayed then that menu is called a flyout. Figure 1 shows the flyout which is displayed on choosing the **Cube** tool from the Command Palette.

Figure 1 *Flyout displayed on choosing the **Cube** tool*

Shortcut Menu

In CINEMA 4D, the shortcut menus provide quick access to the commonly used commands that are related to the current selection of an object. A shortcut menu is displayed on right-clicking on an object, a viewport, and so on, refer to Figure 2. Some of the options in the shortcut menus have an arrow on their right side. If you move the cursor on such options, a cascading menu will be displayed showing some more options related to the selected option, refer to Figure 2.

Button

The item in a dialog box and Attribute Manager that has a rectangular shape is termed as **Button**. For example, **OK** button, **Cancel** button, **Save** button, **Basic** button, **Coord** button, and so on, refer to Figure 3.

Dialog Box

In this book, different terms are used for referring to the components of a dialog box. Refer to Figure 4 for the terminology used.

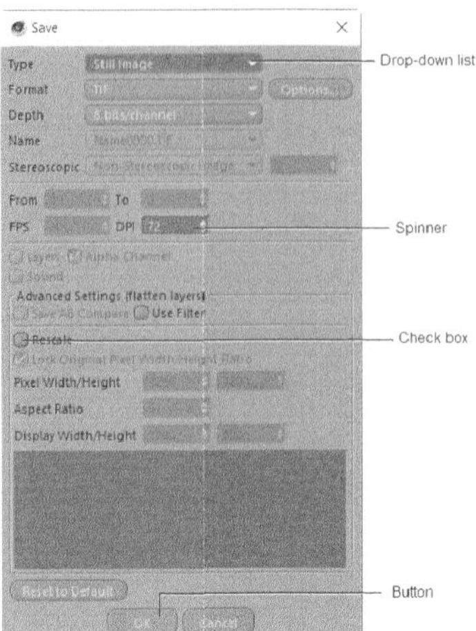

Figure 4 *Terminologies used in a dialog box*

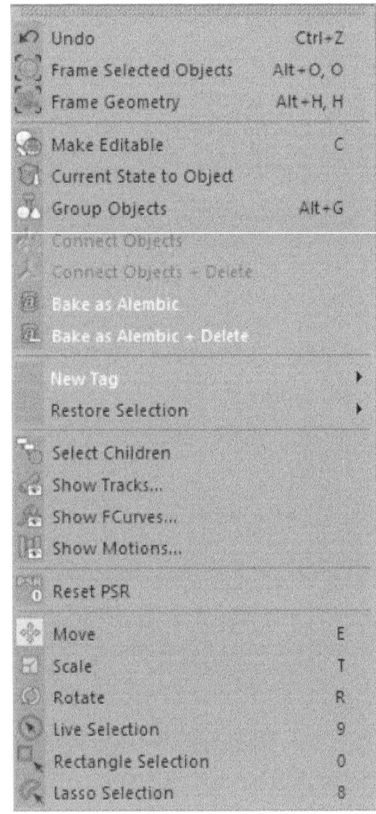

Figure 2 *Shortcut menu displayed on right-clicking in the viewport*

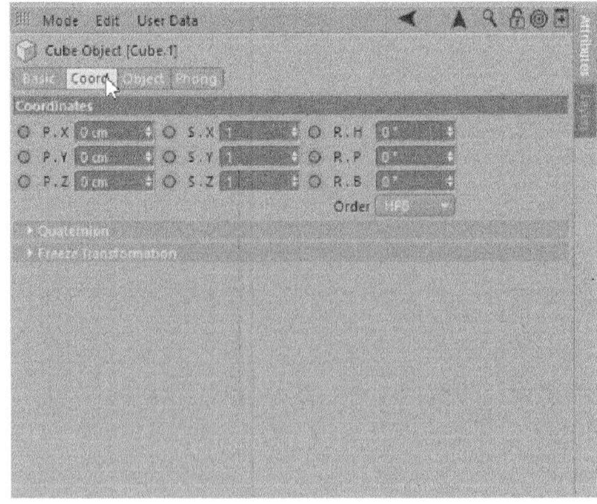

Figure 3 *Choosing the* ***Coord*** *button from the Attribute Manager*

Drop-down List

A drop-down list is the one in which a set of options are grouped together. You can set various parameters using these options. You can identify a drop-down list with a down arrow on it. For example, **Mode** drop-down list, **Type** drop-down list, and so on, refer to Figure 5.

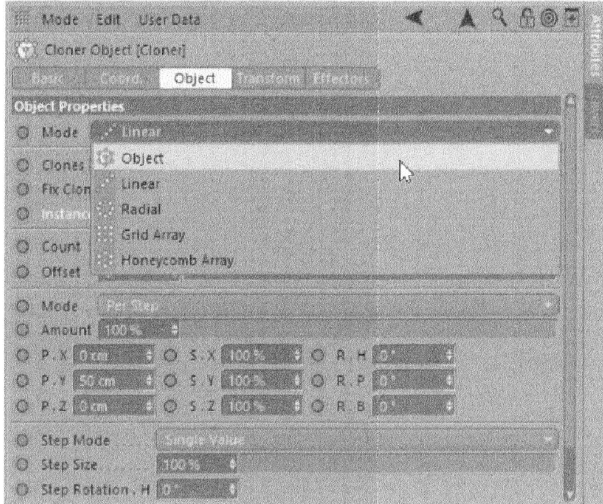

*Figure 5 The **Mode** drop-down list*

Options

Options are the items that are available in shortcut menus, drop-down lists, dialog boxes, and so on, refer to Figure 6.

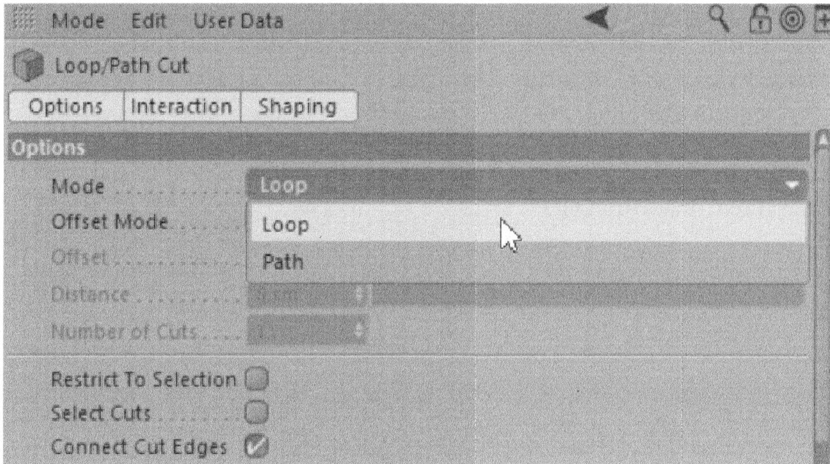

*Figure 6 Selecting the **Loop** option from the **Mode** drop-down list*

Window

A window consists of various components such as tools, buttons, main menu, and so on. Different types of windows available in CINEMA 4D are **XPresso Editor**, **Timeline**, **Render Settings**, and so on. The components of a window differ depending on the type of window, refer to Figure 7.

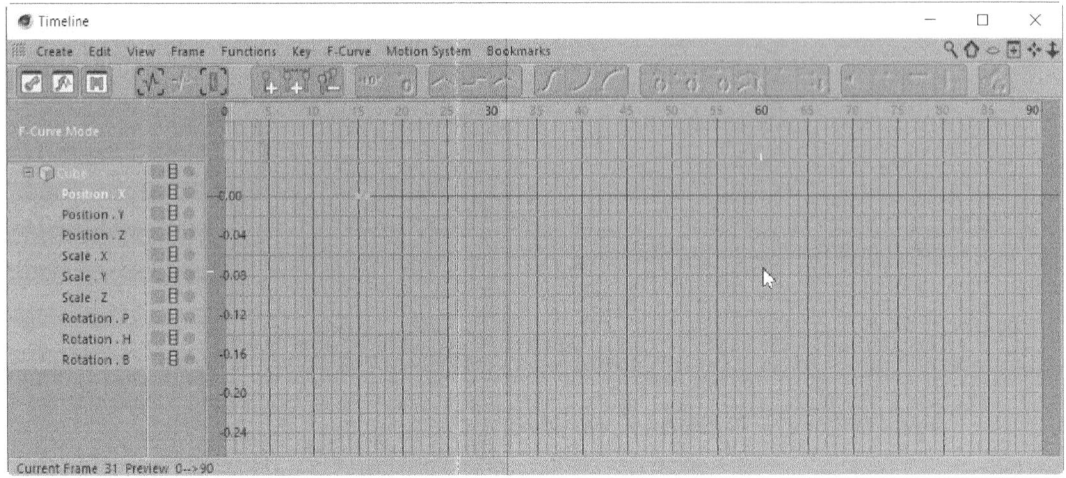

*Figure 7 The **Timeline** window*

Free Companion CD

It has been our constant endeavor to provide you the best textbooks and services at affordable price. In this endeavor, we have come up with a Free Companion CD that will facilitate the process of teaching and learning of MAXON CINEMA 4D R20 Studio. If you purchase this book, you will get access to the files on the companion CD.
The resources like Tutorial files, Part files, Exercise files, Render files, Instructor guide etc. are available in the Free Companion CD.

If you face any problem in accessing these files, please contact us at ***sales@cadcim.com*** or the author at ***stickoo@pnw.edu*** or ***tickoo525@gmail.com***.

Stay Connected

You can now stay connected with us through Facebook and Twitter to get the latest information about our textbooks, videos, and teaching/learning resources. To stay informed of such updates, follow us on Facebook ***(www.facebook.com/cadcim)*** and Twitter (@cadcimtech). You can also subscribe to our YouTube channel ***(www.youtube.com/cadcimtech)*** to get the information about our latest video tutorials.

Chapter 1

Exploring CINEMA 4D R20 Studio Interface

Learning Objectives

After completing this chapter, you will be able to:

- *Work with Viewport Navigation Tools in CINEMA 4D*
- *Understand various terms related to CINEMA 4D interface*
- *Work with tools in CINEMA 4D*

INTRODUCTION

MAXON CINEMA 4D R20 Studio is a high-end 3D application developed by MAXON Computer. This application is used by professional 3D artists to create impressive 3D scenes, VFX, and broadcast artwork. CINEMA 4D comes in four versions: Prime, Visualize, Broadcast, and Studio. CINEMA 4D Prime is used to create stunning 3D graphics. CINEMA 4D Visualize provides fast and easy solution to architects, designers, and photographers for creating realistic animations and better product visualization. It also has the ability to import models from all major 2D and 3D file formats. CINEMA 4D Broadcast is a perfect solution for creating high quality broadcast graphics. CINEMA 4D Studio contains all the features of CINEMA 4D Prime, CINEMA 4D Visualize, and CINEMA 4D Broadcast. Moreover, it includes character animation tools that makes it easier for its users to create rigs and character animations.

MAXON CINEMA 4D is a user-friendly application which is used for sculpting, creating particles using advance particle system, hair system, and for creating motion graphics using MoGraph. In this chapter, you will be introduced to MAXON CINEMA 4D Studio R20 interface elements.

STARTING MAXON CINEMA 4D R20 Studio

To start MAXON CINEMA 4D R20 Studio, click on the icon of this software available on the desktop of your PC; the default interface of MAXON CINEMA 4D R20 Studio will be displayed, as shown in Figure 1-1.

EXPLORING MAXON CINEMA 4D R20 Studio INTERFACE

CINEMA 4D interface consists of various components such as title bar, Viewport, Command Palette, Modes Palette, main menu, and so on, as shown in Figure 1-2. All these components are discussed next.

Viewport

Viewport is a part of the work area where you can create a 3D scene. Every viewport has a grid placed at the center. A grid is a framework of intersecting lines placed perpendicularly in the X-Z plane. At the center point (origin), the X, Y, and Z coordinates will be 0, 0, and 0, respectively.

Note

In CINEMA 4D, the X, Y, and Z axes are displayed in red, green, and blue colors, respectively, refer to Figure 1-2.

When you start CINEMA 4D, the Perspective viewport is displayed by default, as shown in Figure 1-2. This viewport displays objects from a perspective camera. You can also display other viewports such as Top, Right, Bottom, and Front in the work area. These viewports display objects from orthographic camera view and do not display the perspective view. To switch to the 4-view viewport arrangement, hover the cursor over the Perspective viewport and then press the middle-mouse button once. If you need to maximize any of the four viewports, hover the cursor over the required viewport and then press the middle-mouse button once.

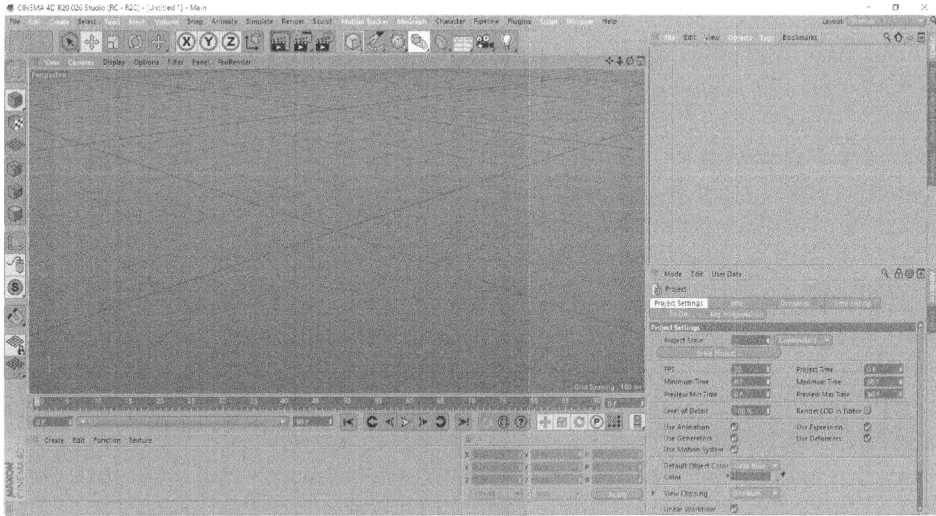

Figure 1-1 The default interface of CINEMA 4D R20 Studio

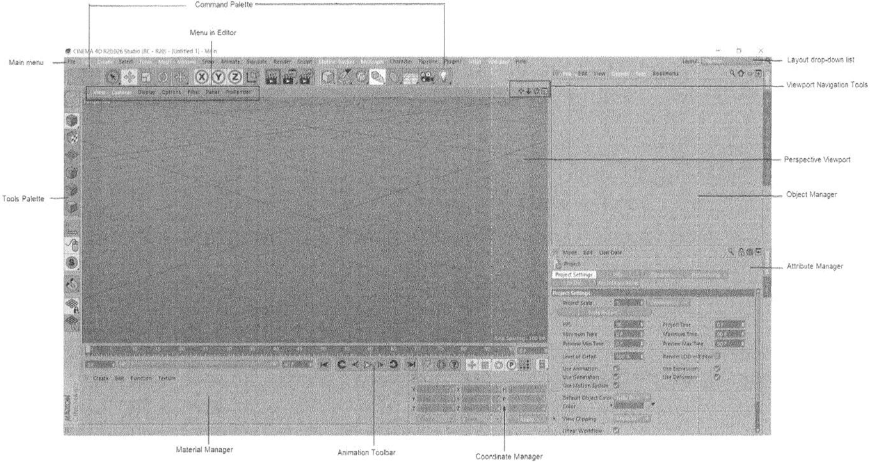

Figure 1-2 Various components of CINEMA 4D R20 Studio interface

Title Bar

The title bar, located at the top of the interface, displays the name and version of the software, and the name of the opened file. A CINEMA 4D file is saved with the *.c4d* extension.

Tip

You can display different viewports by using the functional keys: F1 (Perspective), F2 (Top), F3 (Right), F4 (Front), and the F5 key (for all viewports).

Main Menu

The main menu is located just below the title bar, refer to Figure 1-2. The options in this menu are used to access tools, functions, or commands in CINEMA 4D.

Command Palette

The Command Palette is located below the main menu, refer to Figure 1-2. It is used to invoke the most commonly used tools in CINEMA 4D.

Tools Palette

The Tools Palette is located on the extreme left of the interface, refer to Figure 1-2. It consists of various tools.

Animation Toolbar

The Animation toolbar is located below the viewport area. It consists of all the animation controls that are used to control animation in a scene.

Material Manager

The Material Manager is located at the bottom left corner of the interface. It is used to create materials and shaders used in the scene. In Cinema 4D R20 version, uber material, node material, and some in-built node based materials are added to create complex materials.

Coordinate Manager

The Coordinate Manager is located at the right of the Material Manager. It is used to position, rotate, and scale the objects created in the scene. You need to choose the **Apply** button to apply the values in the spinners of the Coordinate Manager.

Object Manager

The Object Manager is located at the upper right corner of the interface. It consists of a list of objects used in the scene. You can specify tags for objects, rename the objects, and select the objects in the Object Manager. Therefore, it is defined as the control center of the objects created in the scene.

Attribute Manager

The Attribute Manager is used to display the attributes of a selected tool or object in the scene. You can also modify the attributes of the objects and materials in it. Moreover, you can set keys for animation to the attributes that have a circle next to their name. By default, it displays the project settings.

Layers Manager

The Layers Manager is used to manage the objects in layers when you need to work in complex scenes. To invoke the Layers Manager, choose the **Layers** tab in the Attribute Manager. The Layer Manager will be displayed.

Viewport Navigation Tools

The Viewport Navigation Tools are located on the top right corner of each viewport, refer to Figure 1-2. These tools are used to pan, zoom, and rotate the camera in the viewport.

Note

You can maximize a viewport by pressing the middle mouse button inside that viewport.

Menu in editor view

The Menu in editor view is available in every viewport and is used to perform various tasks. It consists of **View**, **Cameras**, **Display**, **Options**, **Filter**, and **Panel** menus, refer to Figure 1-2.

Layout

The **Layout** drop-down list is located on the top right corner of the interface. The options in this drop-down list are used to switch between various layouts available in CINEMA 4D. You can select the required layout from this drop-down list.

Content Browser

The Content Browser is an integral part of CINEMA 4D. It is used to manage scenes, images, materials, shaders, and presets. The Content Browser is docked with the Object Manager in CINEMA 4D interface.

Structure Manager

The Structure Manager is a type of spreadsheet that is used to calculate the data. It displays the data of the polygon objects only. On converting the parametric object into a polygon object, the data of the points, polygons, UVW coordinates, and so on will be displayed in the rows and columns of the Structure Manager. The Structure Manager is docked with the Object Manager and Content Browser in CINEMA 4D interface.

CREATING PROJECT FOLDER WITH ASSETS

When you transfer the scene in Cinema 4D to another computer, make sure texture files are also transferred with the scene in a single project folder. To create this project folder, choose **Save Project with Assets** from the **File** menu; the **Save File** dialog box will be displayed. In this dialog box, navigate to the desired location and enter the name of the folder in the **File name** text box. Next, choose the **Save** button; the project folder will be created at the specified location. This project folder contains a cinema 4D file and a folder named **tex** that contains texture files used in the scene.

HOT KEYS

Table 1-1 displays the hot keys of tools used in CINEMA 4D.

Table 1-1 *The tools and their hot keys*

Tool	**Hot keys**
Undo	CTRL+Z
Redo	CTRL+Y
Move	E
Scale	T
Rotate	R
X-Axis / Heading	X
Y-Axis / Pitch	Y
Z-Axis / Bank	Z
Coordinate System	W
Render View	CTRL+R
Render to Picture Viewer	SHIFT+R
Edit Render Settings	CTRL+B
Make Editable	C
Undo View	CTRL+SHIFT+Z
Redo View	CTRL+SHIFT+Y

Tip

If you want to view the documentation of a tool or option in CINEMA 4D, place the cursor over that tool or option and then press CTRL+F1; the ***Help*** *window will be displayed with the documentation.*

Chapter 2

Working with Splines

Learning Objectives

After completing this chapter, you will be able to:

- *Work with spline primitives*
- *Understand spline modeling techniques*
- *Create geometries using Generators*

INTRODUCTION

In computer graphics, a spline is a line formed by connecting a sequence of vertices lying in 3D space. Although, it is formed in 3D space, it has no depth. A spline is not visible on rendering. You can create complete parametric spline primitives (with pre-defined shapes) as well as empty splines whose shapes can be defined interactively in the viewport. You can use splines to create complex geometries using Generator objects in CINEMA 4D. Generators are CINEMA 4D's most powerful modeling tools.

TUTORIALS

All the files used in the tutorials can be downloaded from the CADSoft website (*www.cadsofttech.com*). These files are compressed in zip file format and are required to be extracted before using them in the tutorials. The path of the files is as follows: *Textbooks > Animation and Visual Effects > MAXON CINEMA 4D > MAXON CINEMA 4D R20 Studio for Novices*

Next, you need to extract the contents of the zip file. To do so, navigate to the *Documents* folder and create a new folder in it with the name *c4dr20*. Next, you need to browse to *\Documents\c4dr20* and create a new folder in it with the name *c02*. Then, extract the contents of the zip file in this folder.

Tutorial 1

In this tutorial, you will create 3D model of a door lock system with the help of splines and Generators. The final output of the model is shown in Figure 2-1.

(Expected time: 35 min)

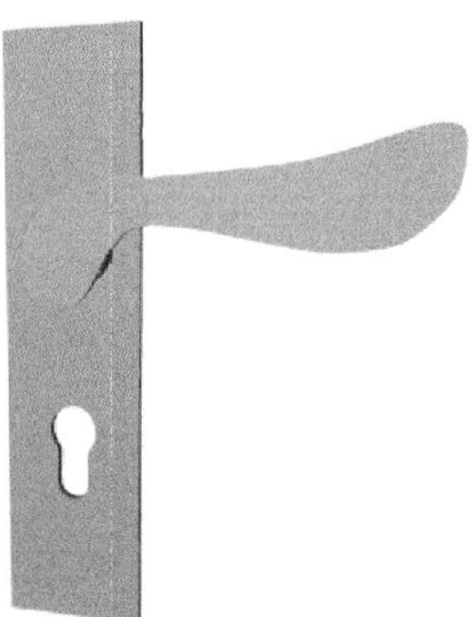

Figure 2-1 *The model of door lock system*

The following steps are required to complete this tutorial:

a. Set the viewport background.
b. Create the base of the door lock system.
c. Create the key hole.
d. Create the handle.
e. Change the background color of the scene.
f. Save and render the scene.

Setting the Viewport Background

In this section, you will set the background image in the Front viewport.

1. Choose **File > New** from the main menu; a new scene is displayed. Next, press the middle mouse button in the Perspective viewport; all viewports are displayed. Next, hover the cursor over the Front viewport and then press MMB to maximize it. Alternatively, choose **Cameras > Front** from the Menu in editor view, as shown in Figure 2-2; the Front viewport is maximized.

2. Choose **Options > Configure** from the Menu in editor view, as shown in Figure 2-3; the **Viewport [Front]** settings are displayed in the Attribute Manager. In the Attribute Manager, choose the **Back** button; the **Back** area is displayed. In this area, choose the browse button next to the **Image** text box, as shown in Figure 2-4; the **Open File** dialog box is displayed. Browse to *\Documents\c4dr20\c02\keyhole.jpg*. Next, choose the **Open** button; the *keyhole.jpg* is opened as the background image in the Front viewport.

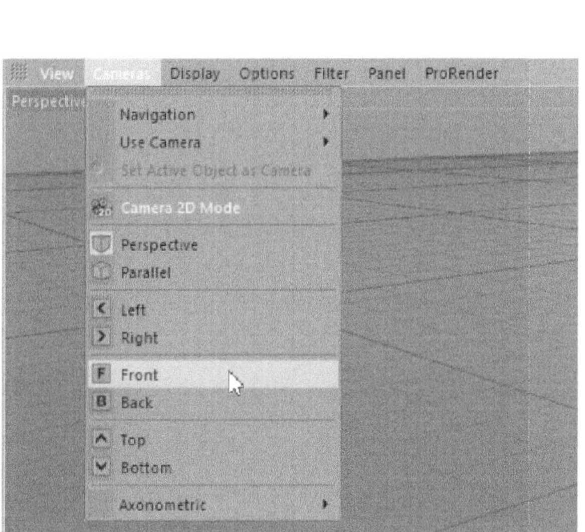

Figure 2-2 *Choosing the* ***Front*** *option from the Menu in editor view*

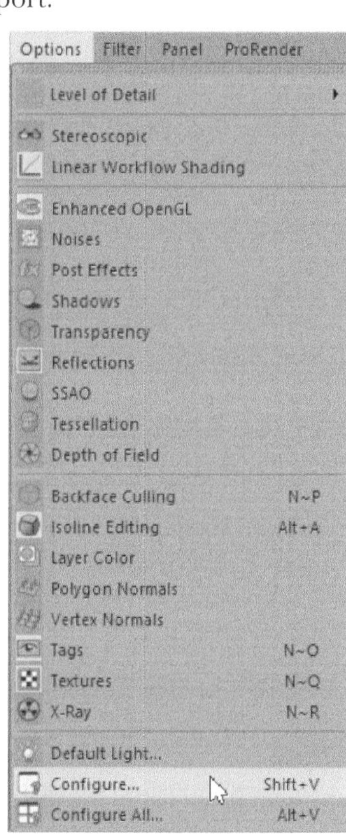

Figure 2-3 *Choosing the* ***Configure*** *option from the Menu in editor view*

3. In the **Back** area, clear the **Keep Aspect Ratio** check box and then set the parameters as follows:

   Offset X: **122** Offset Y: **2** Size X: **445**
   Size Y: **500**

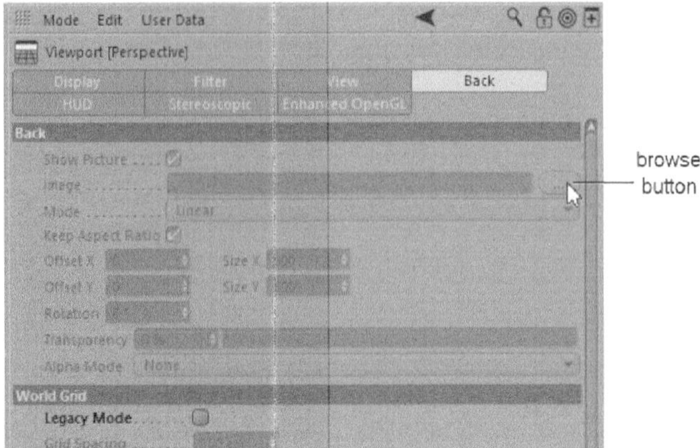

Figure 2-4 Choosing the browse button next to the ***Image*** *text box*

The **Configure** option available in the **Options** menu of the Menu in editor view is used to edit the settings of the respective viewport. It applies to all viewports. The options in the **Back** area are used to place the reference image at the desired location as the viewport background. The **Image** text box displays the location of the loaded file. Any image with a recognizable format can be loaded in CINEMA 4D.

The **Offset X** option is used to move the reference image horizontally.

The **Offset Y** option is used to move the reference image vertically.

The **Size X** and **Size Y** options are used to scale the reference image.

Creating the Base of the Door Lock System

In this section, you will create the base of the door lock system using the **Rectangle** tool.

1. Press F1; the Perspective viewport is maximized. Alternatively, choose **Cameras > Perspective** from the Menu in editor view, refer to Figure 2-2. Choose **Create > Spline** from the main menu; a cascading menu is displayed. Next, choose **Rectangle** from it, as shown in Figure 2-5; a rectangle is created in the Perspective viewport. Also, *Rectangle* is added to the Object Manager.

Figure 2-5 Choosing ***Rectangle*** *from the* ***Create*** *menu*

Note

The spline primitives are parametric in nature as their attributes such as height, radius, and so on can be altered in the Attribute Manager.

2. Make sure that *Rectangle* is selected in the Object Manager. In the Attribute Manager, make sure the **Object** button is chosen and then enter **121** and **465** in the **Width** and **Height** spinners, respectively, of the **Object Properties** area, refer to Figure 2-6.

   By default, the value of these parameters is set to 400. As a result, a square is displayed in the viewport.

Next, you will extrude the rectangle.

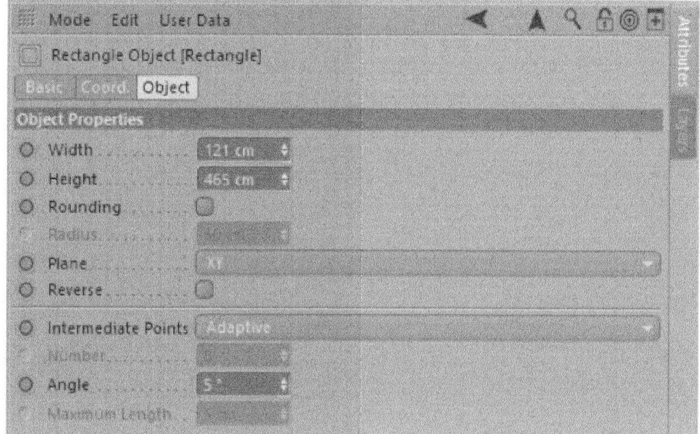

Figure 2-6 *Setting the width and height of the rectangle*

Note

You can change the units of parametric objects. To do so, choose ***Mode > Project*** *in the Attribute Manager; the* ***Project*** *area is displayed in the Attribute Manager. Make sure the* ***Project Settings*** *button is chosen in this area. In the* ***Project Settings*** *area, by default* ***Centimeters*** *is selected in the drop-down list located next to the* ***Project Scale*** *spinner. You can select any other unit from the drop-down list as per your requirement.*

3. Press and hold the left mouse button on the **Subdivision Surface** tool in the Command Palette; a flyout is displayed. Next, choose the **Extrude** tool from it, as shown in Figure 2-7; *Extrude* is added to the Object Manager, refer to Figure 2-8.

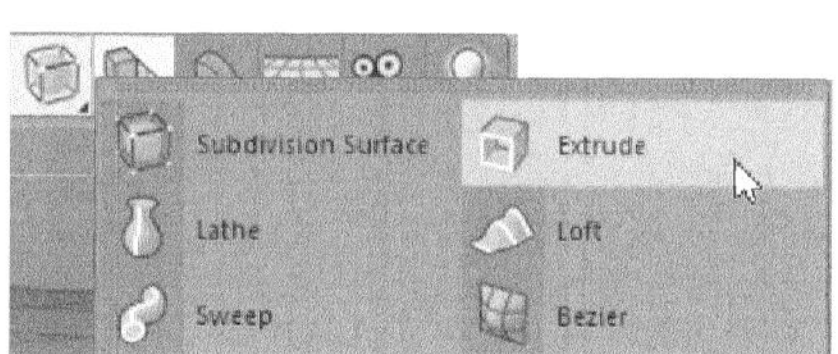

Figure 2-7 *Choosing* ***Extrude*** *from the flyout*

Figure 2-8 *Extrude added to the Object Manager*

4. Select *Rectangle* in the Object Manager. Press and hold the left mouse button on *Rectangle* and drag the cursor to *Extrude* in the Object Manager; *Rectangle* is connected to *Extrude* in the Object Manager. Also, *Rectangle* is extruded in the Perspective viewport, as shown in Figure 2-9.

   On pressing and holding the left mouse button on **Subdivision Surface**, a flyout is displayed with various tools. You can use these tools to create complex models with relatively less number of control points. Models created using these tools can be converted into polygons. The **Extrude** tool is used to extrude the spline in any direction. The effect of this tool is only visible when the spline is connected to the Extrude object.

Creating the Keyhole

In this section, you will create a keyhole using the **Pen** tool.

1. Press F4; the Front viewport is maximized. Choose **Create > Spline** from the main menu; a cascading menu is displayed. Now, choose **Pen** from it, as shown in Figure 2-10. Alternatively, choose the **Pen** tool in the Command Palette; the shape of the cursor changes, as shown in Figure 2-11.

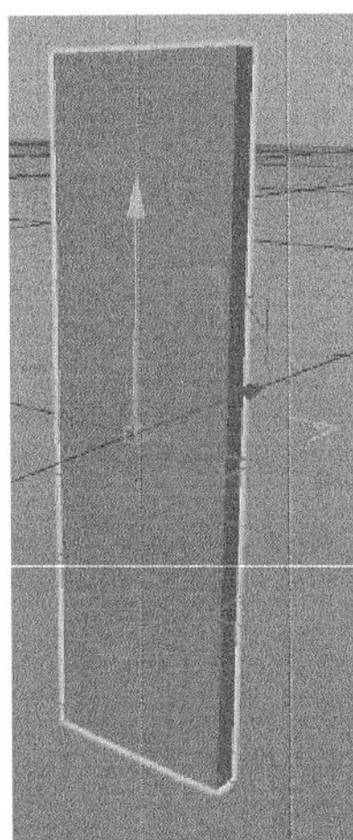

Figure 2-9 Rectangle extruded in the Perspective viewport

Figure 2-10 *Choosing **Pen** from the main menu*

2. In the Front viewport, draw the shape of the keyhole on the reference image, as shown in Figure 2-12. You will notice that *Spline* is also added to the Object Manager.

3. Invoke the **Move** tool from the Command Palette and select the points of *Spline*. Next, edit the shape of *Spline* to give it the shape of a keyhole, as shown in the reference image, refer to Figure 2-12. You can also use the **Pen** tool to move and edit points on the line.

4. Select the *Spline* in the Object Manager. In the Attribute Manager, make sure that the **Object** button is chosen. In the **Object Properties** area, make sure the **Close Spline** check box is selected. Next, choose the **Basic** button; the **Basic Properties** area is displayed. In this area, enter **keyhole** in the **Name** text box; *Spline* is renamed as *keyhole* in the Object Manager, as shown in Figure 2-13.

Note

The spline also closes if you click on the first point of the spline.

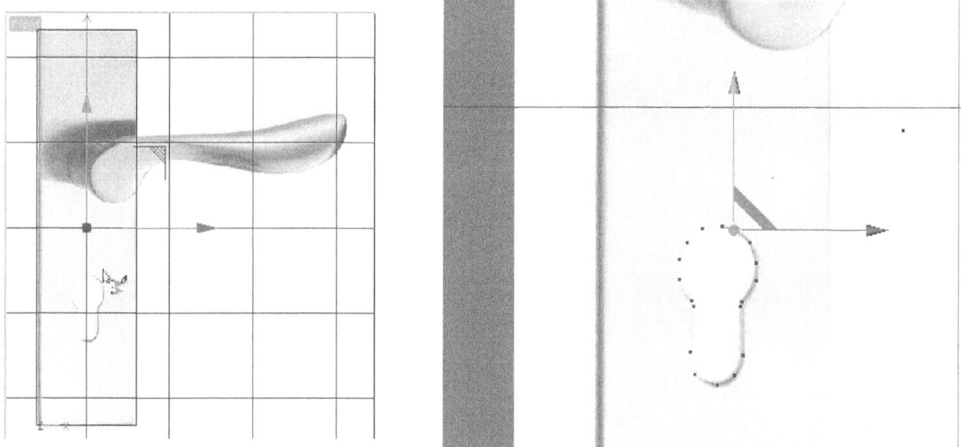

Figure 2-11 The changed shape of the cursor

Figure 2-12 Shape of the keyhole

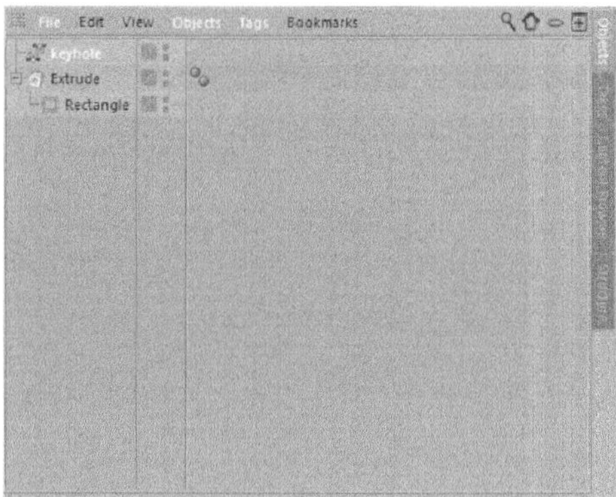

Figure 2-13 *Spline renamed as keyhole*

5. Press F1; the Perspective viewport is maximized. Press and hold the left mouse button on the **Subdivision Surface** tool in the Command Palette; a flyout is displayed. Next, choose **Extrude** from it, as shown in Figure 2-14; *Extrude.1* is added to the Object Manager. Next, drag *keyhole* on *Extrude.1* in the Object Manager; *keyhole* is connected to *Extrude.1*.

6. Select *Extrude.1* in the Object Manager. Next, choose the **Object** button in the Attribute Manager, if it is not already chosen; the **Object Properties** area is displayed. In this area, enter **40** in the Z spinner of the **Movement** parameter; the *keyhole* is extruded.

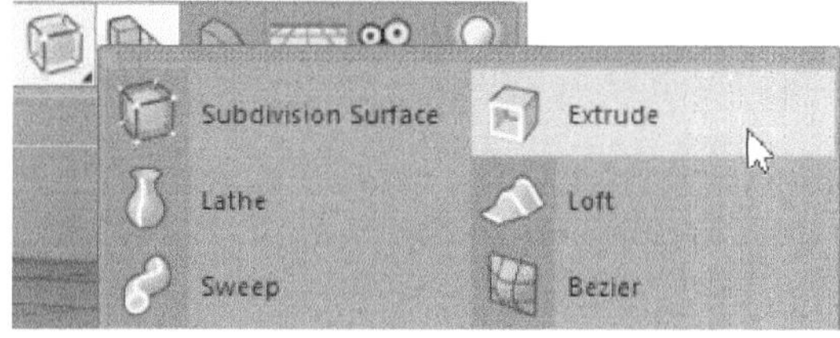

Figure 2-14 *Choosing* **Extrude** *from the flyout*

7. In the Attribute Manager, choose the **Coord** button; the **Coordinates** area is displayed. In this area, enter **-5.409** in the **P . Z** spinner. Figure 2-15 displays *keyhole* in the Perspective viewport.

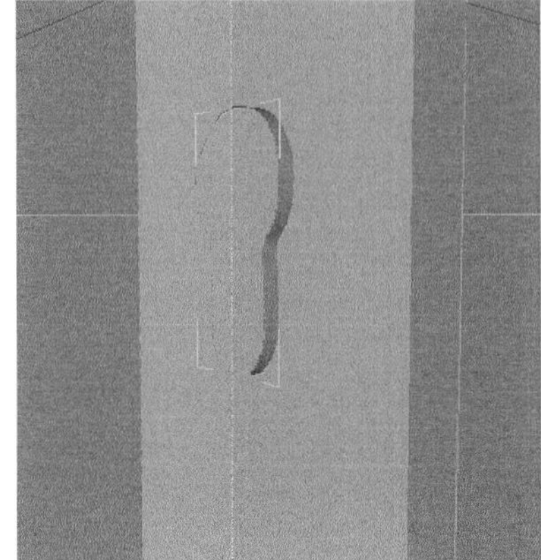

Figure 2-15 *keyhole extruded in the Perspective viewport*

8. Press and hold the left mouse button on the **Instance** tool in the Command Palette; a flyout is displayed. Next, choose **Boole** from the flyout, as shown in Figure 2-16; *Boole* is added to the Object Manager. Now, select *Extrude.1* and drag the cursor to *Boole*; *Extrude.1* is connected to *Boole*.

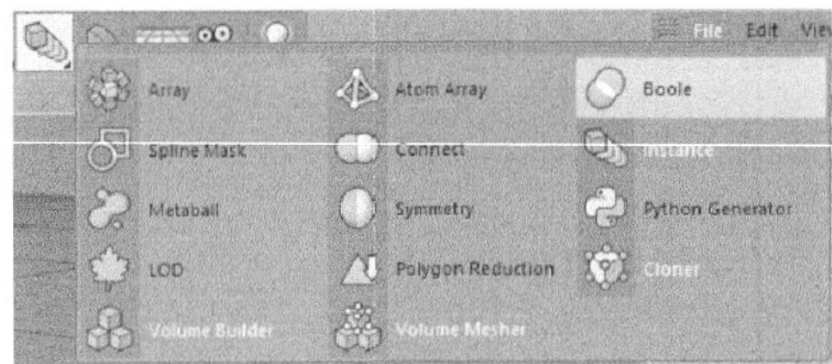

Figure 2-16 *Choosing* ***Boole*** *from the flyout*

9. In the Object Manager, select *Extrude* and press and hold the left mouse button; the shape of the cursor is changed. Next, drag *Extrude* to *Boole*; *Extrude* is connected to *Boole*, as shown in Figure 2-17. Also, *keyhole* is subtracted from *Extrude* and a hole is created in the Perspective viewport, as shown in Figure 2-18.

   The **Boole** tool is used to subtract two or more objects to create a hole in the object. Mostly, this tool is used to perform operations on splines and polygon primitives.

Creating the Handle

In this section, you will create the handle of the door using the **Pen** tool.

1. Press F4; the Front viewport is maximized. **Choose Create > Spline from the main menu; a cascading menu is displayed. Choose Pen** from it; the shape of the cursor is changed. Alternatively, choose the **Pen** tool from the Command Palette.

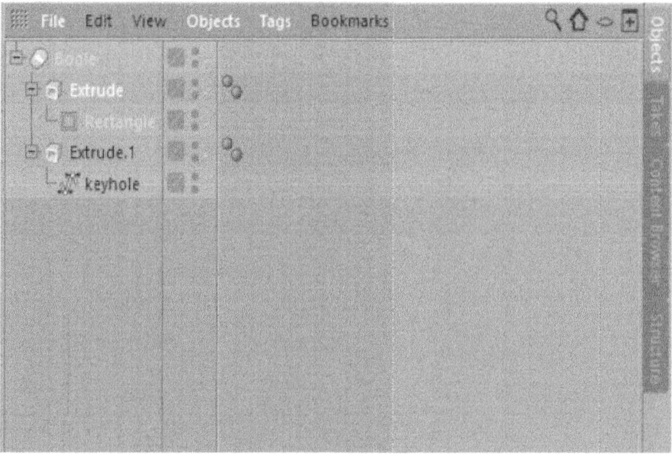

Figure 2-17 *Extrude connected to Boole*

Figure 2-18 *The hole created in the Perspective viewport*

2. In the Front viewport, draw the shape of the door handle on the reference image, refer to Figure 2-19. You will notice that *Spline* is added to the Object Manager. Make sure that the **Close Spline** check box is selected in the **Object Properties** area in the Attribute Manager.

3. In the Attribute Manager, choose the **Basic** button; the **BasicProperties** area is displayed. In this area, type **Handle** in the **Name** text box; the name of *Spline* changes to *Handle* in the Object Manager.

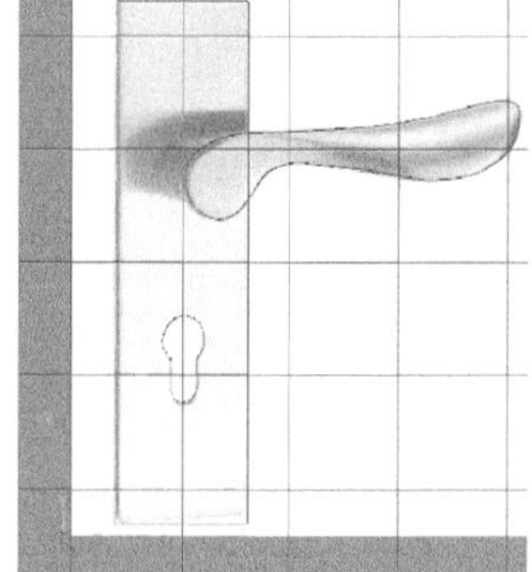

Figure 2-19 *Handle placed in the front viewport*

Figure 2-19 displays *Handle* placed in the Front viewport.

4. Press F1; the Perspective viewport is maximized. Next, press and hold the left mouse button on the **Subdivision Surface** tool in the Command Palette; a flyout is displayed. Next, choose **Extrude** from it; *Extrude* is added to the Object Manager.

Now, select *Handle* in the Object Manager and drag *Handle* to *Extrude*; *Handle* is connected to *Extrude* and is extruded in the Perspective viewport, as shown in Figure 2-20.

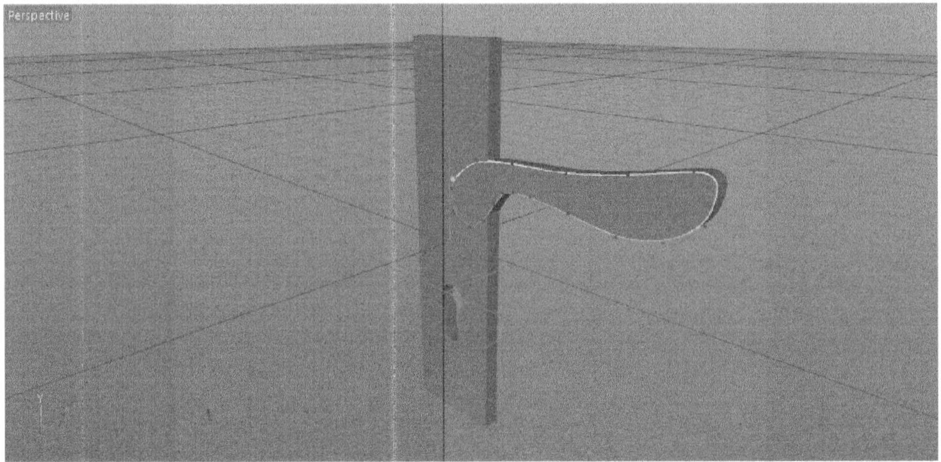

Figure 2-20 *Handle extruded in the Perspective viewport*

5. In the Attribute Manager, choose the **Coord** button; the **Coordinates** area is displayed. In this area, set the parameters as follows:

   P . X: **-30.7** P . Y: **18.1** P . Z: **-45**

   P . X, **P . Y**, and **P . Z** parameters are used to specify the position values of X, Y, and Z axes. The **S . X**, **S . Y**, and **S . Z** parameters are used to specify the scale values of X, Y, and Z axes. Similarly, the **R . X**, **R . Y**, and **R . Z** parameters are used to specify the rotational values of X, Y, and Z axes.

   Next, you will create the joint behind the handle and the base of the door.

6. Press F2; the Top viewport is maximized. Next, choose **Create > Spline** from the main menu; a cascading menu is displayed. Choose **Circle** from it, as shown in Figure 2-21; a circle is created in the Top viewport and *Circle* is added to the Object Manager.

Figure 2-21 *Choosing* ***Circle*** *from the main menu*

7. Make sure that *Circle* is selected in the Object Manager. Next, in the Attribute Manager, choose the **Basic** button. In the **Basic Properties** area, type **Joint** in the **Name** text box; *Circle* is renamed as *Joint* in the Attribute Manager. Next, choose the **Coord** button; the **Coordinates** area is displayed. In this area, set the parameters as follows:

   P . Y: **81.591** R . P: **90**

8. Choose the **Object** button in the Attribute Manager; the **Object Properties** area is displayed. In this area, enter **20** in the **Radius** spinner.

9. Press F1; the Perspective viewport is maximized. Make sure that *Joint* is selected in the Object Manager. Now, create a copy of *Joint* by pressing both the CTRL key and the left mouse button. Now, drag the cursor and release the left mouse button; a copy of *Joint* is created in the Object Manager with the name *Joint.1*. You can also create a copy in the viewport by CTRL dragging.

10. Make sure that *Joint.1* is selected in the Object Manager. In the Attribute Manager, make sure that the **Coordinates** area is displayed and enter **-24.05** in the **P . Z** spinner. Figure 2-22 shows the position of *Joint* and *Joint.1* in the Perspective viewport.

    Next, you will create the surface of the joints.

11. Press and hold the left mouse button on the **Subdivision Surface** tool in the Command Palette; a flyout is displayed. Next, choose the **Loft** tool from it; *Loft* is added to the Object Manager.

12. Press F5; all viewports are displayed. Select *Joint* and *Joint.1* in the Object Manager by using the SHIFT key and then press and hold the left mouse button and drag the cursor on *Loft*; the *Joint* and *Joint.1* are connected to the *Loft* in the Object Manager. Also, a surface is created. Figure 2-23 displays the surface in all viewports.

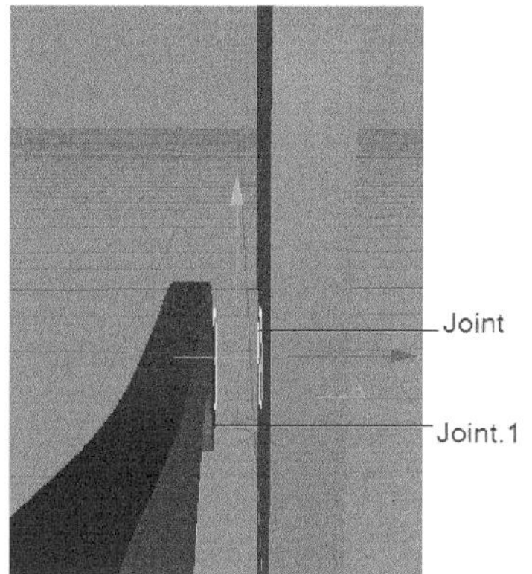

***Figure 2-22** The position of Joint and Joint.1 displayed in the Perspective viewport*

    Next, you will group the surfaces together.

13. In the Object Manager, select *Boole*, *Extrude*, and *Loft* by using the CTRL key. Next, choose **Group Objects** from the **Objects** menu in the Object Manager, refer to Figure 2-24; all selected objects are grouped and *Null* is added to the Object Manager. Rename *Null* as **Door Lock** by double-clicking its label in the Object Manager.

Changing the Background Color of the Scene

In this section, you will change the background color of the scene.

1. Choose **Create > Environment** from the main menu; a cascading menu is displayed. Choose the **Background** option from it, as shown in Figure 2-25; *Background* is added to the Object Manager.

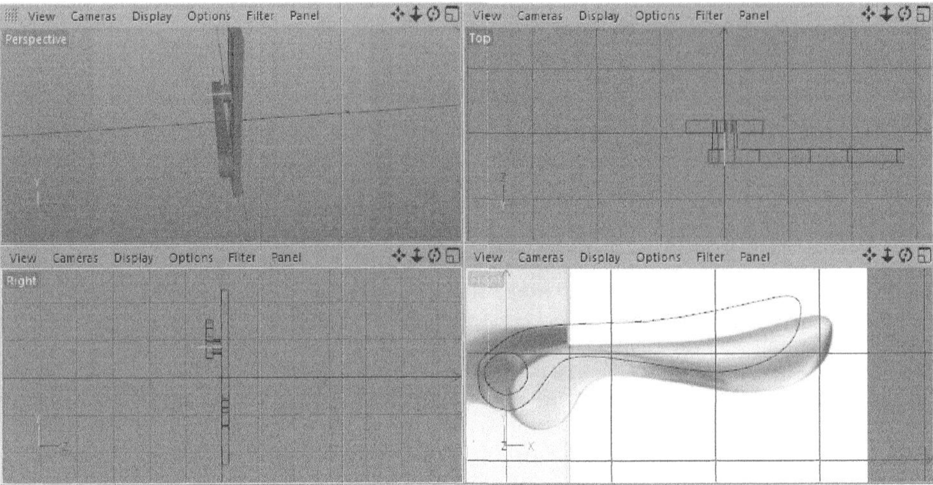

Figure 2-23 *Joint and Joint.1 lofted to create a surface*

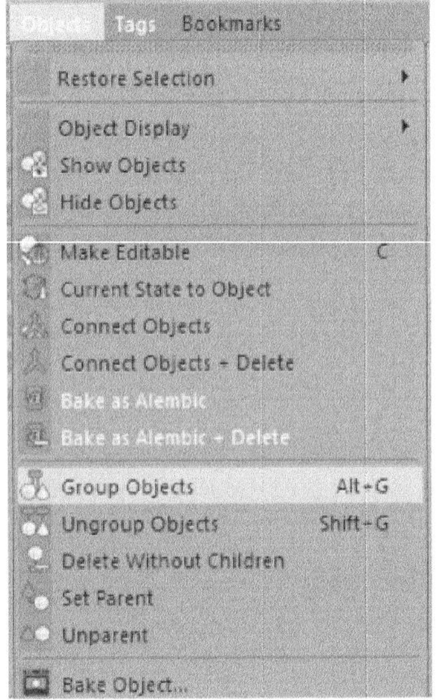

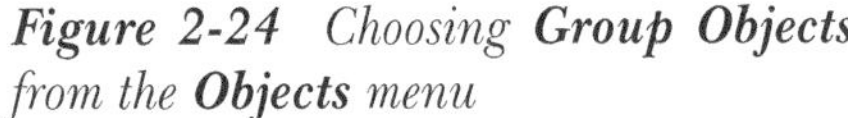
Figure 2-24 *Choosing **Group Objects** from the **Objects** menu*

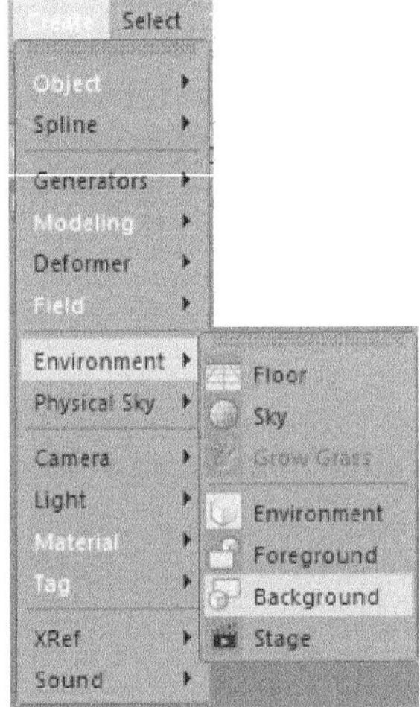

Figure 2-25 *Choosing the **Background** option from the main menu*

The **Background** option is used to change the background with the color or image which is only visible in the render view.

Next, you will change the background color to white.

2. Make sure *Background* is selected in the Object Manager, as shown in Figure 2-26. In the Attribute Manager, choose the **Basic** button; the **Basic Properties** area is displayed. In this area, select **On** from the **Use Color** drop-down list. On doing so, the **Display Color** parameter is activated, as shown in Figure 2-27. By default, the white color is selected in this spinner. As a result, the background color changes to white.

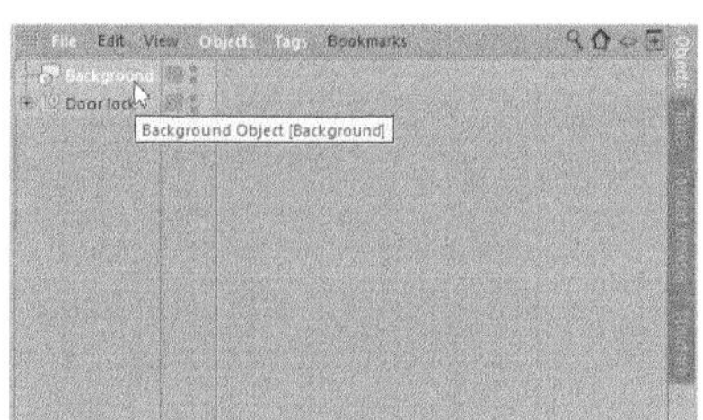

*Figure 2-26 The **Background** Object selected in the Object Manager*

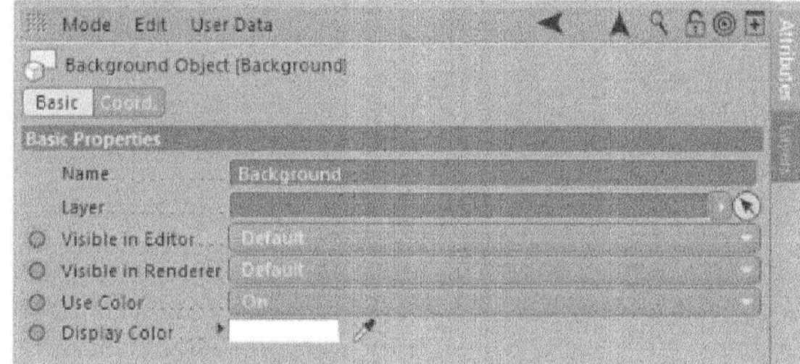

*Figure 2-27 The **Display Color** parameter activated*

The options in the **Use Color** drop-down list are used to determine whether the selected objects in the viewport use the color assigned to them or not. You need to select the **On** option from the **Use Color** drop-down list to ensure that the display color is used even if the materials are applied to it.

Saving and Rendering the Scene

In this section, you will save and render the scene. You can also view the final render of the scene by downloading the file *c02_cinema4d_r20_rndr.zip* from *www.cadsofttech.com*. The path of the file is mentioned at the beginning of the chapter.

1. Choose **File > Save** from the main menu; the **Save File** dialog box is displayed. In this dialog box, browse to the location *\Documents c4dr20\c02*.

2. Enter **c02tut1** in the **File name** text box and then choose the **Save** button.

3. In the Perspective viewport, set the camera angle using the Viewport Navigation Tools located at the top right of the Perspective viewport. Next, choose the **Render to Picture Viewer** tool from the Command Palette. Alternatively, press SHIFT+R; the **Picture Viewer** window is displayed, as shown in Figure 2-28.

   The **Render to Picture Viewer** tool is used to render the scene in the **Picture Viewer** window. The **Picture Viewer** window is also known as the output window in CINEMA 4D. It is used to view the output of the scene as well as to save it.

   Next, you will save the rendered image.

4. In the **Picture Viewer** window, choose **File > Save as**, as shown in Figure 2-29; the **Save** dialog box is displayed, as shown in Figure 2-30.

   The **Save as** option is used to save a scene or an image sequence in the format based on your requirement. The **Save** dialog box is displayed with specific parameters which helps you in saving the still image or image sequence in an uncompressed format.

5. In the **Save** dialog box, select **JPEG** from the **Format** drop-down list and then choose the **OK** button; the **Save Dialog** dialog box is displayed. Next, browse to *\Documents c4dr20\c02*. In the **File Name** text box, type **c02_tut1_rndr**. Next, choose the **Save** button; the rendered image is saved at the desired location.

The output of the model is shown in Figure 2-1.

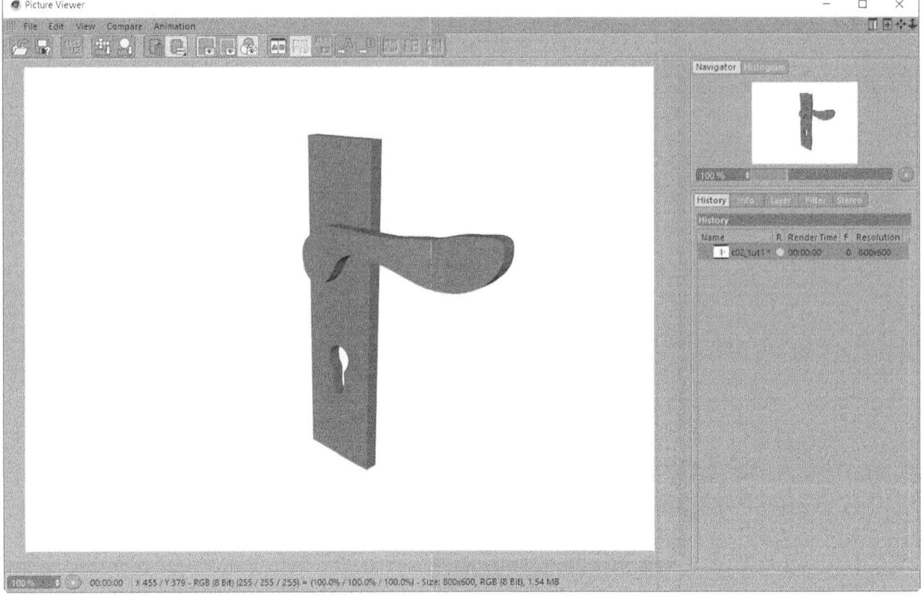

Figure 2-28 *The* ***Picture Viewer*** *window*

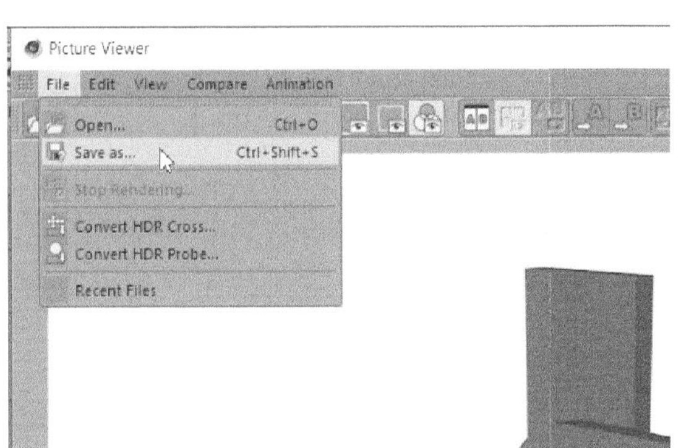

Figure 2-29 *Choosing the* ***Save as*** *option from the* ***File*** *menu*

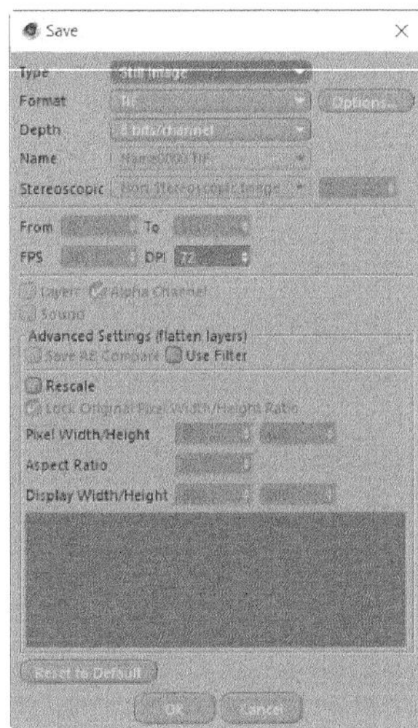

Figure 2-30 *The* ***Save*** *dialog box*

Tutorial 2

In this tutorial, you will create a hand bag with the help of splines and generators. The final output of the model is shown in Figure 2-31. **(Expected time: 25 min)**

Figure 2-31 *The model of a hand bag*

The following steps are required to complete this tutorial:

a. Create the shape of the hand bag.
b. Create the handles of the hand bag.
c. Create text on the hand bag.
d. Change the background color of the scene.
e. Save and render the scene.

Creating the Shape of the Hand Bag

In this section, you will create the shape of the hand bag using the **Spline** tool.

1. Choose **File > New** from the menu bar; a new scene is started. Next, choose **Create > Spline** from the main menu; a cascading menu is displayed. Choose **Rectangle** from the menu; a rectangle is created in the Perspective viewport and *Rectangle* is added to the Object Manager.

2. Make sure that *Rectangle* is selected in the Object Manager. In the Attribute Manager, choose the **Object** button; the **Object Properties** area is displayed. In this area, set the values of the parameters as follows:

   Width: **980** Height: **340**

3. In the **Object Properties** area, select the **Rounding** check box and enter **55** in the **Radius** spinner. Next, select the **XZ** option from the **Plane** drop-down list.

4. In the Attribute Manager, choose the **Coord** button; the **Coordinates** area is displayed. In this area, set the parameters as follows:

   P . X: **1.6** P . Z: **-4**

After entering the values, *Rectangle* is placed in the Perspective viewport, as shown in Figure 2-32.

5. Make sure that *Rectangle* is selected in the Object Manager. Press and hold the left mouse button and the CTRL key and then drag and drop the cursor in the empty space above it; the copy of *Rectangle* is created in the Perspective viewport and added to the Object Manager with the name *Rectangle.1*, as shown in Figure 2-33.

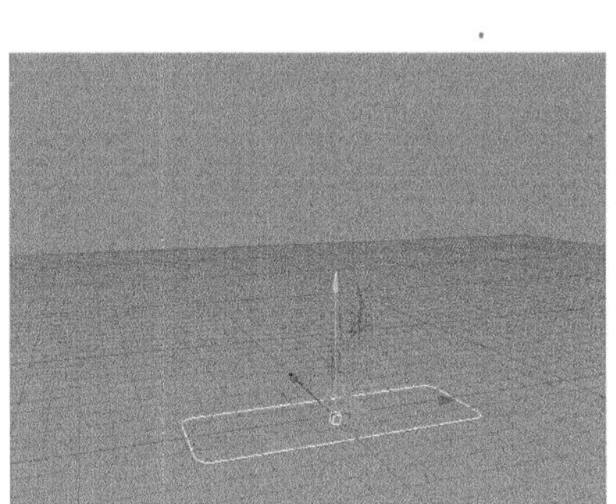

Figure 2-32 *Rectangle placed in the Perspective viewport*

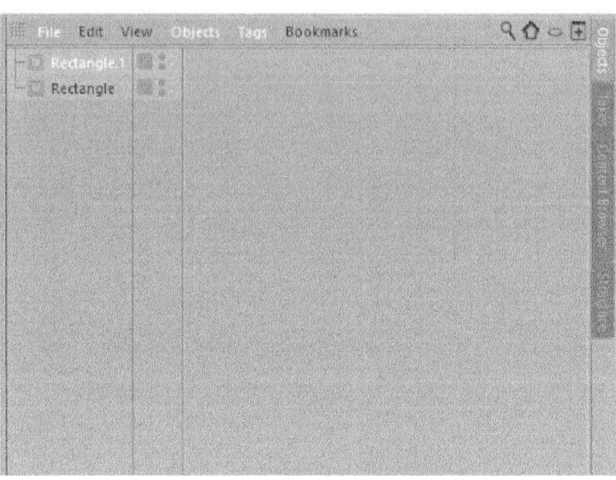

Figure 2-33 *Rectangle.1 added to the Object Manager*

6. Make sure that *Rectangle.1* is selected in the Object Manager. In the Attribute Manager, make sure that the **Object** button is chosen. In the **Object Properties** area, set the parameters as follows:

   Width: **730** Height: **129**

7. In the Attribute Manager, choose the **Coord** button; the **Coordinates** area is displayed. In this area, enter **286.8** in the **P . Y** spinner.

   After entering the values, *Rectangle.1* is placed in the Perspective viewport, as shown in Figure 2-34.

8. Make sure that *Rectangle.1* is selected in the Object Manager. Press and hold the left mouse button and the CTRL key and then drag and drop the cursor in the empty space; a copy of the *Rectangle.1* is created and added to the Object Manager with the name *Rectangle.2*, as shown in Figure 2-35.

9. Make sure that *Rectangle.2* is selected in the Object Manager. In the Attribute Manager, make sure that the **Object** button is chosen. In the **Object Properties** area, set the parameters as follows:

   Width: **815** Height: **165**

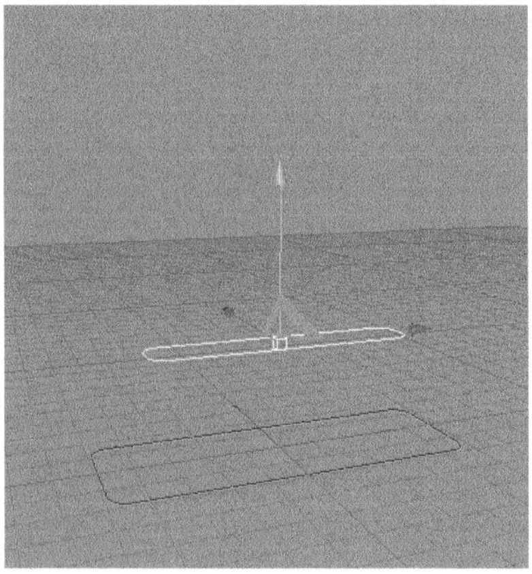

Figure 2-34 *Rectangle.1 placed in the Perspective viewport*

Make sure that the **Rounding** check box is selected and enter **82.5** in the **Radius** spinner.

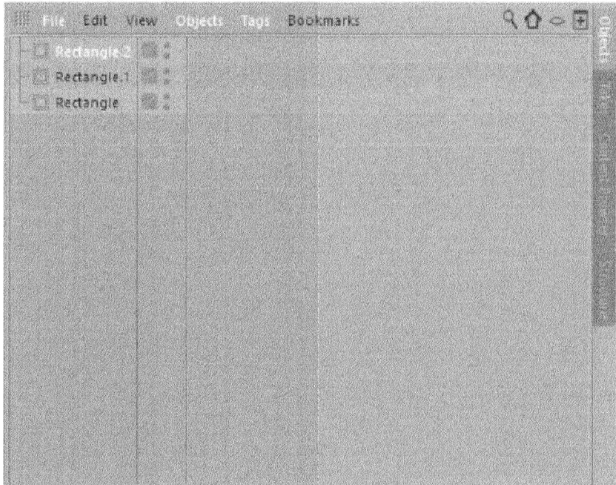

Figure 2-35 *Rectangle.2 added to the Object Manager*

10. In the Attribute Manager, choose the **Coord** button; the **Coordinates** area is displayed. In this area, enter **-3.66** in the **P . Y** spinner. After entering the values, *Rectangle.2* is placed in the Perspective viewport, as shown in Figure 2-36.

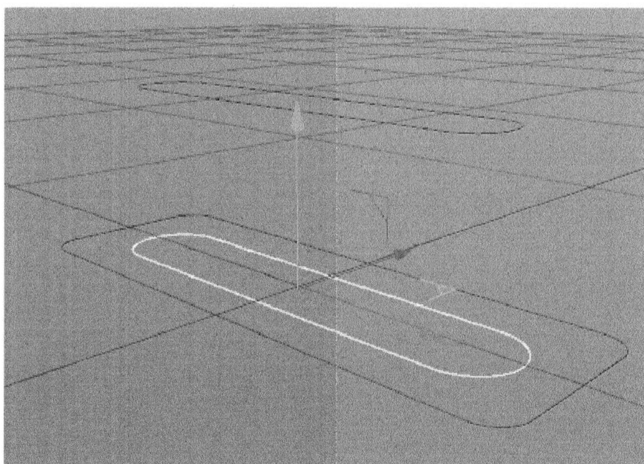

Figure 2-36 *Rectangle.2 placed in the Perspective viewport*

11. Make sure that *Rectangle.2* is selected in the Object Manager. Next, press and hold the left mouse button and the CTRL key and then drag and drop the cursor in the empty space; a copy of *Rectangle.2* is created and added to the Object Manager with the name *Rectangle.3*, as shown in Figure 2-37.

12. Make sure that *Rectangle.3* is selected in the Object Manager. In the Attribute Manager, make sure that the **Object** button is chosen. In the **Object Properties** area, set the parameters as follows:

    Width: **527** Height: **55**

    Clear the **Rounding** check box.

13. In the Attribute Manager, choose the **Coord** button; the **Coordinates** area is displayed. In this area, set the parameters as follows:

    P . X: **-1.9**   P . Y: **647.4**

    After entering the values, *Rectangle.3* is placed in the Perspective viewport, as shown in Figure 2-38.

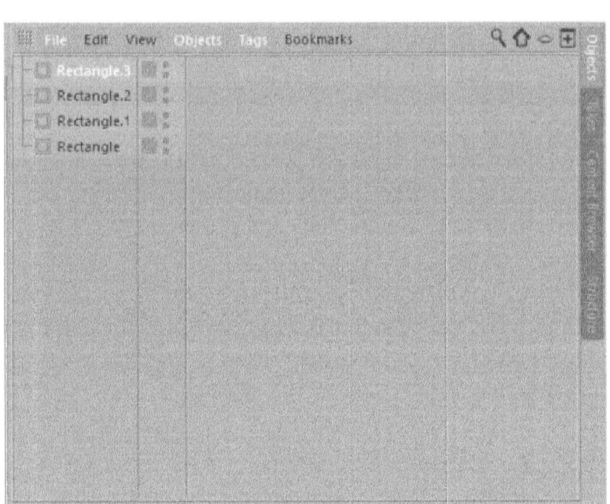

Figure 2-37 *Rectangle.3 added to the Object Manager*

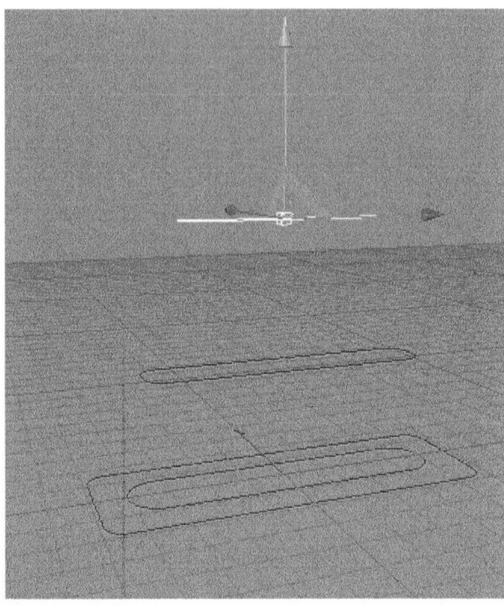

Figure 2-38 *Rectangle.3 placed in the Perspective viewport*

14. Press and hold the left mouse button on the **Subdivision Surface** tool in the Command Palette; a flyout is displayed. Choose the **Loft** tool from the flyout, as shown in Figure 2-39; *Loft* is added to the Object Manager.

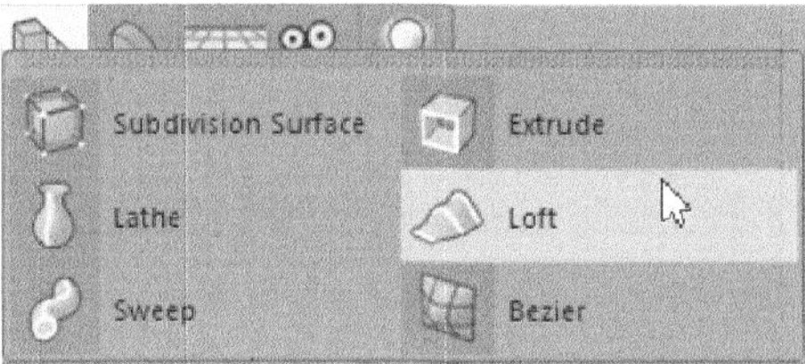

Figure 2-39 *Choosing* ***Loft*** *from the flyout*

15. In the Object Manager, select *Rectangle*.2. Next, drag and drop *Rectangle.2* on *Loft*; *Rectangle.2* is connected to *Loft*, as shown in Figure 2-40. Also, *Rectangle*.2 is lofted with a surface in the Perspective viewport.

16. Connect *Rectangle.1*, *Rectangle.3*, and *Rectangle* to *Loft* in the Object Manager in the order as shown in Figure 2-41; a lofted surface resembling the shape of a hand bag is created in the Perspective viewport, as shown in Figure 2-42.

Figure 2-40 Rectangle.2 connected to Loft in the Object Manager

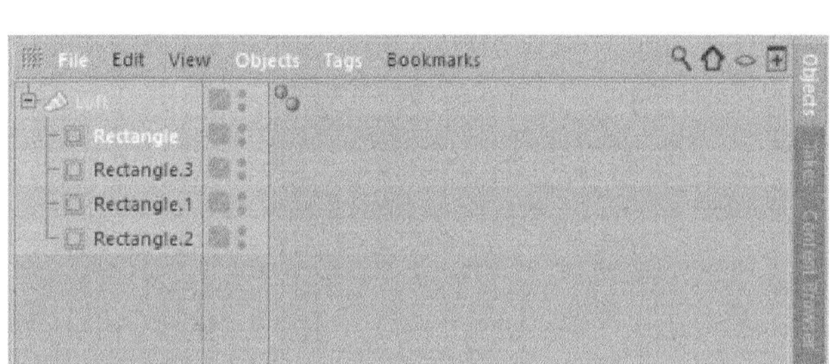

Figure 2-41 Rectangle, Rectangle.1, and Rectangle.3 connected to Loft

Figure 2-42 All rectangles lofted in the Perspective viewport

Creating the Handles of the Hand Bag

In this section, you will create the handles of the bag using the **Lathe** tool.

1. Choose **Create > Spline** from the main menu; a cascading menu is displayed. Choose **Circle** from it; a circle is created in the Perspective viewport and *Circle* is added to the Object Manager.

2. Make sure *Circle* is selected in the Object Manager. In the Attribute Manager, make sure that the **Object** button is chosen. In the **Object Properties** area, enter **8** in the **Radius** spinner. Also, make sure that the **XY** option is selected in the **Plane** drop-down list. Next, choose the **Coord** button; the **Coordinates** area is displayed. In the **Coordinates** area, set the parameters as follows:

   P . X: **242.63** P . Y: **293.5** P . Z: **-110.8**

3. Press and hold the left mouse button on the **Subdivision Surface** tool in the Command Palette; a flyout is displayed. Choose the **Lathe** tool from the flyout, as shown in Figure 2-43; *Lathe* is added to the Object Manager, refer to Figure 2-44.

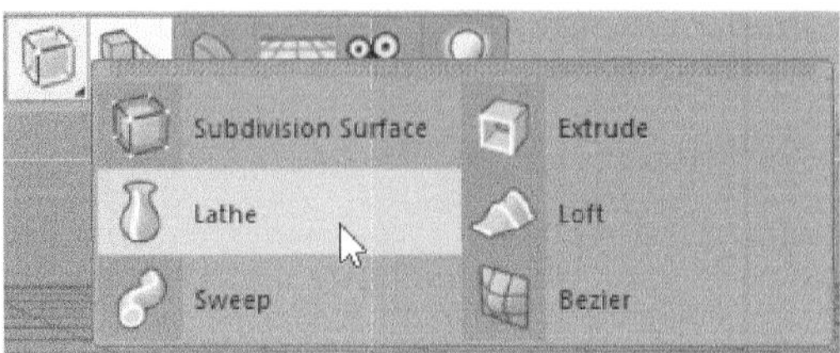

Figure 2-43 *Choosing* ***Lathe*** *from the flyout*

4. In the Object Manager, drag *Circle* and drop it on *Lathe*; *Circle* is connected to *Lathe*, as shown in Figure 2-44.

   The **Lathe** tool is used to rotate the profile curve on the Y-axis of the local axis system of the shape. It is used to generate a revolved surface.

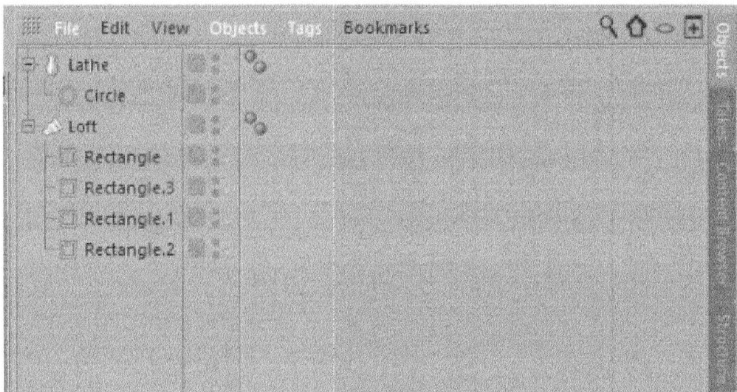

Figure 2-44 *Circle connected to Lathe in the Object Manager*

5. Select *Lathe* in the Object Manager. In the Attribute Manager, choose the **Object** button; the **Object Properties** area is displayed. In this area, enter **75** in the **Subdivision** spinner and **227** in the **Angle** spinner.

6. Choose the **Coord** button; the **Coordinates** area is displayed. In this area, set the parameters as follows:

P . X: **5.715**	P . Y: **634.142**	P . Z: **291.176**
S . X: **0.87**	S . Z: **1.62**	R . H: **90**
R . P: **90**	R . B: **-90**	

   Figure 2-45 displays the hand bag with its handle. Next, you will create a copy of the handle.

7. Select *Lathe* in the Object Manager. Press and hold the left mouse button along with the CTRL key; the shape of the cursor is changed, as shown in Figure 2-46. Next, drag *Lathe* in the empty space above it and then release the left mouse button; a copy of *Lathe* is added with the name *Lathe.1* to the Object Manager.

Figure 2-45 *The handle of the hand bag created*

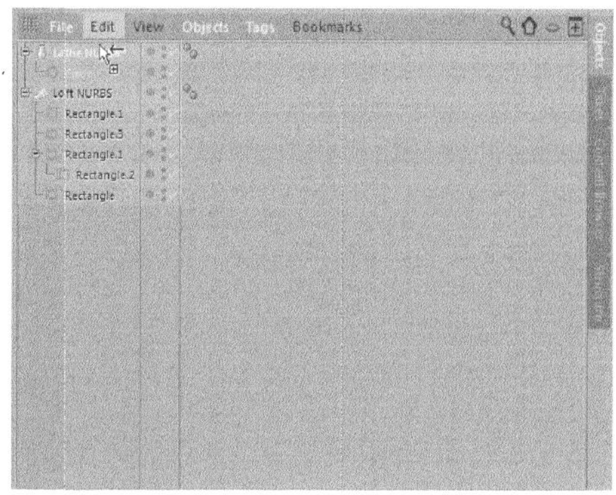

Figure 2-46 *The changed shape of the cursor in the Object Manager*

8. Make sure that *Lathe.1* is selected in the Object Manager and the **Coord** button is chosen in the Object Manager. In the **Coordinates** area of the Attribute Manager, enter **282.25** in the **P . Z** spinner.

Creating Text on the Hand Bag

In this section, you will create text on the hand bag using the **Extrude** tool.

1. Press and hold the left mouse button on the **Pen** tool in the Command Palette; a flyout is displayed. Choose the **Text** tool from the flyout; *Text* is created in the Perspective viewport and added to the Object Manager.

2. Make sure that *Text* is selected in the Object Manager. In the Attribute Manager, choose the **Object** button. In the **Object Properties** area, set the parameters as follows:

   Text: **S&S** Height: **274** Horizontal Spacing: **5**
   Vertical Spacing: **11**

   The **Text** edit box in the **Object Properties** area is used to write the text in the viewport. You can also type multiple lines. The **Height** parameter is used to determine the height of the text displayed in the viewport. The **Horizontal Spacing** parameter is used to determine the horizontal spaces or gaps between the characters. The **Vertical Spacing** parameter is used to determine the vertical spaces or gaps between the characters.

3. In the Attribute Manager, choose the **Coord** button; the **Coordinates** area is displayed. In this area, set the parameters as given next:

   P . X: **-249.402** P . Y: **354.604**
   P . Z: **-109.475** R . P: **-12**

The text is placed in the Perspective viewport, as shown in Figure 2-47. Next, you will extrude the text.

Figure 2-47 *The text placed in the Perspective viewport*

4. Press and hold the left mouse button on the **Subdivision Surface** tool in the Command Palette; a flyout is displayed. Choose the **Extrude** tool from it; *Extrude* is added to the Object Manager.

5. In the Object Manager, drag *Text* and drop it on *Extrude*; *Text* is connected to *Extrude*, as shown in Figure 2-48. Also, *Text* is extruded in the Perspective viewport, refer to Figure 2-49.

Changing the Background Color of the Scene

To change the background color of the scene to white in the final output, follow the steps given in Tutorial 1 of Chapter 2.

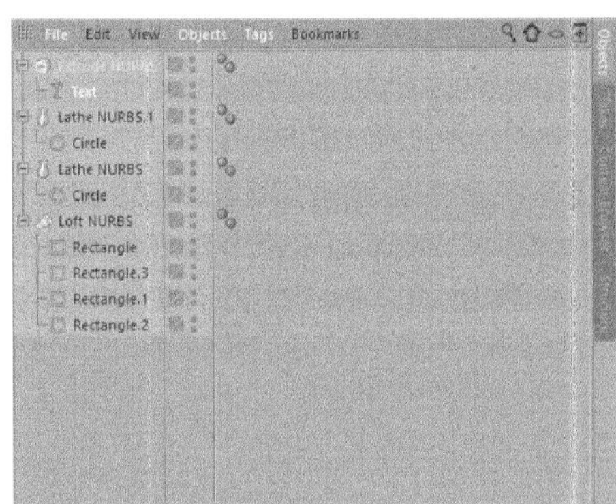

Figure 2-48 *Text connected to Extrude in the Object Manager*

Figure 2-49 *The extruded text on the hand bag*

Saving and Rendering the Scene

In this section, you will save and render the scene. You can also view the final render of the scene by downloading the file *c02_cinema4d_r20_rndr.zip* from *www.cadsofttech.com*. The path of the file is mentioned at the beginning of the chapter.

1. Choose **File > Save** from the main menu; the **Save File** dialog box is displayed. In this dialog box, browse to the location *\Documents\c4dr20\c02*.

2. Enter **c02tut2** in the **File name** text box and then choose the **Save** button.

3. In the Perspective viewport, set the camera angle using the Viewport Navigation Tools located on the extreme top right of the Perspective viewport. Next, you need to render the scene. For rendering, refer to Tutorial 1.

   Figure 2-31 displays the final output.

EXERCISE

The rendered output of the model used in the following exercise can be accessed by downloading the *c02_cinema4d_r20_exr.zip* file from *www.cadsofttech.com*. The path of the file is as follows: *Textbooks > Animation and Visual Effects > MAXON CINEMA 4D > MAXON CINEMA 4D R20 Studio for Novices*

Exercise 1

Using various Generators and spline modeling tools, create the model of a chair, as shown in Figure 2-50. **(Expected time: 25 min)**

Figure 2-50 *The model of a chair*

This page is intentionally left blank

Chapter 3

Introduction to Polygon Modeling

Learning Objectives

After completing this chapter, you will be able to:

- *Create polygon primitives*
- *Work with various polygon modeling tools*

INTRODUCTION

In the previous chapters, you learned to create 3D objects and shapes using the spline modeling techniques. In CINEMA 4D, you can modify the objects at an advanced level by converting them into editable polygons. The converted objects consist of sub-objects that can be modified using the **Move**, **Rotate**, and **Scale** tools. The sub-objects are points, edges, and polygons. In this chapter, you will learn to modify the objects at an advanced level by converting them into polygons.

TUTORIALS

All the files used in the tutorials can be downloaded from the CADSoft website (*www.cadsofttech.com*). These files are compressed in zip file format and are required to be extracted before using them in the tutorials. The path of the files is as follows: *Textbooks > Animation and Visual Effects > MAXON CINEMA 4D > MAXON CINEMA 4D R20 Studio for Novices*

Next, you need to browse to *\Documents\c4dR20* and create a new folder in it with the name *c03*. Next, extract the contents of the zip file in this folder.

Tutorial 1

In this tutorial, you will create 3D model of a computer mouse, as shown in Figure 3-1, using the polygon modeling techniques. **(Expected time: 35 min)**

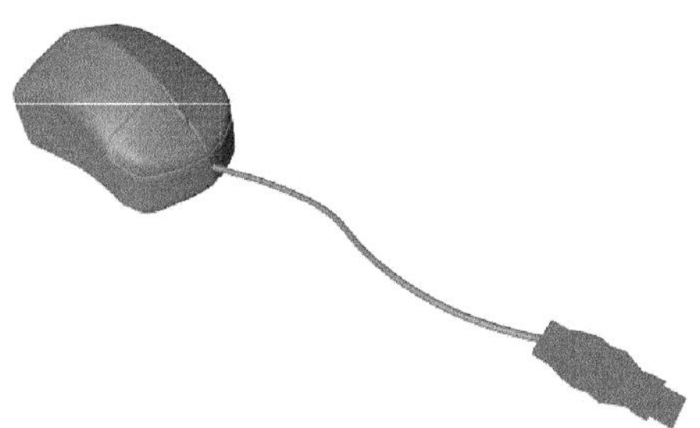

Figure 3-1 *The model of a computer mouse*

The following steps are required to complete this tutorial:

a. Create the body of the computer mouse.
b. Create the left-click and right-click buttons of the mouse.
c. Create the scroll wheel of the mouse.
d. Create the bottom of the mouse.
e. Create the USB cable of the mouse.
f. Change the background color of the scene.
g. Save and render the scene.

Creating the Body of the Computer Mouse

In this section, you will create the body of the computer mouse using the **Cube** tool.

1. Choose **Create > Object** from the main menu; a cascading menu is displayed. Next, choose **Cube** from it; a cube is created in the Perspective viewport, as shown in Figure 3-2, and *Cube* is added to the Object Manager.

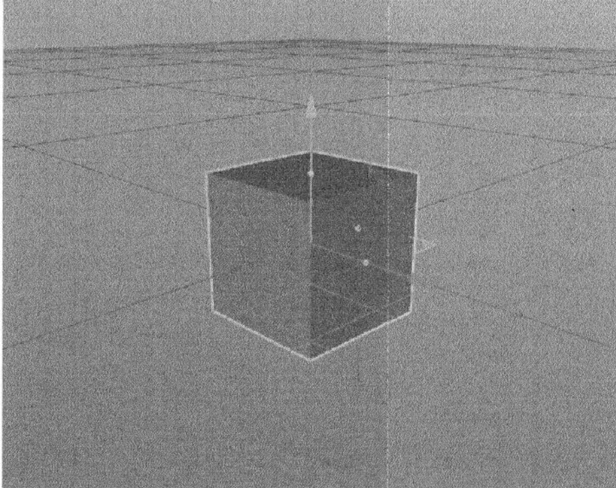

Figure 3-2 *Cube created in the Perspective viewport*

2. In the Attribute Manager, make sure the **Object** button is chosen. In the **Object Properties** area, set the parameters as follows:

Size . X: **91**	Size . Y: **37**	Size . Z: **137**
Segments X: **6**	Segments Y: **4**	Segments Z: **6**

   The **Size . X**, **Size . Y**, and **Size . Z** parameters in the **Object Properties** area are used to set width, height, and depth, respectively of the cube.

3. In the Attribute Manager, choose the **Basic** button; the **Basic Properties** area is displayed. In this area, enter **Computer mouse** in the **Name** text box; *Cube* is renamed as *Computer mouse* in the Object Manager.

4. Make sure *Computer mouse* is selected in the Object Manager and choose the **Make Editable** tool from the Modes Palette; *Computer mouse* is converted into a polygon object. 

Note

After converting Computer mouse into a polygon object, you will notice that when you hover the cursor over it, the name of the Computer mouse changes to ***Polygon Object [Computer mouse]*** *on hovering the cursor on it. Also, the icon of the Cube object changes into a triangle.*

5. Press F2; the Top viewport is maximized. Choose the **Points** tool from the Modes Palette; the *Computer mouse* is displayed in the points mode.

6. Invoke the **Live Selection** tool from the Command Palette. The shape of the cursor changes. To increase or decrease the size of the cursor, press the } or { key, respectively. In the Attribute Manager, make sure the **Options** button is chosen. In the **Options** area, clear the **Only Select Visible Elements** check box, if not already cleared.

   The **Only Select Visible Elements** check box is cleared to select the polygons that are behind the visible sub-objects.

7. Using the **Live Selection** tool and the SHIFT key, select the corner points of *Computer mouse*, as shown in Figure 3-3.

8. Invoke the **Scale** tool from the Command Palette and scale the selected points uniformly in the Top viewport, as shown in Figure 3-4.

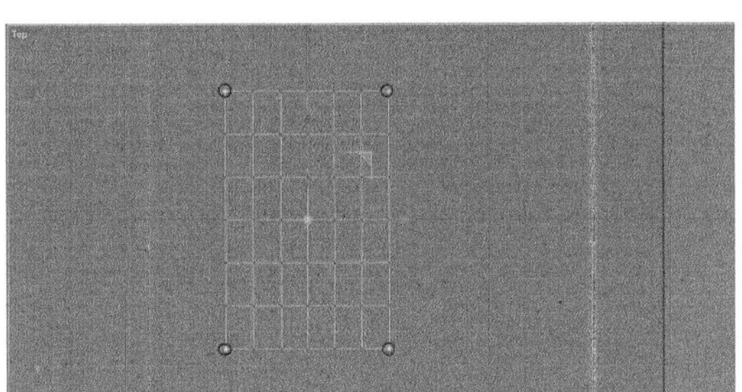

Figure 3-3 *The corner points of Computer mouse to be selected*

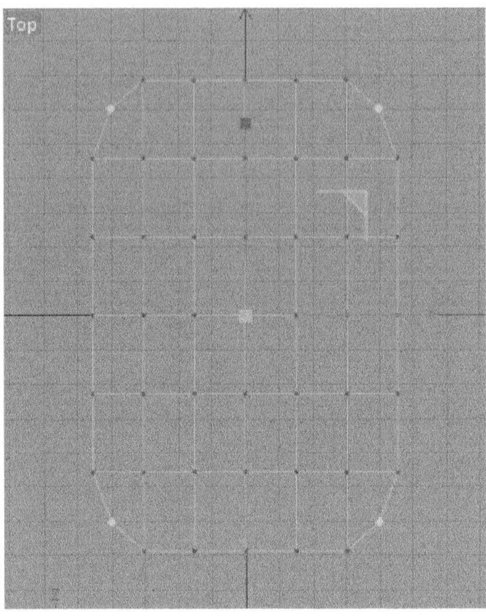

Figure 3-4 *Scaling the selected points of Computer mouse*

9. Deselect the corner points of *Computer mouse* by clicking on the empty area of the viewport. Invoke the **Live Selection** tool from the Command Palette and select the center points of *Computer mouse* in the Top viewport by dragging the cursor on them, as shown in Figure 3-5.

10. Invoke the **Scale** tool from the Command Palette and scale the selected points in the Top viewport, as shown in Figure 3-6.

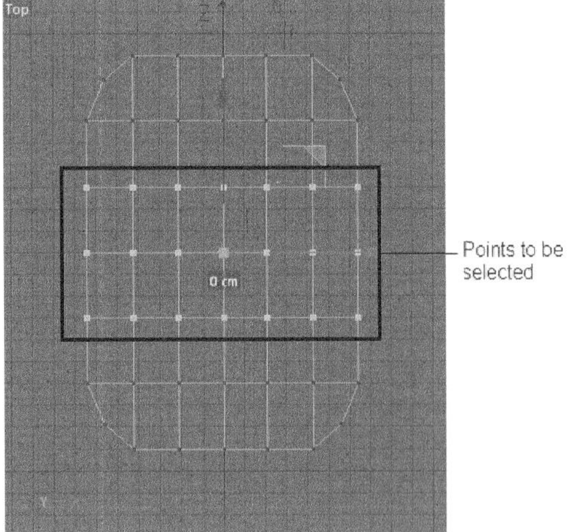

Figure 3-5 *The points to be selected*

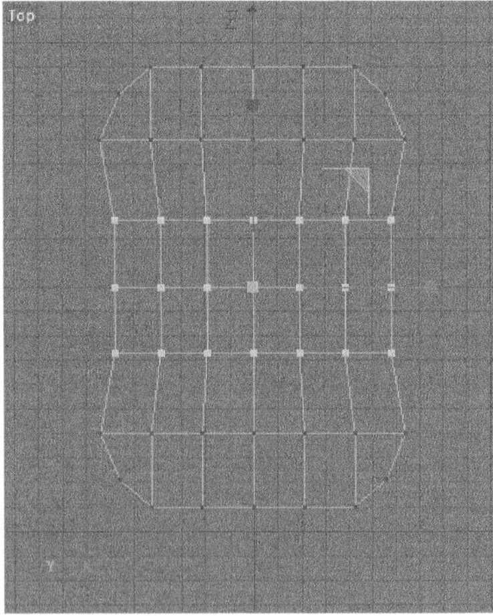

Figure 3-6 *Scaling the selected points of Computer mouse*

11. Press and hold the 9 key on the main keyboard to temporarily invoke the **Live Selection** tool and then select the center points of *Computer mouse* in the Top viewport, as shown in Figure 3-7. Now, release the 9 key.

    On releasing the 9 key, the **Scale** tool is activated which is the last used tool.

12. Scale the selected points inward in the Top viewport, as shown in Figure 3-8.

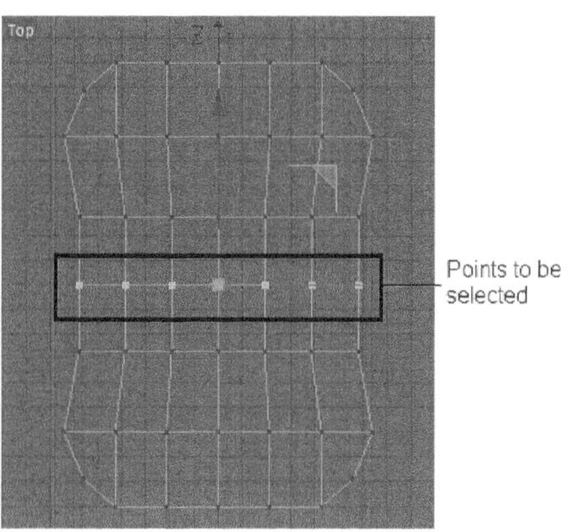

Figure 3-7 *The center points to be selected*

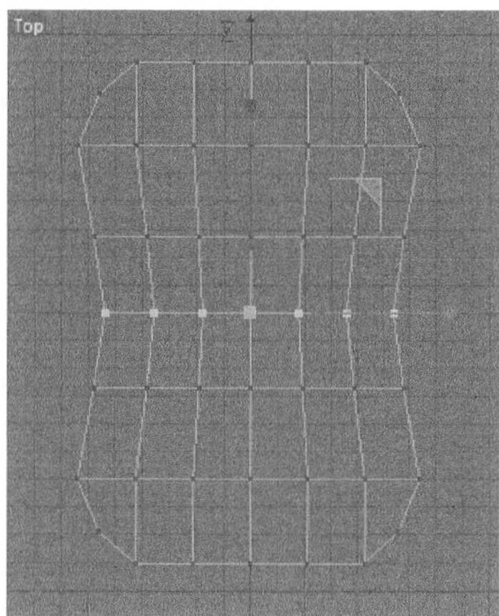

Figure 3-8 *Scaling the selected points of Computer mouse*

13. Press and hold the 9 key and select the top and bottom points of *Computer mouse* by using the SHIFT key, as shown in Figure 3-9. Next, release the 9 and SHIFT keys. Now, scale the selected points along the Z-axis, as shown in Figure 3-10.

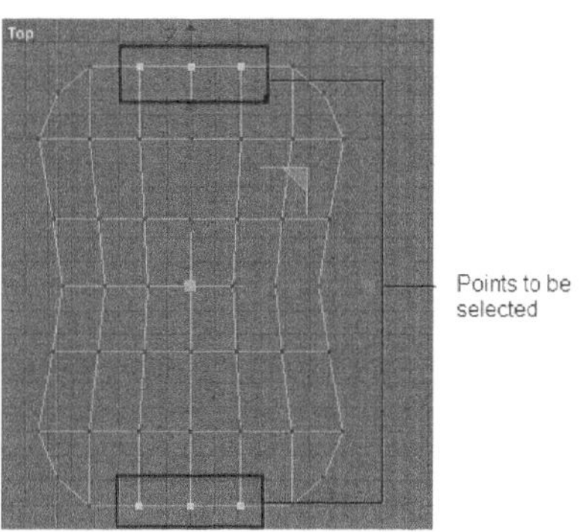

Figure 3-9 *The selected points of Computer mouse*

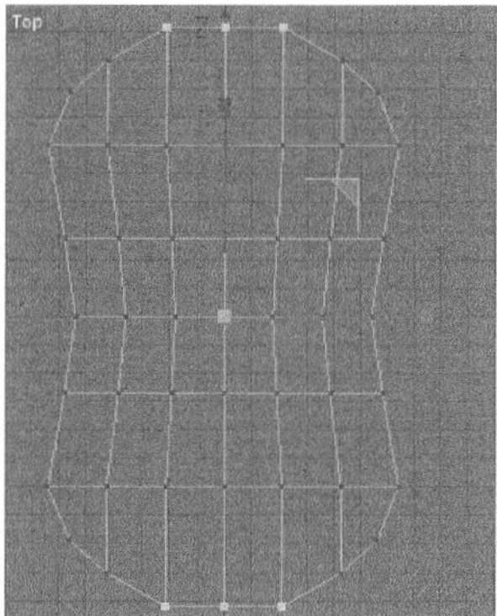

Figure 3-10 *Scaling the selected points of Computer mouse*

14. Press and hold the 9 key and select the top and bottom center points of *Computer mouse* using the SHIFT key, as shown in Figure 3-11.

15. Scale the selected points along the Z-axis in the Top viewport, as shown in Figure 3-12.

16. Press F3; the Right viewport is maximized. Invoke the **Live Selection** tool from the Command Palette. In the Attribute Manager, make sure the **Options** button is chosen. In the **Options** area, make sure that the **Only Select Visible Elements** check box is cleared.

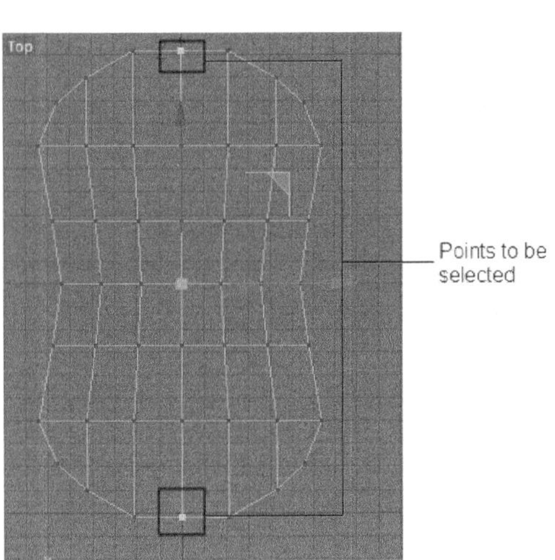

Figure 3-11 *The top and bottom center points of Computer mouse selected*

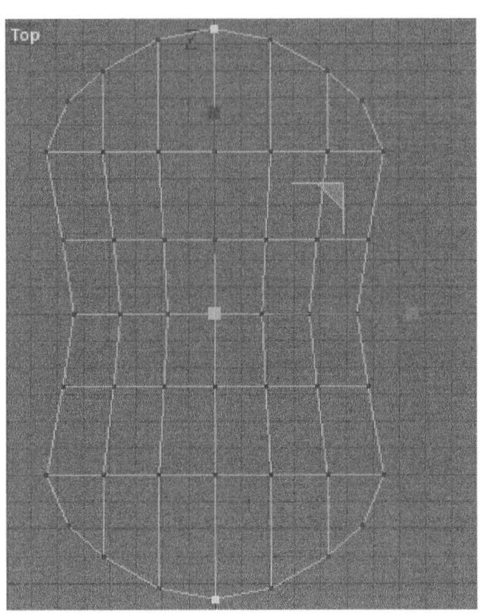

Figure 3-12 *Scaling the selected points of Computer mouse*

17. Using the **Live Selection** tool, select the center points of *Computer mouse* in the Right viewport, as shown in Figure 3-13. Next, move the selected points upward in the Right viewport, as shown in Figure 3-14.

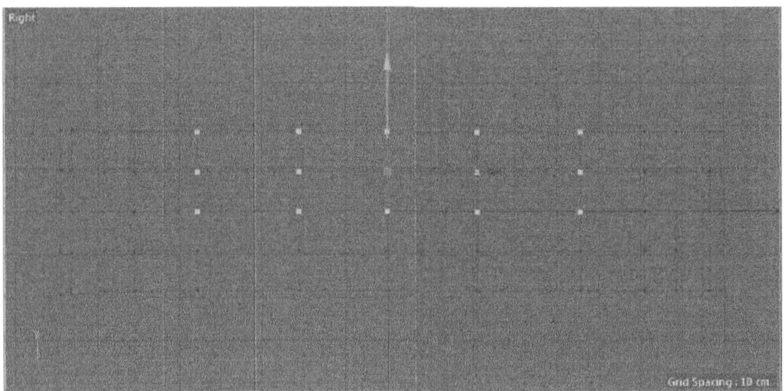

Figure 3-13 *The points to be selected*

18. Select the top points of *Computer mouse* in the Right viewport, as shown in Figure 3-15. Next, move the selected points upward in the Right viewport, as shown in Figure 3-16.

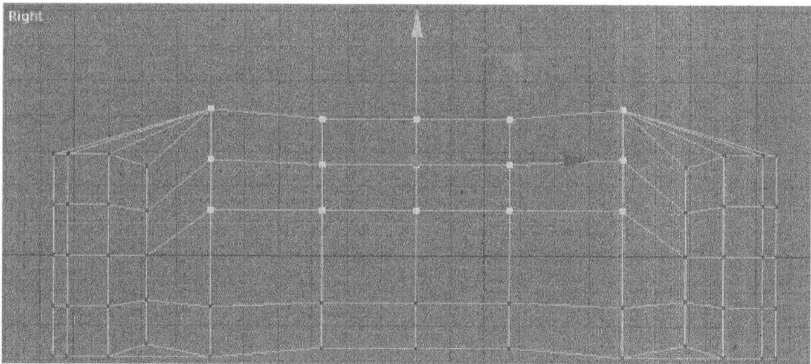

Figure 3-14 *Moving the selected points of Computer mouse*

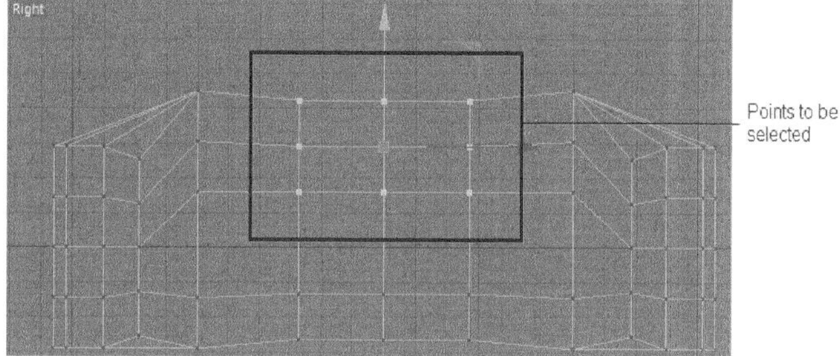

Figure 3-15 *The selected points of Computer mouse*

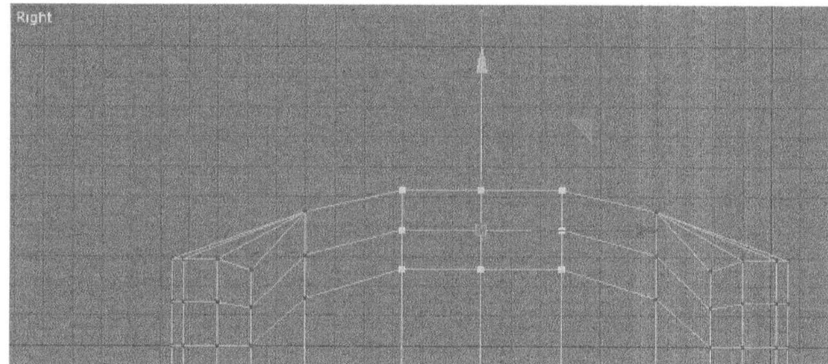

Figure 3-16 *Moving the selected points of Computer mouse*

19. Select the top center points of *Computer mouse*, as shown in Figure 3-17. Move the selected points upward in the Right viewport, as shown in Figure 3-18.

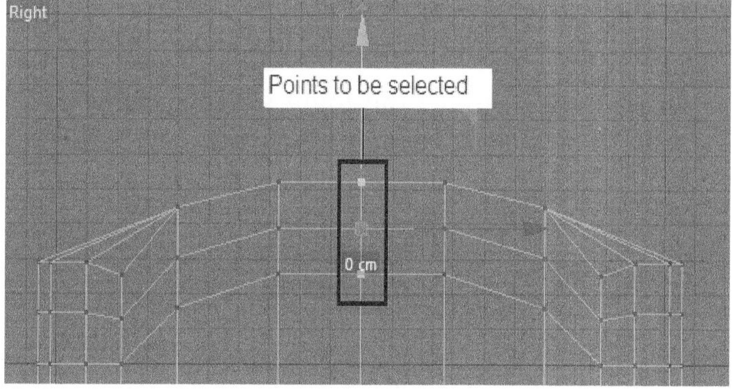

Figure 3-17 *The top center points of Computer mouse selected*

20. Select the points of *Computer mouse* in the Right viewport, as shown in Figure 3-19.

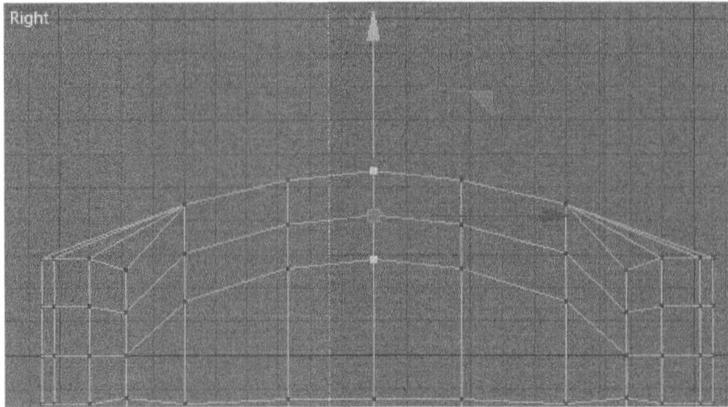

Figure 3-18 *Moving the selected points of Computer mouse*

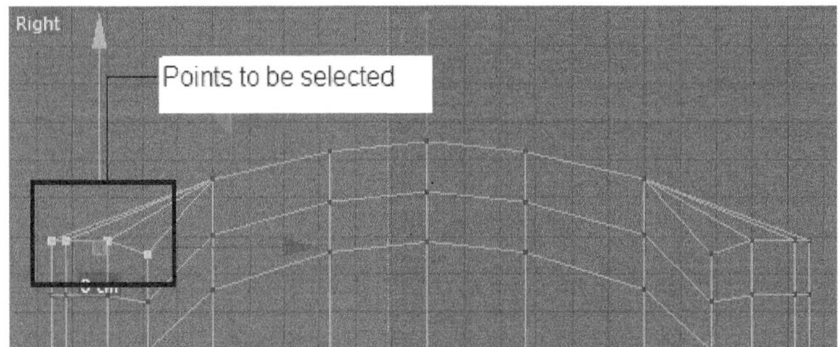

Figure 3-19 *The points to be selected*

21. Invoke the **Rotate** tool from the Command Palette and rotate the selected points along the YZ axis in the Right viewport, as shown in Figure 3-20.

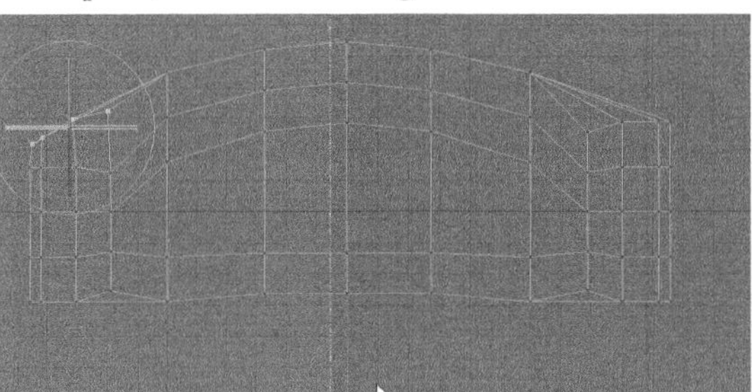

Figure 3-20 *Rotating the selected points of Computer mouse*

22. Select the points of *Computer mouse* in the Right viewport using the 9 key, as shown in Figure 3-21. Next, rotate the selected points along the YZ axis in the Right viewport, as shown in Figure 3-22.

23. Press F4; the Front viewport is maximized. Invoke the **Live Selection** tool from the Command Palette. In the Attribute Manager, make sure the **Options** button is chosen. In the **Options** area, make sure that the **Only Select Visible Elements** check box is cleared.

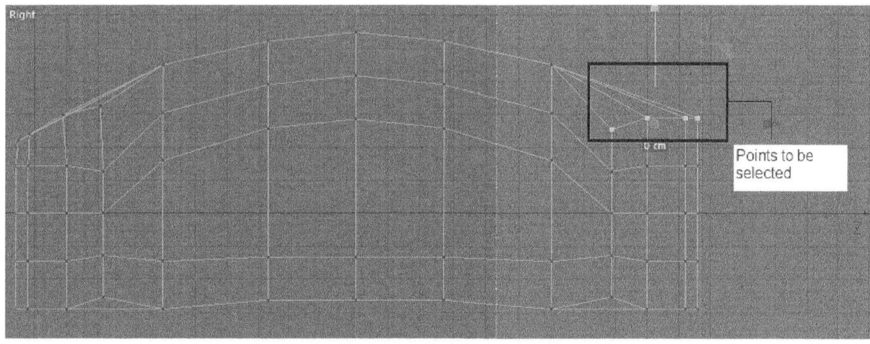

Figure 3-21 The points to be selected

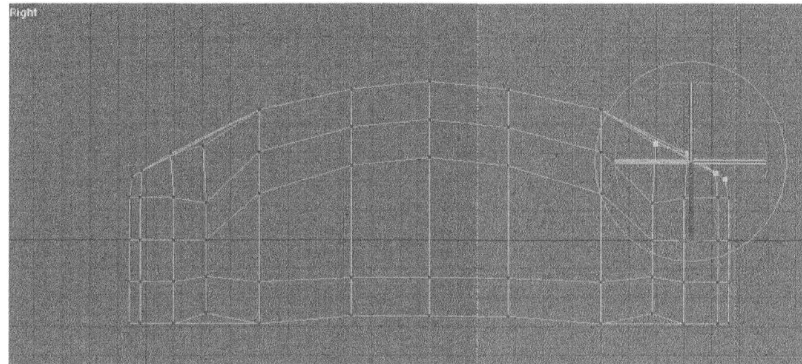

Figure 3-22 Rotating the selected points of Computer mouse

24. Select the center points of *Computer mouse* in the Front viewport, as shown in Figure 3-23. Next, move the selected points upward in the Front viewport, as shown in Figure 3-24.

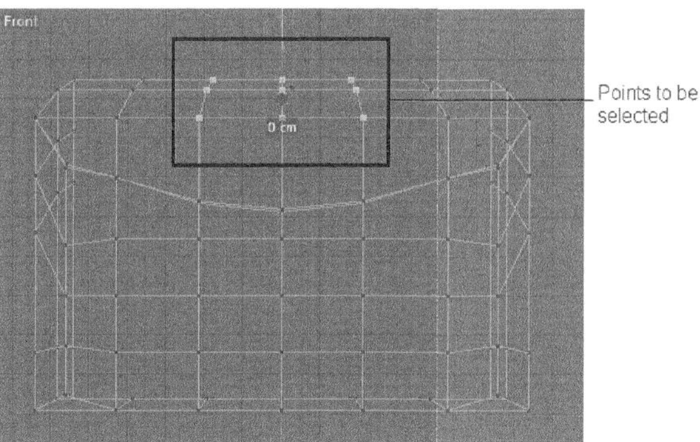

Figure 3-23 The points to be selected

25. Select the points of *Computer mouse* using the 9 key, as shown in Figure 3-25. Next, move the selected points upward in the Front viewport, as shown in Figure 3-26.

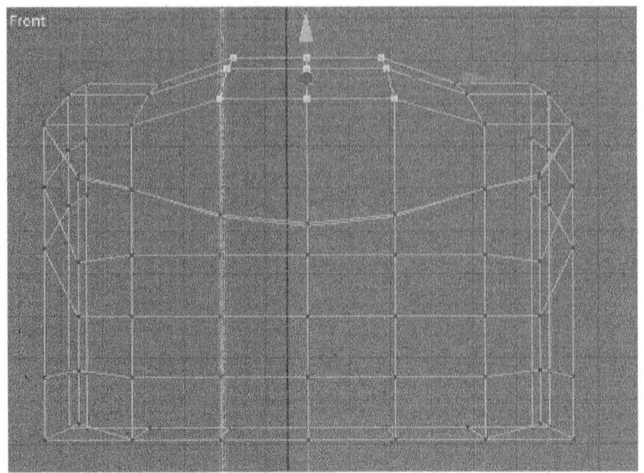

Figure 3-24 Moving the selected points upward

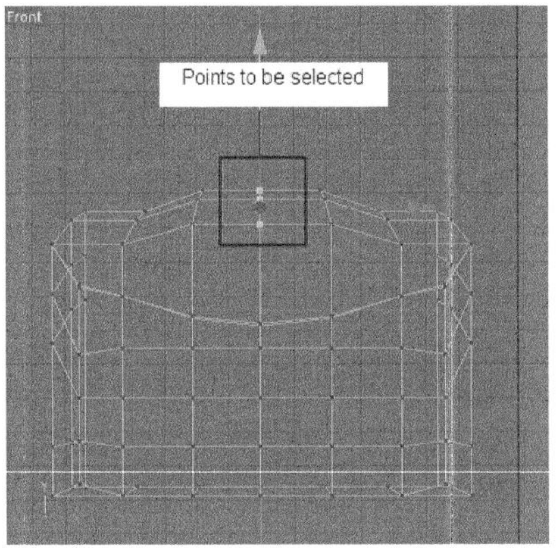

Figure 3-25 The selected points of Computer mouse

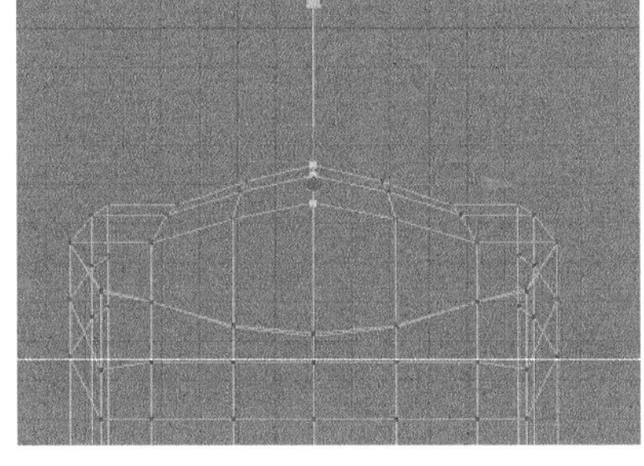

Figure 3-26 Moving the selected points of Computer mouse

26. Select the points of *Computer mouse* using the 9 and SHIFT keys, as shown in Figure 3-27. Next, move the selected points upward in the Front viewport, as shown in Figure 3-28.

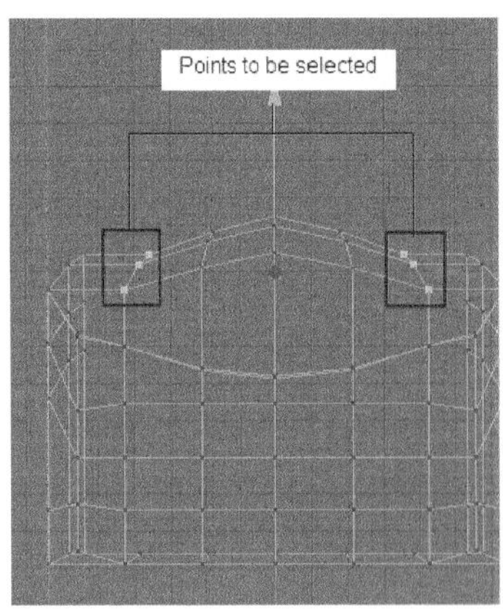

Figure 3-27 The points to be selected

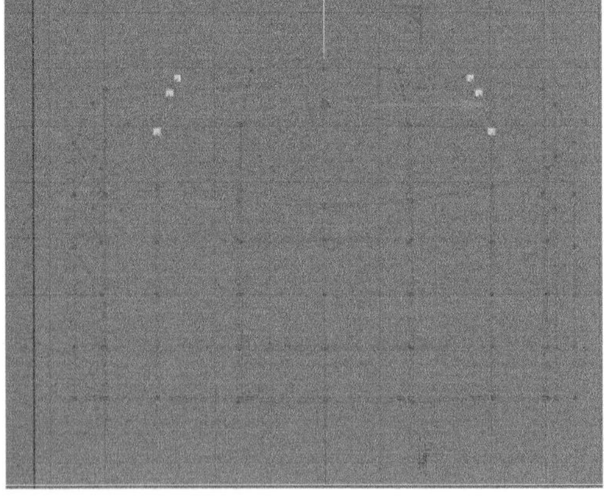

Figure 3-28 Moving the selected points of Computer mouse

27. Press F1; the Perspective viewport is maximized. Choose the **Edges** tool from the Modes Palette; *Computer mouse* is displayed in the edge mode.

28. Select the edges of *Computer mouse* in the Top viewport using the 9 and SHIFT keys, as shown in Figure 3-29.

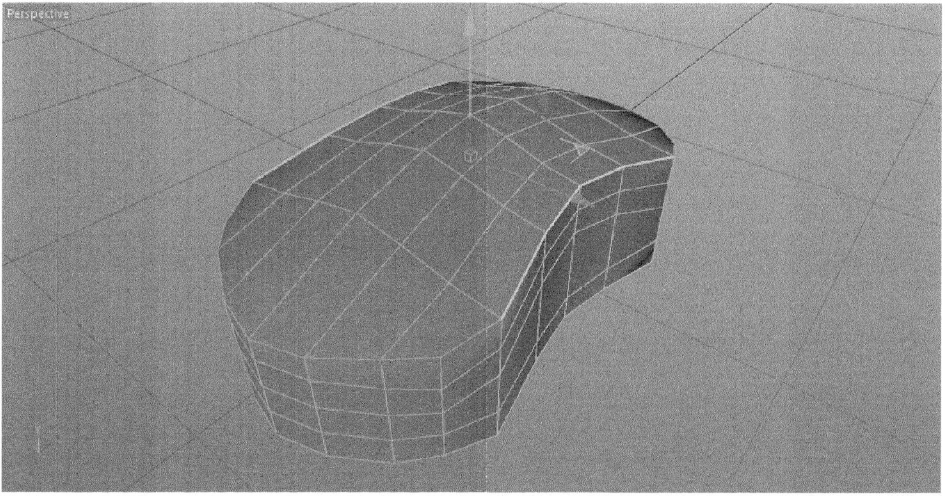

Figure 3-29 *The selected edges in the Perspective viewport*

29. Invoke the **Scale** tool from the Command Palette and scale down the selected edges to 95 percent along the x-axis, as shown in Figure 3-30.

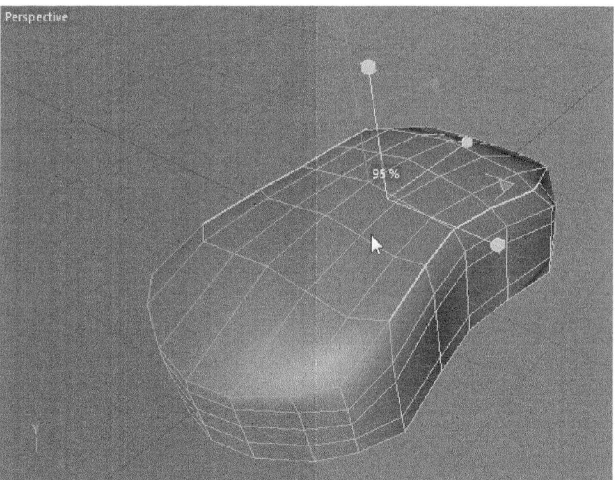

Figure 3-30 *Scaling down the edges of Computer mouse in the Perspective viewport*

30. Press F3; the Right viewport is maximized. Choose the **Points** tool from the Modes Palette; the *Computer mouse* is displayed in the points mode.

31. Select the points of *Computer mouse* in the Right viewport using the 9 key, as shown in Figure 3-31.

32. Invoke the **Move** tool from the Command Palette and move the selected points upward in the Right viewport, as shown in Figure 3-32.

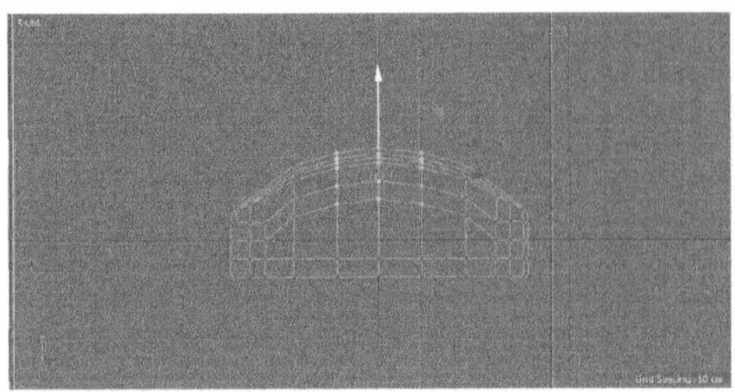

Figure 3-31 *The points to be selected*

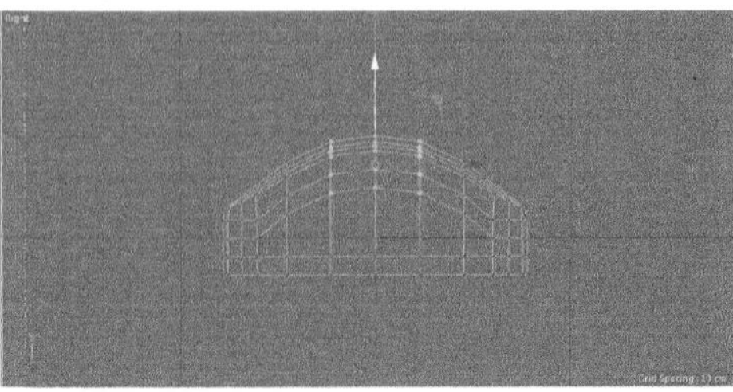

Figure 3-32 *Moving the selected points of Computer mouse*

33. Select the center points of *Computer mouse* using the 9 key, as shown in Figure 3-33.

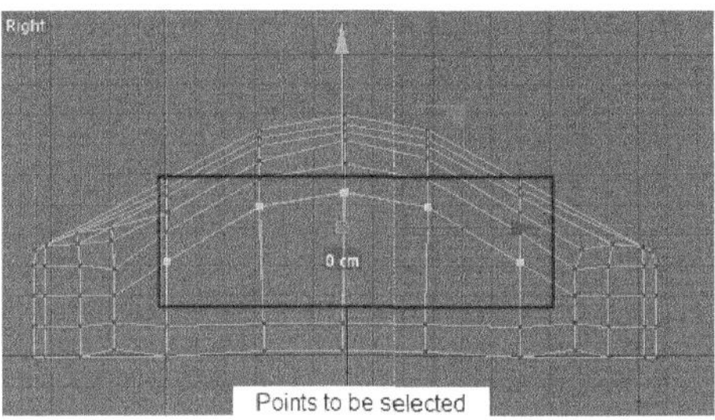

Figure 3-33 *The points to be selected*

34. Invoke the **Scale** tool from the Command Palette. Scale the selected points downward along the Y-axis and then move them downwards to get a straight line in the Right viewport, as shown in Figure 3-34.

35. Select the points of *Computer mouse* using the 9 key, as shown in Figure 3-35. Next, scale the selected points along the Y axis to 87.2 percent in the Right viewport, as shown in Figure 3-36.

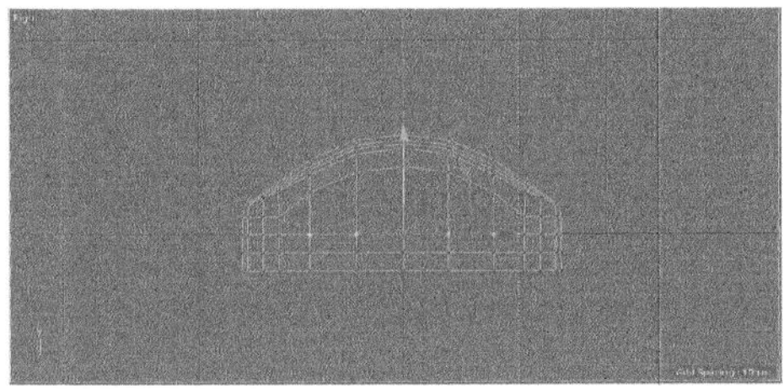

Figure 3-34 *Scaling and moving the points of Computer mouse*

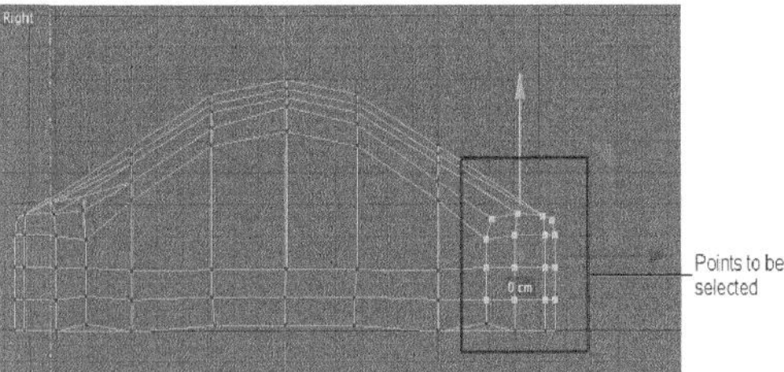

Figure 3-35 *The points of Computer mouse to be selected*

36. Invoke the **Move** tool from the Command Palette and move the selected points downward in the Right viewport, as shown in Figure 3-37.

Figure 3-36 Scaling the points of Computer mouse

Figure 3-37 Moving the selected points in the Right viewport

37. Select the bottom points of *Computer mouse* using the 9 key, refer to Figure 3-38. Next, invoke the **Scale** tool and scale the selected points to get a straight line in the Right viewport, if they are not straight, as shown in Figure 3-38.

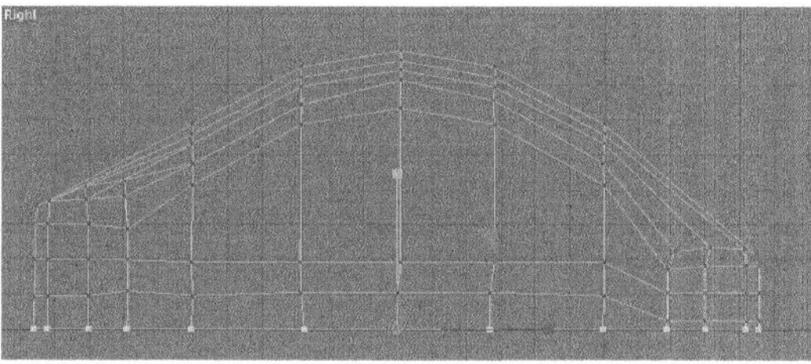

Figure 3-38 Scaling the points of Computer mouse

Creating the Left-Click and Right-Click Buttons of the Mouse

In this section, you will create the left-click and the right-click buttons of *Computer mouse*.

1. Press F1; the Perspective viewport is maximized. Choose the **Edges** tool from the Modes Palette; the *Computer mouse* is displayed in the edge mode.

2. Right-click in the empty area of the Perspective viewport; a shortcut menu is displayed. Choose **Loop/Path Cut** from the shortcut menu; the **Loop/Path Cut** tool settings are displayed in the Attribute Manager. In the **Options** area, make sure **Loop** is selected in the **Mode** drop-down list.

3. Make sure the **Enable Snap** tool is deactivated in the Modes Palette. In the **Options** area, make sure the **Restrict to Selection** check box is cleared and then click on the right of the middle edge loop of the *Computer mouse* in the Perspective viewport, as shown in Figure 3-39; a new edge is created next to it, as shown in Figure 3-40.

   When you create an edge loop using the **Loop/Path Cut** tool, you can interactively slide the edge loop using the slider that appears at the top of the viewport, as shown in Figure 3-41.

4. Again, create three new edge loops using the **Loop/Path Cut** tool, refer to Figures 3-42 and 3-43.

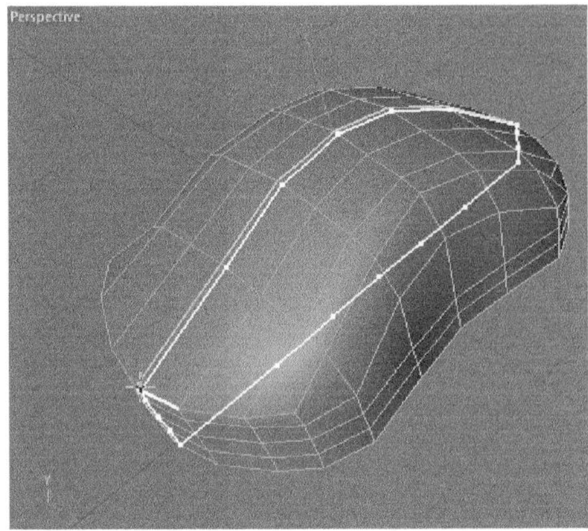

Figure 3-39 Clicking on the right of the middle edge loop

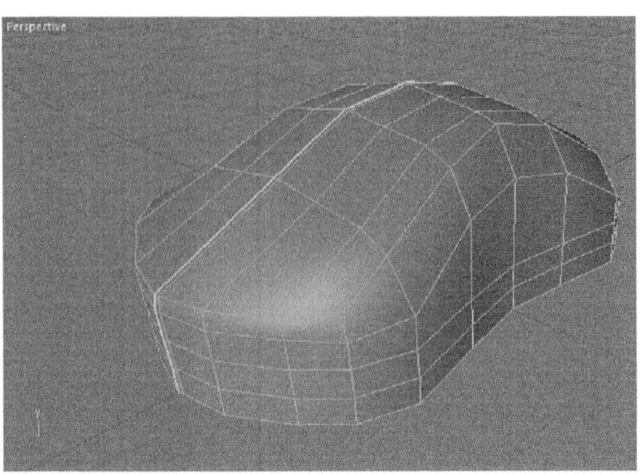

Figure 3-40 A new edge loop added to the Computer mouse

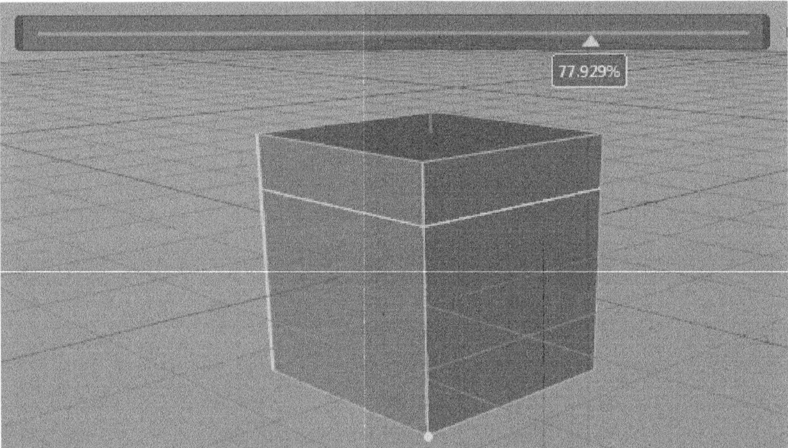

Figure 3-41 The slider displayed at the top of the viewport

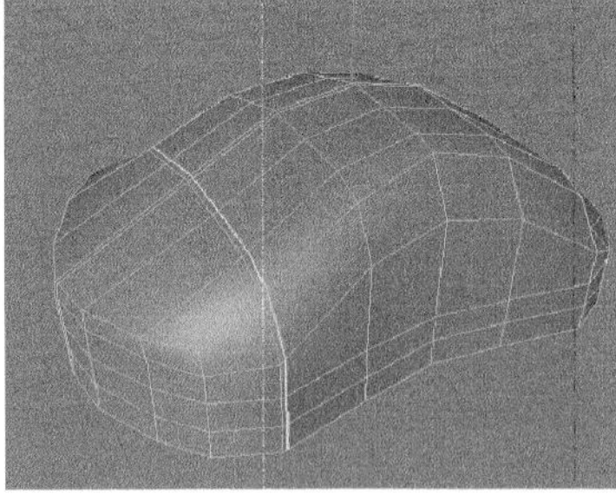

Figure 3-42 A new edge added to Computer mouse

5. Choose the **Live Selection** tool from the Command Palette and then choose the **Polygons** tool from the Modes Palette; the *Computer mouse* is displayed in the polygon mode. In the

Attribute Manager, choose the **Options** button; the **Options** area is displayed. In this area, select the **Only Select Visible Elements** check box, if not already selected. Next, using the **Live Selection** tool, select the polygons of *Computer mouse* in the Perspective viewport, as shown in Figure 3-44. If required, decrease the size of the selection cursor.

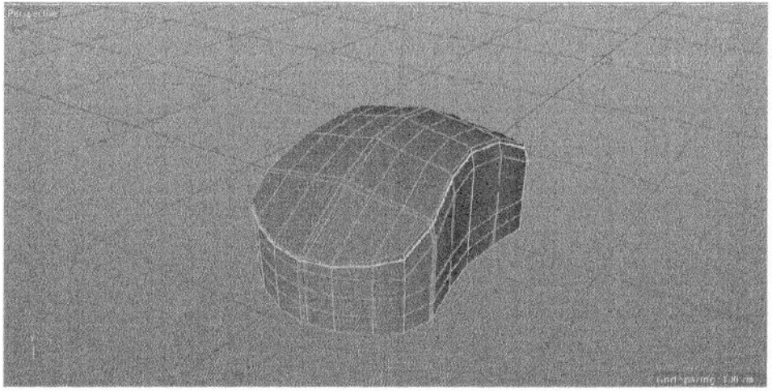

Figure 3-43 *A new edge added to Computer mouse*

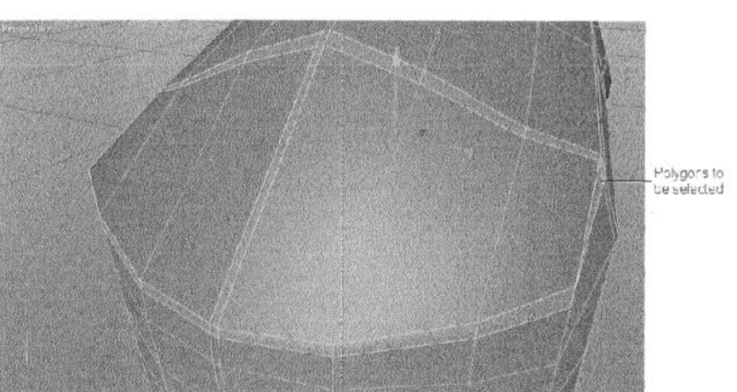

Figure 3-44 *The polygons selected*

6. In the Perspective viewport, right-click on the selected polygons of *Computer mouse*; a shortcut menu is displayed. Choose **Extrude** from the shortcut menu; the **Extrude** tool settings are displayed in the Attribute Manager. Choose the **Options** button; the **Options** area is displayed. Specify the value **-1** in the **Offset** spinner and then press ENTER; the selected polygons of *Computer mouse* are extruded, as shown in Figure 3-45.

7. Right-click on the empty area of the Perspective viewport; a shortcut menu is displayed. Choose **Loop/Path Cut** from the shortcut menu; the **Loop/Path Cut** tool settings are displayed in the Attribute Manager. In the **Options** area, make sure that **Loop** is selected in the **Mode** drop-down list.

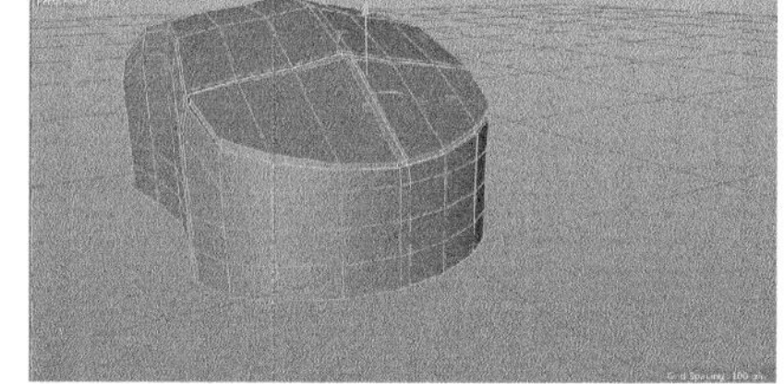

Figure 3-45 *The extruded polygons of Computer mouse*

8. Using the **Loop/Path Cut** tool, create an edge, refer to Figure 3-46.

9. Add two more edges, refer to Figures 3-47 and 3-48. Figure 3-49 shows the edges.

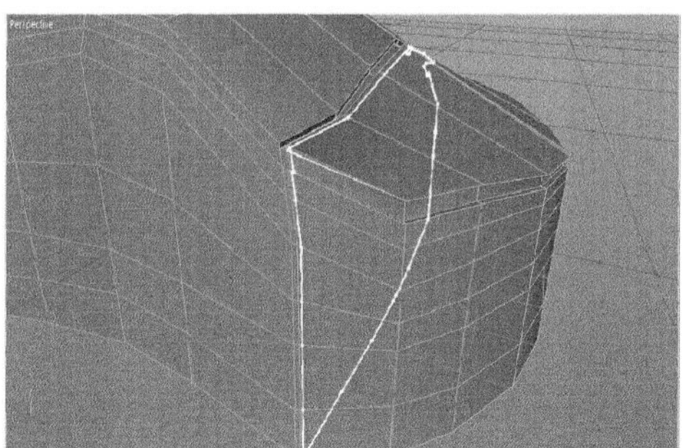

Figure 3-46 *An edge loop added to Computer mouse*

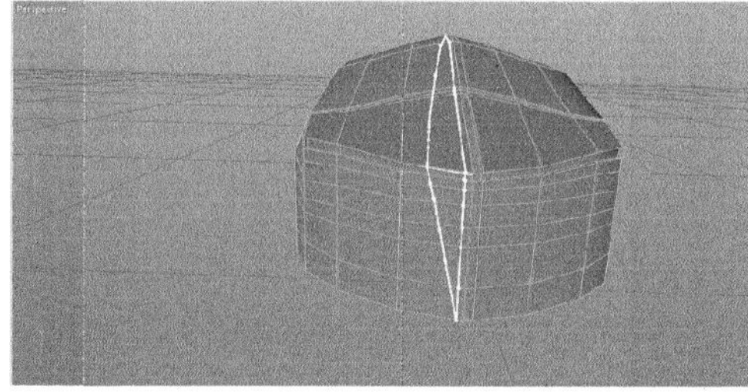

Figure 3-47 *An edge loop added to Computer mouse*

10. To smoothen the surface of the Computer mouse, choose the **Subdivision Surface** tool from the Command Palette; **Subdivision Surface** is added to the Object Manager. Next, select *Computer mouse* in the Object Manager and press and hold the left mouse button and then

drag it on the **Subdivision Surface**; the *Computer mouse* is connected to the **Subdivision Surface** and the smoothened result is displayed, as shown in Figure 3-50.

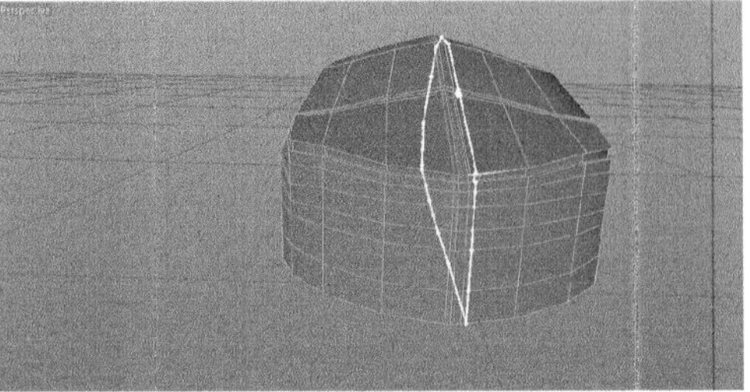

Figure 3-48 *An edge loop added to Computer mouse*

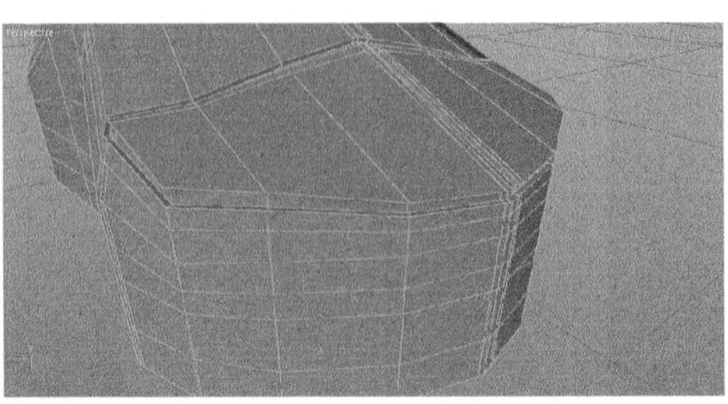

Figure 3-49 *The edges added to Computer mouse*

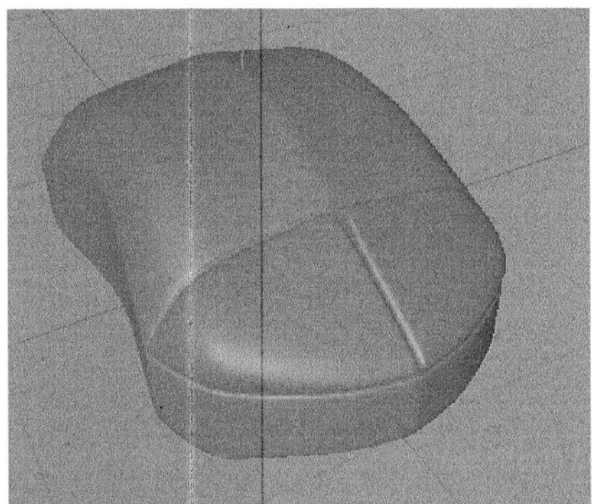

Figure 3-50 *The smoothened Computer mouse*

Creating the Scroll Wheel of the Mouse

In this section, you will create the scroll wheel of the *Computer mouse*.

1. Choose **Create > Object** from the main menu; a cascading menu is displayed. Next, choose **Torus** from it; a torus is created in the Perspective viewport and *Torus* is added to the Object Manager.

2. In the Attribute Manager, choose the **Basic** button; the **Basic Properties** area is displayed. In this area, enter **Scroll wheel** in the **Name** text box; *Torus* is renamed as *Scroll wheel* in the Object Manager.

3. In the Attribute Manager, choose the **Object** button; the **Object Properties** area is displayed. In this area, set the parameters as follows:

   Ring Radius: **6** Pipe Radius: **2** Pipe Segments: **7**
   Orientation: **-X**

4. Make sure that *Scroll wheel* is selected in the Object Manager. Invoke the **Move** tool from the Command Palette and place *Scroll wheel* on *Computer mouse*, as shown in Figure 3-51.

Creating the Bottom of the Mouse

In this section, you will create the bottom of *Computer mouse*.

1. Choose **Cameras** in Menu in editor view in the Perspective viewport; a flyout is displayed. Choose **Bottom** from the flyout; the Bottom viewport is displayed.

2. Select the *Computer mouse* in the Object Manager. Make sure the **Polygons** tool is chosen from the Modes Palette; the *Computer mouse* is displayed in the polygon mode. Make sure the **Live Selection** tool is chosen from the Standard palette. In the Attribute Manager, choose the **Options** button; the **Options** area is displayed. In this area, make sure the **Only Select Visible Elements** check box is selected. Select the polygons of *Computer mouse*, as shown in Figure 3-52.

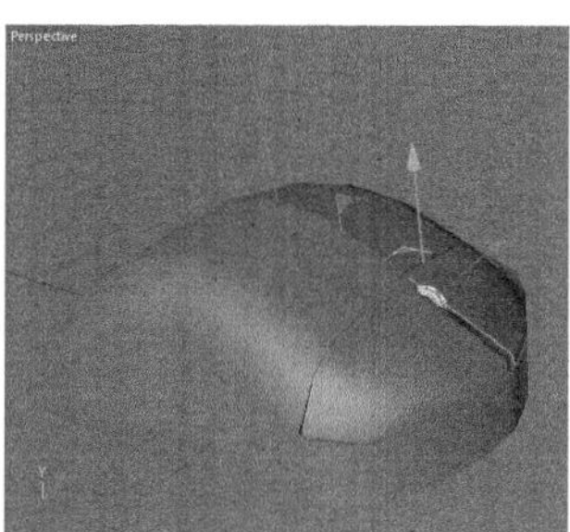

Figure 3-51 *The Scroll wheel placed on Computer mouse*

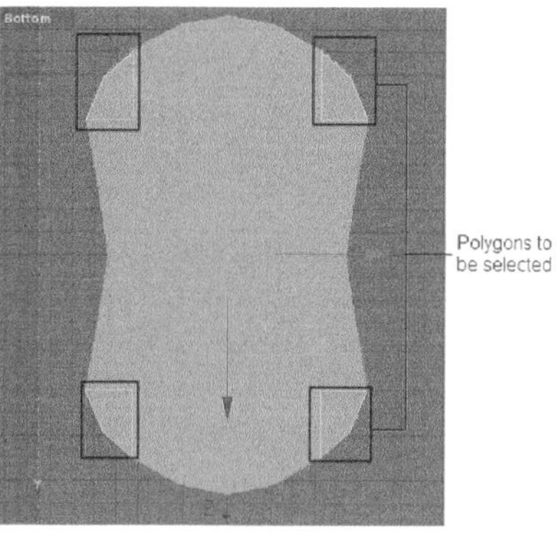

Figure 3-52 *The selected polygons of Computer mouse*

3. In the Bottom viewport, right-click on the selected polygons of *Computer mouse*; a shortcut menu is displayed. Choose **Extrude Inner** from the shortcut menu; the **Extrude Inner** tool settings are displayed in the Attribute Manager. Choose the **Options** button; the **Options** area is displayed. Specify the value **3** in the **Offset** spinner and then press ENTER; the selected polygons of the *Computer mouse* are extruded.

4. In the Perspective viewport, right-click on the selected polygons of *Computer mouse*; a shortcut menu is displayed. Choose **Extrude** from the shortcut menu; the **Extrude** tool settings are displayed in the Attribute Manager. Choose the **Options** button; the **Options** area is displayed. Specify the value **1.5** in the **Offset** spinner and then press ENTER; the selected polygons of the *Computer mouse* are extruded.

5. Choose **Cameras** from the Menu in editor view; a flyout is displayed. Choose **Perspective** from the flyout; the Perspective viewport is maximized.

Creating the USB Cable of the Mouse

In this section, you will create the USB cable of *Computer mouse* using the **Sweep NURBS** tool.

1. Choose **Create > Spline** from the main menu; a cascading menu is displayed. Next, choose **Circle** from it; a circle is created in the Perspective viewport and *Circle* is added to the Object Manager.

2. Make sure that *Circle* is selected in the Object Manager. In the Attribute Manager, make sure the **Object** button is chosen. In the **Object Properties** area, enter **2** in the **Radius** spinner.

3. In the Attribute Manager, choose the **Coord** button; the **Coord** area is displayed. In this area, enter **-80** in the **P . Z** spinner; the *Circle* is positioned in the Perspective viewport.

4. Press F2; the Top viewport is maximized. Choose **Create > Spline** from the main menu; a cascading menu is displayed. Choose **Pen** from it. Next, create a curve in the Top viewport, as shown in Figure 3-53. Press ESC to exit the **Pen** tool.

5. Press and hold the left mouse button on the **Subdivision Surface** tool from the Command Palette; a flyout is displayed. Choose the **Sweep** tool from the flyout; the *Sweep* is added to the Object Manager.

6. In the Object Manager, press and hold the left mouse button on *Spline* and drag it to *Sweep*; the *Spline* is connected to *Sweep*. Next, press and hold the left mouse button on *Circle* and drag it to *Sweep*; *Circle* is connected to *Sweep*. You will notice that a wire is created in the Top viewport.

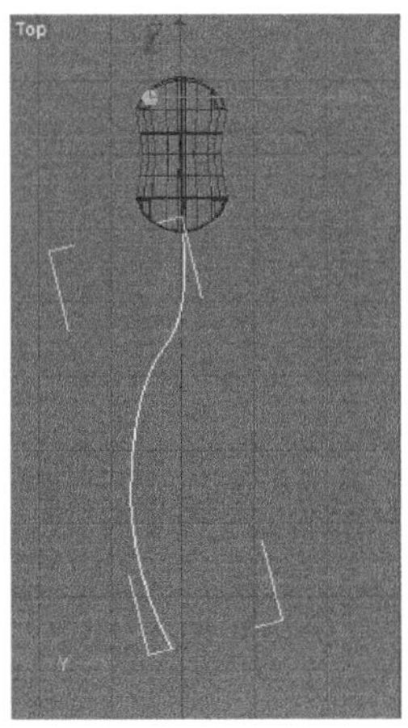

Figure 3-53 *Spline created in the Top viewport*

Next, you will create the USB port of *Computer mouse*.

7. Choose **Create > Object** from the main menu; a cascading menu is displayed. Next, choose **Cube** from it; a cube is created in the Top viewport and a *Cube* is added to the Object Manager.

8. Make sure that *Cube* is selected in the Object Manager. In the Attribute Manager, choose the **Object** button; the **Object Properties** area is displayed. In this area, set the parameters as follows:

Size . X: **28**	Size . Y: **8**	Size . Z: **62**
Segments X: **10**	Segments Y: **10**	Segments Z: **10**

9. Invoke the **Move** tool from the Command Palette and move *Cube* in the Top viewport to place it, as shown in Figure 3-54.

10. Make sure *Cube* is selected in the Object Manager. Next, choose the **Make Editable** tool from the Modes Palette; the *Cube* is converted into a polygonal object.

11. Choose the **Edges** tool from the Modes Palette; the *Cube* is displayed in the edge mode. Choose the **Live Selection** tool from the Command Palette. In the Attribute Manager, make sure the **Only Select Visible Elements** check box is cleared in the **Options** area. Next, select the edges of *Cube* in the Top viewport, as shown in Figure 3-55.

12. Invoke the **Scale** tool from the Command Palette and scale down the selected edges to 70 percent uniformly.

13. Choose the **Points** tool from the Modes Palette; *Cube* is displayed in the points mode. Select the points of *Cube* using the 9 and SHIFT keys, as shown in Figure 3-56.

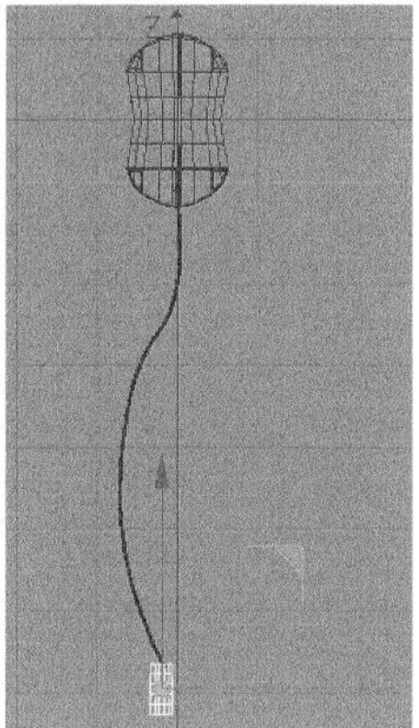

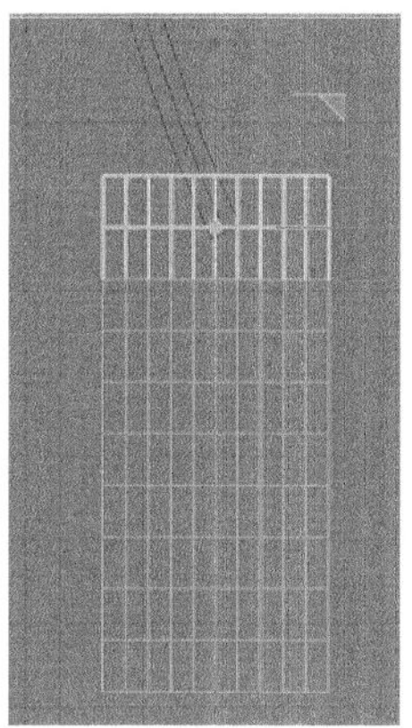

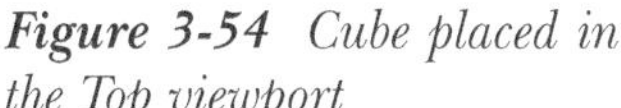

Figure 3-54 *Cube placed in the Top viewport*

Figure 3-55 *The edges to be selected in the Top viewport*

14. Scale down the selected points along the X axis to get the shape, as shown in Figure 3-57.

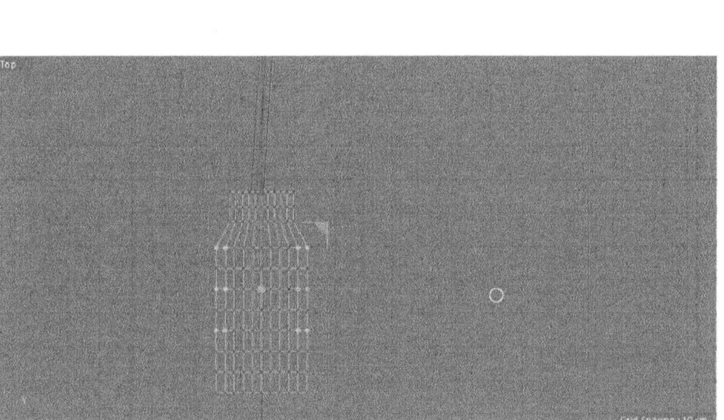

Figure 3-56 *The points to be selected*

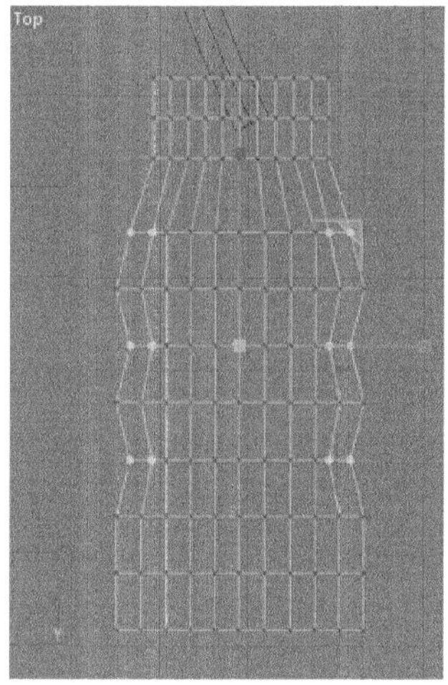

Figure 3-57 *Scaling the selected points*

15. Choose the **Edges** tool from the Modes Palette; *Cube* is displayed in the edge mode. Choose the **Live Selection** tool from the Command Palette. In the Attribute Manager, select the **Only Select Visible Elements** check box in the **Options** area. Select the edges of *Cube* in the Top viewport, as shown in Figure 3-58.

16. Scale down the selected edges along the X and Y axis to get the shape, as shown in Figure 3-59.

17. Press F1; the Perspective viewport is maximized. Choose the **Polygons** tool from the Modes Palette; *Cube* is displayed in the polygon mode. Select the polygons of *Cube* using the 9 key, as shown in Figure 3-60. Make sure the **Only Selected Visible Elements** check box is cleared.

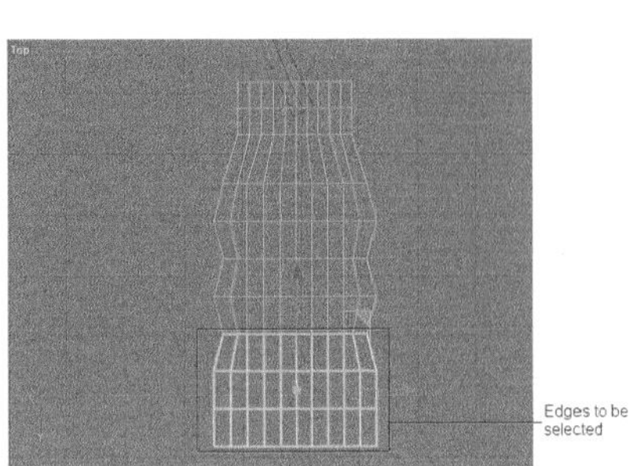

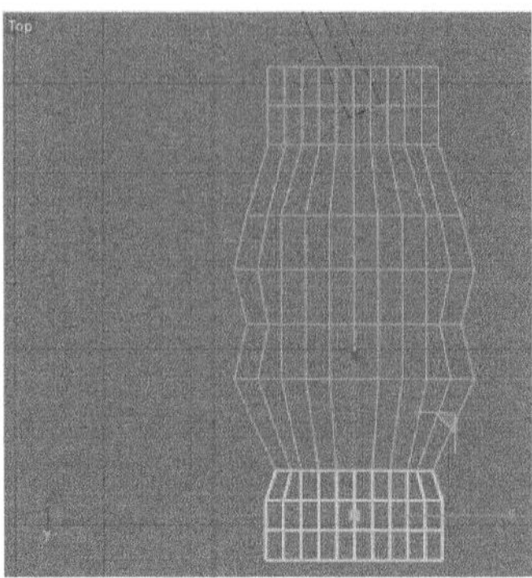

Figure 3-58 *The edges selected*

Figure 3-59 *Scaling the selected edges*

18. Right-click on the selected polygons of *Computer mouse*; a shortcut menu is displayed. Choose **Extrude** from the shortcut menu; the **Extrude** tool settings are displayed in the Attribute Manager. In the **Extrude** tool settings area, specify the value **10** in the **Offset** spinner and then press ENTER; the selected polygons of *Computer mouse* are extruded, as shown in Figure 3-61.

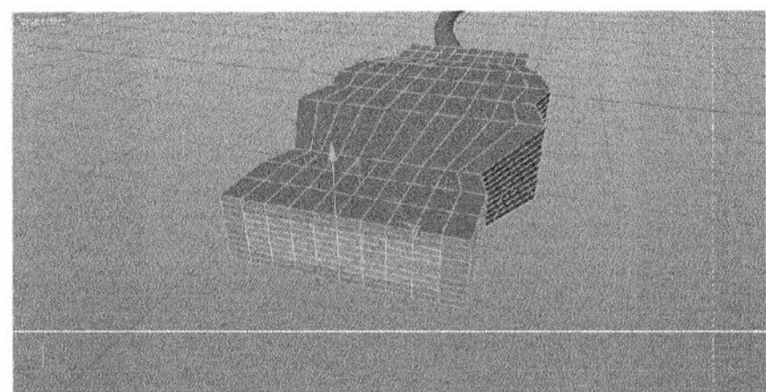

Figure 3-60 *The polygons to be selected*

Figure 3-61 *The extruded edge loop*

19. Choose the **Polygons** tool from the Modes Palette. Right-click on the Perspective viewport; a shortcut menu is displayed. Choose **Loop/Path Cut** from the shortcut menu; the **Loop/Path Cut** tool settings are displayed in the Attribute Manager. In the Attribute Manager, make sure **Loop** is selected in the **Mode** drop-down list. Next, add two edges, as shown in Figure 3-62.

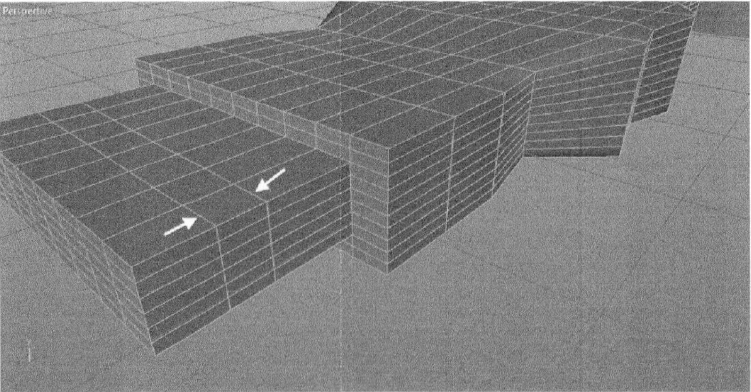

Figure 3-62 *The edges to be added*

20. Choose the **Polygons** tool from the Modes Palette; *Cube* is displayed in the polygon mode. Select the polygons of *Cube* using the **Live Selection** tool, as shown in Figure 3-63. Next, delete the selected polygons of *Cube*, refer to Figure 3-64.

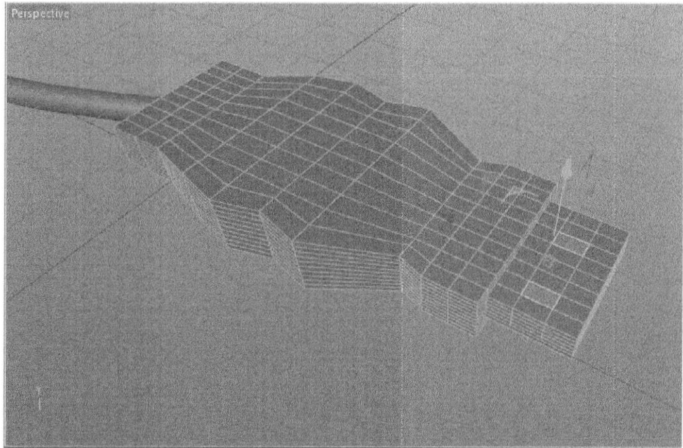

Figure 3-63 *The polygons to be selected*

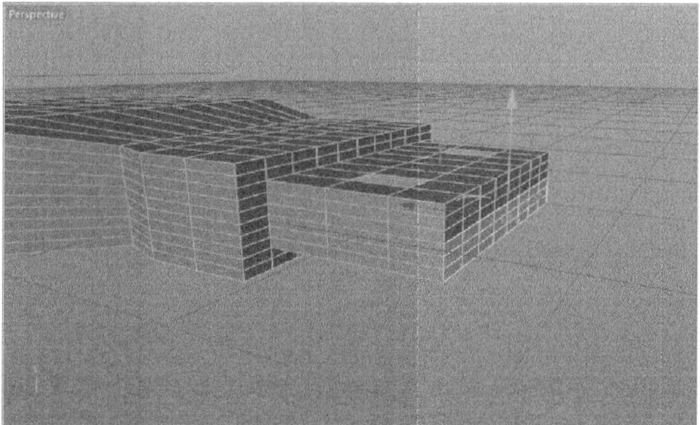

Figure 3-64 *The selected polygons*

21. Again, select the polygons of *Cube* using the **Live Selection tool**, as shown in Figure 3-64. Next, delete the selected polygons of *Cube*, refer to Figure 3-65.

Changing the Background Color of the Scene

To change the background color of the scene to white in the final output, follow the steps given in Tutorial 1 of Chapter 2.

Saving and Rendering the Scene

In this section, you will save and render the scene. You can also view the final render of the scene by downloading the file *c03_cinema4d_R20_rndr.zip* from *www.cadsofttech.com*. The path of the file is mentioned at the beginning of the chapter.

1. Choose **File > Save** from the main menu; the **Save File** dialog box is displayed. In this dialog box, browse to the location *\Documents\c4dR20\c03*.

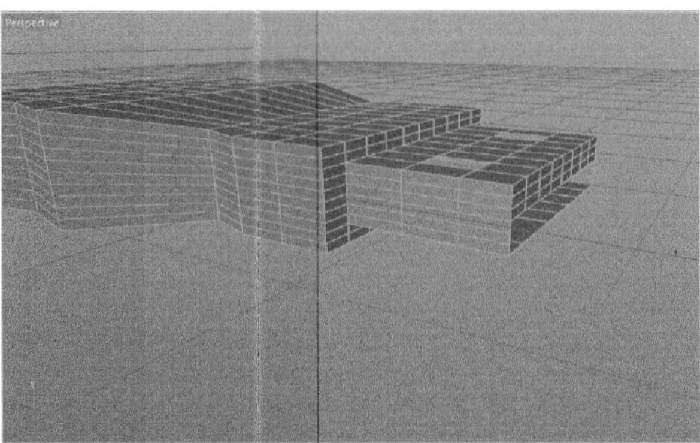

Figure 3-65 The deleted polygons

2. Enter **c03tut1** in the **File name** text box and then choose the **Save** button.

3. In the Perspective viewport, set the camera angle using the Viewport Navigation Tools. Next, choose the **Render to Picture Viewer** tool from the Command Palette. Alternatively, press SHIFT+R; the **Picture Viewer** window is displayed.

4. In the **Picture Viewer** window, choose **File > Save as**; the **Save** dialog box is displayed.

5. In the **Save** dialog box, choose the **OK** button; the **Save Dialog** dialog box is displayed. Next, browse to *\Documents\c4dR20\c03*. In the **File Name** text box, type **c03_tut1_rndr**. Next, choose the **Save** button; the file is saved at the desired location.

   Figure 3-1 displays the final output.

Tutorial 2

In this tutorial, you will create the model of a vase, as shown in Figure 3-66, using the **Cloner**, **Volume Builder**, and **Volume Mesher** tools. **(Expected time: 20 min)**

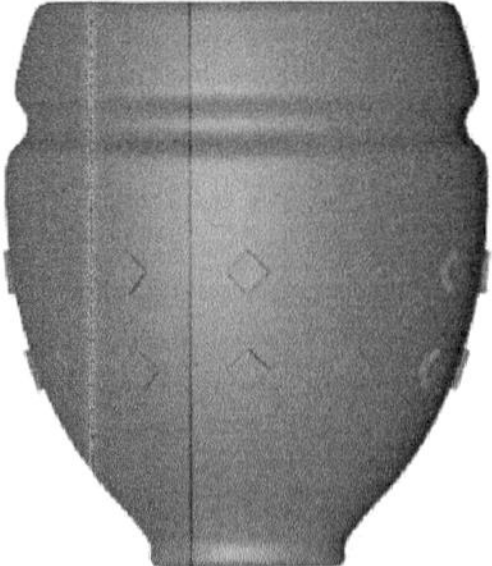

Figure 3-66 Model of a vase

The following steps are required to complete this tutorial:

a. Create the vase.
b. Create groove on the vase.

c. Create design on the vase.
c. Change the background color of the scene.
d. Save and render the scene.

Creating the Vase

In this section, you will create vase using the **Sphere** tool.

1. Press F4; the Front viewport is activated. Choose **Create > Object** from the main menu; a cascading menu is displayed. Next, choose **Sphere** from it; a sphere is created in the Front viewport and *Sphere* is added to the Object Manager. Choose **Display > Gouraud Shading** from the Menu in editor view; *Sphere* is displayed in the shading mode.

2. In the Attribute Manager, choose the **Basic** button; the **Basic Properties** area is displayed. In this area, enter **vase** in the **Name** text box; *Sphere* is renamed as *vase* in the Object Manager.

3. Make sure *vase* is selected in the Object Manager. In the Attribute Manager, choose the **Object** button; the **Object Properties** area is displayed. In the **Object Properties** area, set the parameters as follows:

   Radius: **200** Segments: **48**

4. Choose the **Coord.** button and enter **1.5** in the **S.Y** spinner; *vase* is displayed as shown in Figure 3-67.

5. Make sure *vase* is selected in the Front viewport. Now, choose the **Make Editable** tool from the Modes Palette; *vase* is converted into a polygonal object.

6. Choose the **Live Selection** tool from the Command Palette and then choose the **Polygons** tool from the Modes Palette; *vase* is displayed in the polygon mode. In the Attribute Manager, make sure the **Options** button is chosen. In the **Options** area, clear the **Only Select Visible Elements** check box. Next, choose the **Live Selection** tool and select the polygons of *vase* in the Front viewport, as shown in Figure 3-68. If required, decrease the size of the cursor for selection.

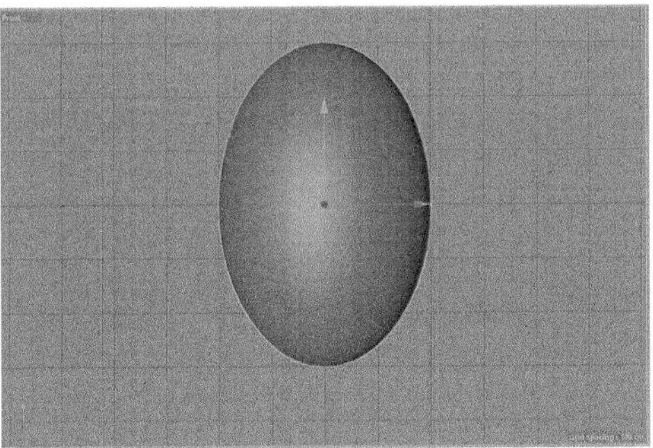

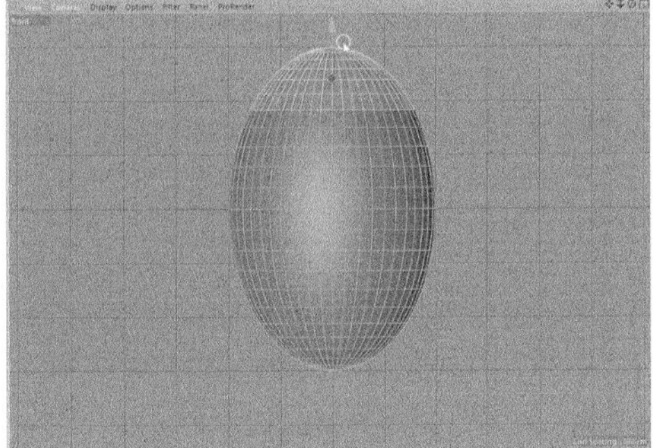

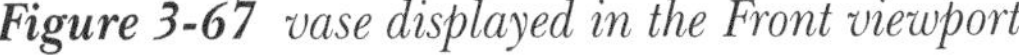

Figure 3-67 *vase displayed in the Front viewport*

Figure 3-68 *Selected Polygons*

7. Scale down the selected polygons uniformly, refer to Figure 3-69. Next scale the polygons only in Y-axis to set them on the upper edge of *vase*, refer to Figure 3-70.

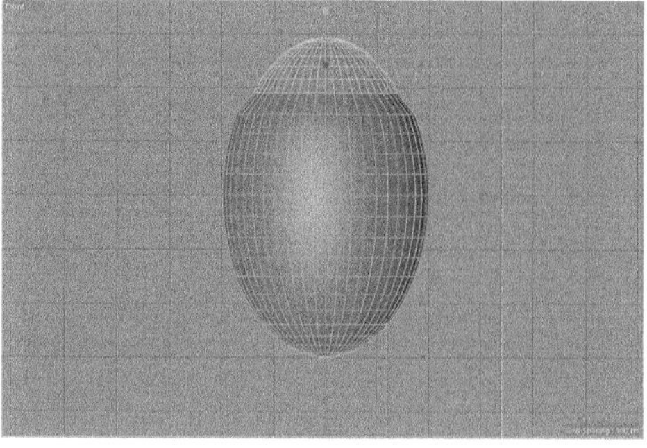

Figure 3-69 Selected polygons scaled uniformly

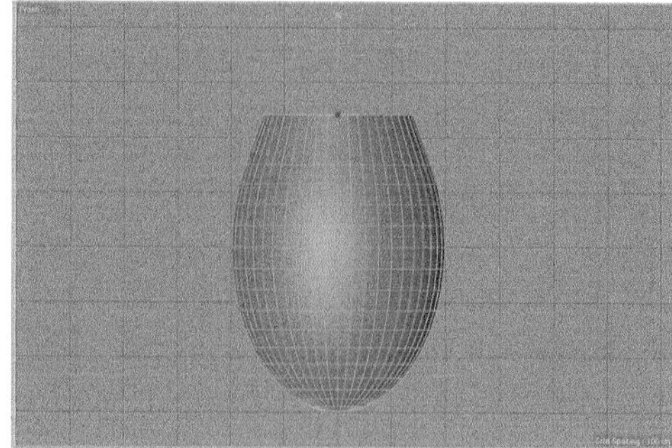

Figure 3-70 Selected Polygons scaled in Y-axis

8. Choose the **Move** tool from the Command Palette and move the selected polygons downword, as shown in Figure 3-71.

9. Right-click in the Front viewport; a shortcut menu is displayed. Choose **Extrude** from the shortcut menu; the **Extrude** tool settings are displayed in the Attribute Manager. In the **Extrude** tool settings area, make sure the **Options** button is chosen. In the **Options** area, sset -230 as the value in the Offset spinner and then press the ENTER key; the selected polygons are extruded in the Perspective viewport, as shown in Figure 3-72.

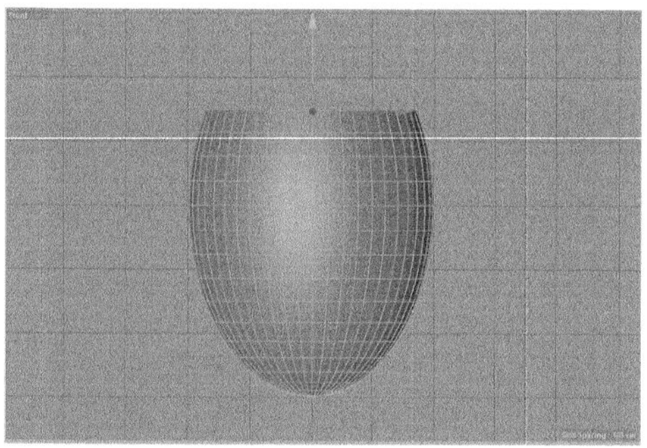

Figure 3-71 Selected polygons moved downwords

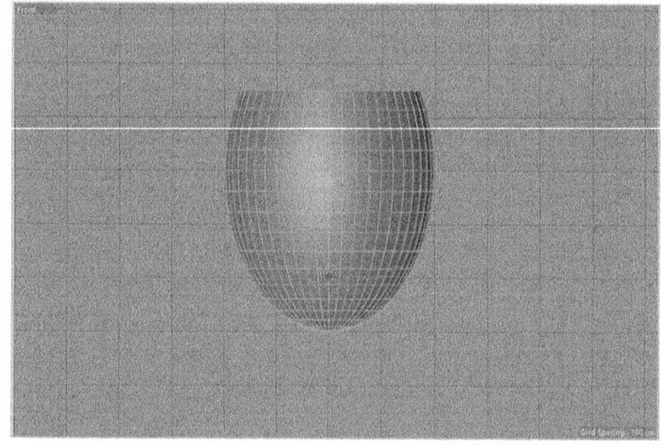

Figure 3-72 Selected Polygons Extruded

10. Choose the **Live Selection** tool and select the bottommost polygons of *vase*, as shown in Figure 3-73. Next, activate the **Scale** tool and scale these polygons in Y-axis as shown in Figure 3-74.

11. Make sure the scaled polygons are selected. Next, right-click in the Front viewport; a shortcut menu is displayed. Choose **Bevel** from the shortcut menu; the **Bevel** tool settings are displayed in the Attribute Manager. In the **Bevel** tool settings area, make sure the **Tool Option** button is chosen. Next, set **-40** in the **Offset** spinner and **4** in the **Subdivision** spinner and then press the ENTER key; the selected polygons are beveled in the Perspective viewport, as shown in Figure 3-75.

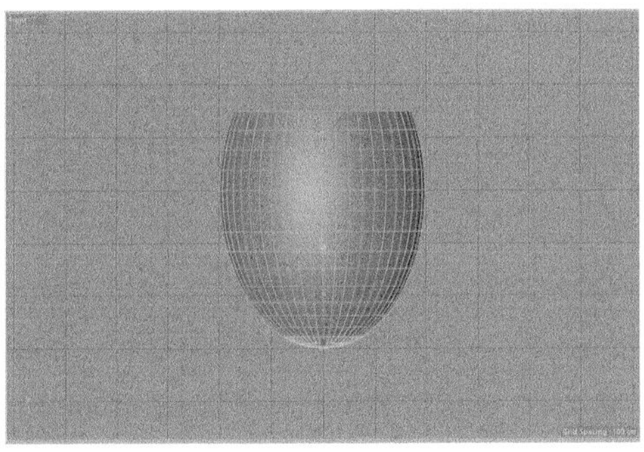

Figure 3-73 Bottommost polygons selected

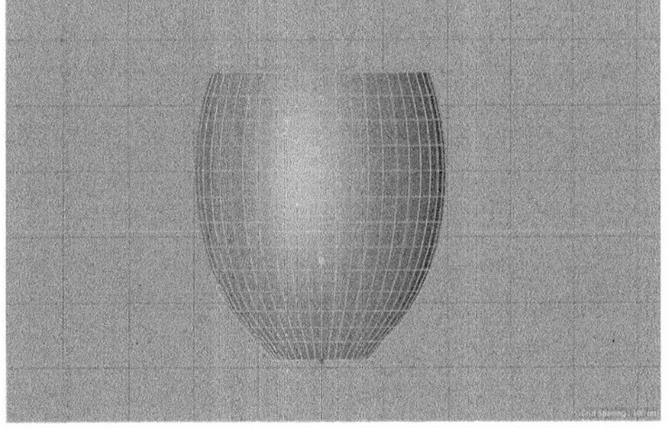

Figure 3-74 Selected polygons scaled in y-axis

Creating Groove on the Vase

In this section, you will create groove on vase using the **Torus**, **Volume Builder**, and **Volume Mesher** tools.

1. Choose **Create > Object** from the main menu; a cascading menu is displayed. Next, choose **Torus** from it; a torus is created in the Front viewport and *Torus* is added to the Object Manager.

2. Double-click on *Torus* in the Object Manager; a text box is displayed. Enter **ring** in the text box; *Torus* is renamed as *ring*.

3. Make sure *ring* is selected in the Object Manager. In the Attribute Manager, choose the **Object** button; the **Object Properties** area is displayed. In the **Object Properties** area, enter **20** in the **Pipe Radius** spinner.

4. Choose the **Coord.** button and enter **51** in the **P.Y** spinner; *Torus* is moved upwards, as shown in Figure 3-76.

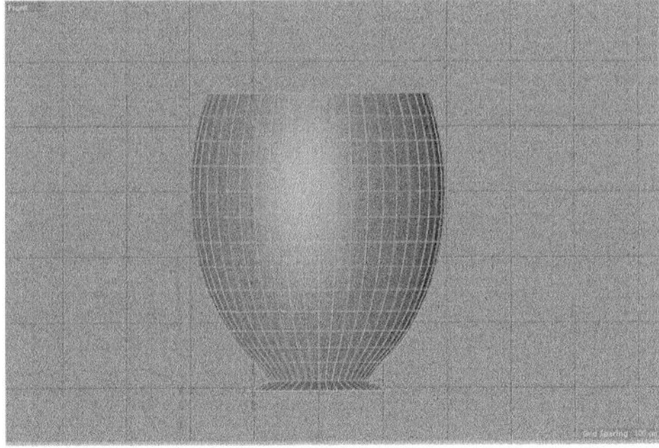

Figure 3-75 Selected polygons beveled

Figure 3-76 Torus moved upwards

5. Choose **Volume > Volume Builder** from the main menu, as shown in Figure 3-77; *Volume Builder* is added to the Object Manager.

6. Select *vase* in the Object Manager. Next, press and hold the left mouse button and then drag it on *Volume Builder*; *vase* is connected to *Volume Builder*. Next, select *ring* in the Object Manager and press and hold the left mouse button and then drag it on *Volume Builder; ring* is also connected to *Volume Builder.* Notice that vase and ring turns white and are converted to voxel objects, refer to Figure 3-78.

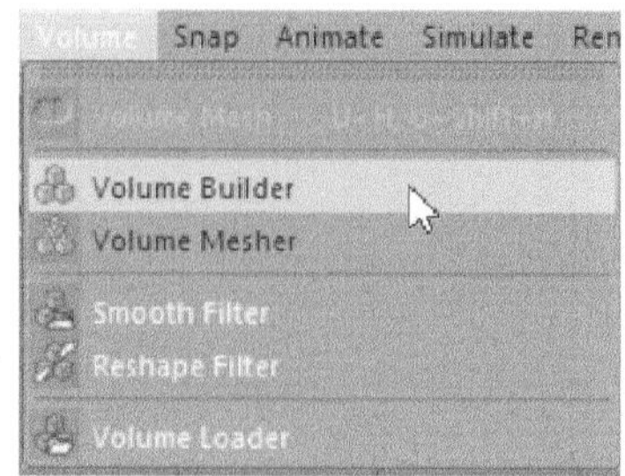

Figure 3-77 *Choosing* ***Volume Builder*** *from the* ***Volume*** *menu*

7. Select *Volume Builder* in the Object Manager. In the Attribute Manager, make sure the **Object** button is chosen. In the **Object Properties** area, enter **1** in the **Voxel Size** spinner; *vase* and *ring* are smoothened comparatively, refer to Figure 3-79.

Figure 3-78 *Voxel objects displayed*

Figure 3-79 *Voxel objects smoothened*

8. Select **Subtract** from the **Mode** drop-down list located next to *ring*, as shown in Figure 3-80; groove is created on *vase*, as shown in Figure 3-81.

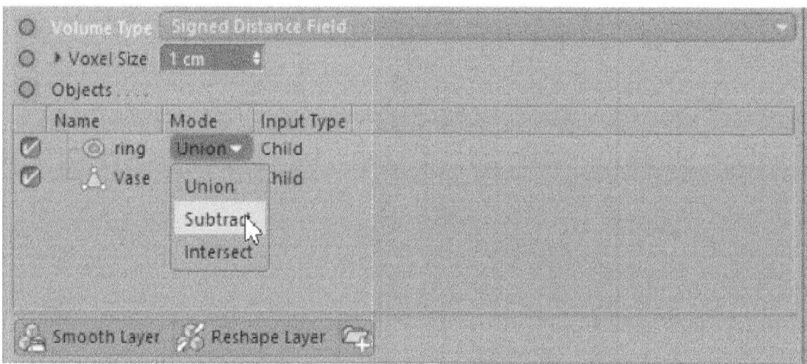

Figure 3-80 *Choosing* ***Subtract*** *from the* ***Mode*** *drop-down list*

9. Choose **Volume > Volume Mesher** from the main menu; *Volume Mesher* is added to the Object Manager.

10. Select *Volume Builder* in the Object Manager. Next, press and hold the left mouse button and then drag it on *Volume Mesher*; *Volume Builder* is connected to *Volume Mesher* and *vase* is converted to polygon object. Also, notice that *vase* turns dark grey, refer to Figure 3-82.

Next, you will smoothen *vase*.

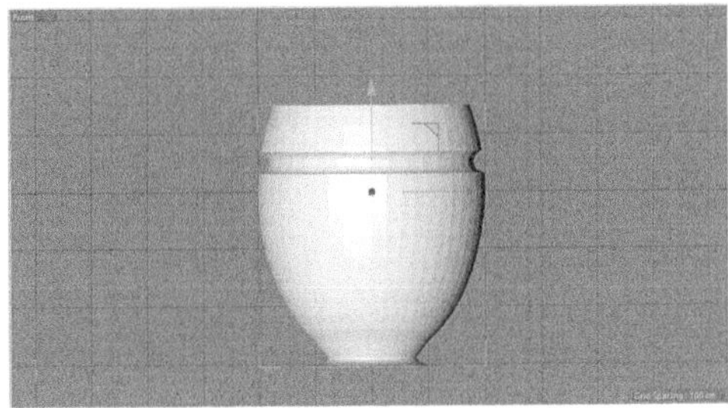

Figure 3-81 Groove created on vase

Figure 3-82 vase turns dark grey

11. Select *Volume Builder* in the Object Manager. In the Attribute Manager, make sure the **Object** button is chosen. In the **Objects** area, select **ring** from the list displayed and then choose the **Smooth Layer** button; **Smooth Layer** is added to the list in the **Objects** area, as shown in Figure 3-83.

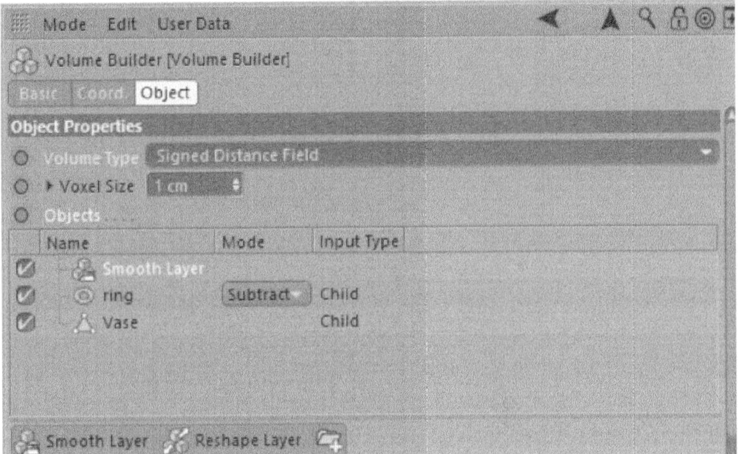

Figure 3-83 ***Smooth Layer*** *added to the* ***Objects*** *area*

12. In the Attribute Manager, make sure **Smooth Layer** is selected in the **Objects** area. In the **Filter** area, enter **4** in the **Voxel Distance** spinner and enter **2** in the **Iterations** spinner; *vase* is smoothened, as shown in Figure 3-84.

Creating Design on the Vase

In this section, you will create design on vase using the **Cloner**, **Volume Builder**, and **Volume Mesher** tools.

1. Choose **Create > Object** from the main menu; a cascading menu is displayed. Next, choose **Cube** from the cascading menu; a cube is created in the Front viewport and *Cube* is added to the Object Manager.

2. Make sure *Cube* is selected in the Object Manager. In the **Object Properties** area of the Attribute Manager, enter **25** in the **Size.X**, **Size.Y** spinners, and **10** in the **Size.Z** spinner.

3. Choose **MoGraph > Cloner** from the main menu, as shown in Figure 3-85; *Cloner* is added to the Object Manager.

Figure 3-84 vase smoothened

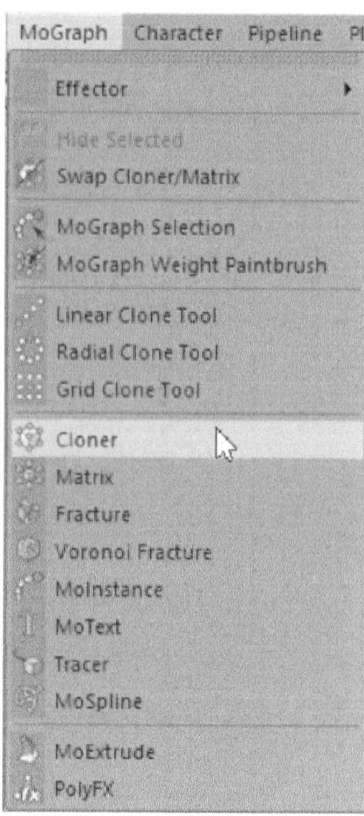

*Figure 3-85 Choosing **Cloner** from the **MoGraph** menu*

4. Select *Cube* in the Object Manager. Next, press and hold the left mouse button and then drag it on *Cloner*; *Cube* is connected to *Cloner*.

5. Select *Cloner* in the Object Manager. In the Attribute Manager, make sure the **Object** button is chosen. In the **Object Properties** area, select **Radial** from the **Mode** drop-down list and **XZ** from the **Plane** drop-down list. Also, enter **12** and **194** in the **Count** and **Radius** spinners, respectively.

6. In the Attribute Manager, choose the **Transform** button and enter **-67** in the **P.Y** spinner in the **Transform** area. Next, enter **-6** and **-45** in the **R.P** and **R.B** spinners, respectively. *Cloner* is placed on *vase* as shown in Figure 3-86.

7. Make sure that *Cloner* is selected in the Object Manager. Now, create a copy of *Cloner* by pressing both the CTRL key and the left mouse button. Now, drag the cursor and release the left mouse button; a copy of *Cloner* is created in the Object Manager with the name *Cloner.1*.

8. Make sure *Cloner.1* is selected in the Object Manager. In the Attribute Manager, choose the **Object** button. Next, enter **174** in the **Radius** spinner.

9. Choose the **Transform** button and enter **-145** in the **P.Y** spinner. Also, enter **-20** in the **R. P** spinner; *Cloner.1* is placed on *vase* as shown in Figure 3-87.

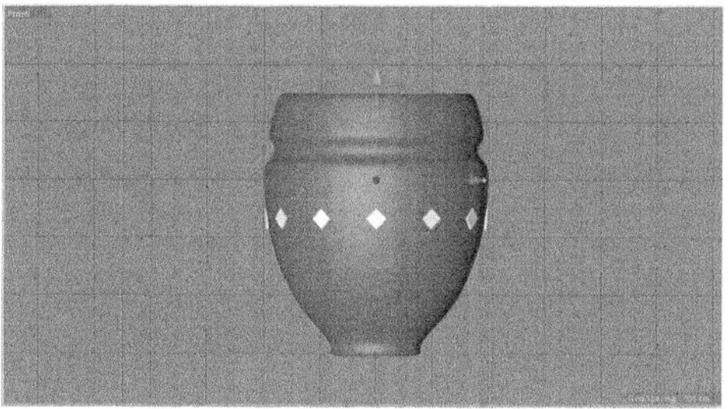

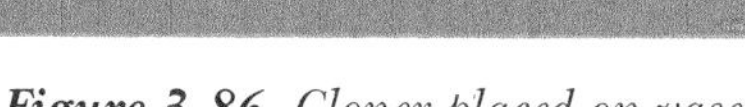

Figure 3-86 *Cloner placed on vase*

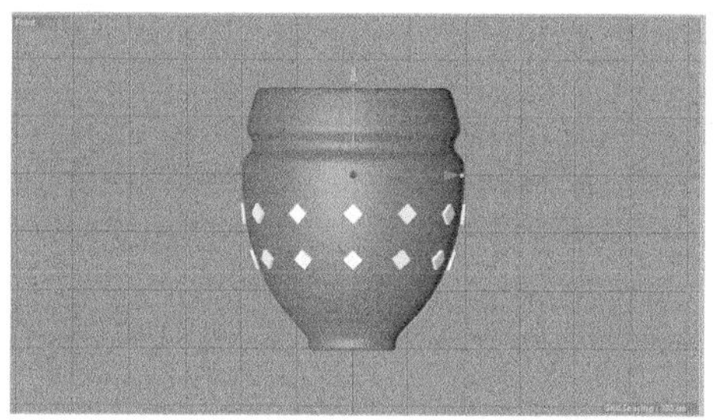

Figure 3-87 *Cloner.1 placed on vase*

10. Select *Cloner* in the Object Manager. Next, press and hold the left mouse button and then drag it on *Volume Builder*; *Cloner* is connected to *Volume Builder*. Next, select *Cloner.1* in the Object Manager and press and hold the left mouse button and then drag it on *Volume Builder; Cloner.1* is also connected to *Volume Builder. Figure 3-88* shows vase displayed in the viewport and Figure 3-89 shows list of all the objects in the Object Manager.

Figure 3-88 *vase displayed in the viewport*

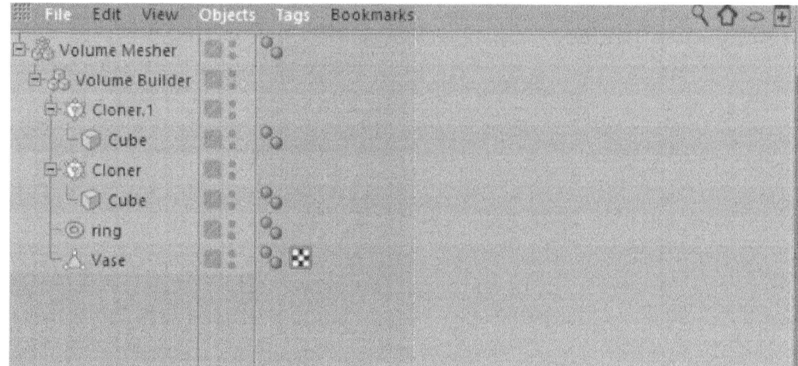

Figure 3-89 *List of all the objects in the Object Manager*

Changing the Background Color of the Scene

To change the background color of the scene to white in the final output, follow the steps given in Tutorial 1 of Chapter 2.

Saving and Rendering the Scene

In this section, you will save and render the scene. You can also view the final render of the model by downloading the file *c03_cinema4d_r20_rndr.zip* from *www.cadsofttech.com*. The path of the file is mentioned at the beginning of the chapter.

1. Choose **File > Save** from the main menu; the **Save File** dialog box is displayed. In this dialog box, browse to the location *\Documents\c4dR20\c03*.

2. Enter **c03tut2** in the **File name** text box and then choose the **Save** button.

3. In the Perspective viewport, set the camera angle using the Viewport Navigation Tools located at the extreme top right of the Perspective viewport. Next, choose the **Render to Picture Viewer** tool from the Command Palette. Alternatively, press SHIFT+R; the **Picture Viewer** window is displayed.

4. In the **Picture Viewer** window, choose **File > Save as**; the **Save** dialog box is displayed.

5. In the **Save** dialog box, choose the **OK** button; the **Save Dialog** dialog box is displayed. Next, browse to *\Documents\c4dR20\c03*. In the **File Name** text box, type **c03_tut2_rndr**. Next, choose the **Save** button; the file is saved at the desired location.

   Figure 3-66 displays the final output.

EXERCISE

The rendered output of the model used in the exercise can be accessed by downloading the *c03_cinema4d_R20_exr.zip* file from *www.cadsofttech.com*. The path of the file is as follows: *Textbooks > Animation and Visual Effects > MAXON CINEMA 4D > MAXON CINEMA 4D R20 Studio for Novices*

Exercise 1

Using the polygon modeling tools, create the model of the chair, as shown in Figure 3-90.

(Expected time: 30 min)

Figure 3-90 *The model of a chair*

Chapter 4

Sculpting

Learning Objectives

After completing this chapter, you will be able to:

- *Use various sculpting tools and brushes*
- *Sculpt polygon objects*

INTRODUCTION

Sculpting is a traditional modeling method which is entirely different from the NURBS and polygon modeling. It is very much similar to clay modeling and has tools that are used in other conventional modeling methods. In this chapter, you will learn the techniques to create models using the sculpting brushes.

TUTORIAL

All the files used in the tutorials can be downloaded from the CADSoft website (www.*cadsofttech*.com). These files are compressed in zip file format and are required to be extracted before using them in the tutorials. The path of the files is as follows: *Textbooks > Animation and Visual Effects > MAXON CINEMA 4D > MAXON CINEMA 4D R20 Studio for Novices*

Next, you need to browse to *\Documents\c4dR20* and create a new folder in it with the name *c04*. Next, extract the contents of the zip file in this folder.

Tutorial 1

In this tutorial, you will create the model of a candle, as shown in Figure 4-1.

(Expected time: 30 min)

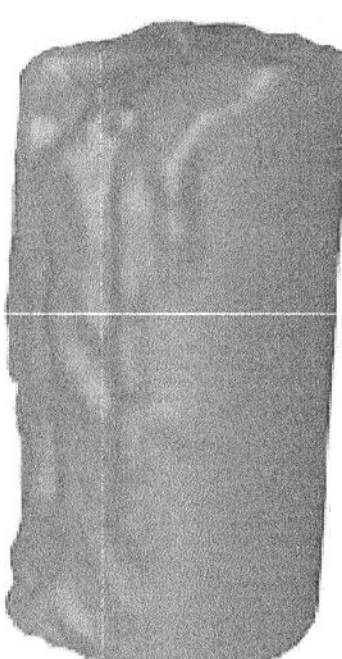

Figure 4-1 *The model of a candle*

The following steps are required to complete this tutorial:

a. Create the base of the candle.
b. Sculpt the candle.
c. Create the wick of the candle.
d. Change the background color of the scene.
e. Save and render the scene.

Creating the Base of the Candle

In this section, you will create the base of the candle using the **Cylinder** tool.

1. Choose **Create > Object** from the main menu; a cascading menu is displayed. Choose **Cylinder** from it; a cylinder is created in the Perspective viewport and the *Cylinder* object is added to the Object Manager.

2. Press SHIFT+V; the **Viewport [Perspective]** area is displayed in the Attribute Manager. Make sure the **Sel.: Bounding Box** check box is selected from the **Active Object** area.

   The **Sel.: Bounding Box** check box is used to toggle the display of the selection outline in the viewport.

3. Make sure *Cylinder* is selected in the Object Manager. In the Attribute Manager, make sure the **Object** button is chosen. In the **Object Properties** area, set the parameters as follows:

   Radius:**100** Height: **366** Height Segments: **100**
   Rotation Segments:**100**

   The **Rotation Segments** option is used to determine the number of subdivisions of cylinder along its circumference. More the number of subdivisions, smoother will be the cylinder.

4. In the Attribute Manager, choose the **Caps** button; the **Caps** area is displayed. In this area, make sure the **Caps** check box is selected. Next, enter **36** in the **Segments** spinner.

   The **Segments** spinner located below the **Caps** check box is used to determine the number of subdivisions vertically.

5. In the **Caps** area, select the **Fillet** check box and then set the parameters as follows:

   Segments: **36** Radius: **7**

6. In the Attribute Manager, choose the **Basic** button; the **Basic Properties** area is displayed. In this area, enter **Candle** in the **Name** text box; the cylinder is renamed as *Candle* in the Object Manager.

7. Make sure *Candle* is selected in the Object Manager and choose the **Make Editable** tool from the Modes Palette; the *Candle* is converted into a polygonal object.

8. Choose the **Polygons** tool from the Modes Palette; the *Candle* is displayed in the polygon mode in the viewport.

9. Press F2; the Top viewport is maximized. Invoke the **Live Selection** tool from the Command Palette. In the Attribute Manager, choose the **Options** button if it is not chosen; the **Options** area is displayed. In this area, make sure the **Only Select Visible Elements** check box is selected.

10. Select the polygons in the Top viewport, as shown in Figure 4-2.

11. Press F1; the Perspective viewport is maximized. Make sure the polygons of *Candle* are selected in the Perspective viewport. Next, move the selected polygons of *Candle* downward, as shown in Figure 4-3.

12. Invoke the **Scale** tool from the Command Palette and uniformly scale down the selected polygons of *Candle*, as shown in Figure 4-4.

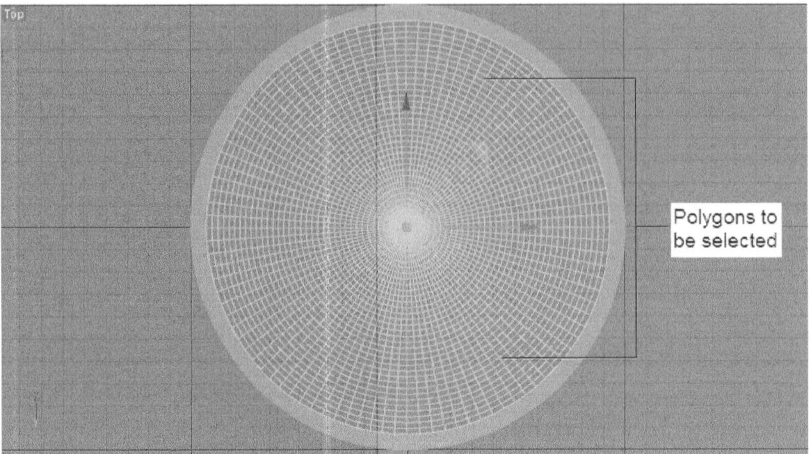

Figure 4-2 The polygons to be selected

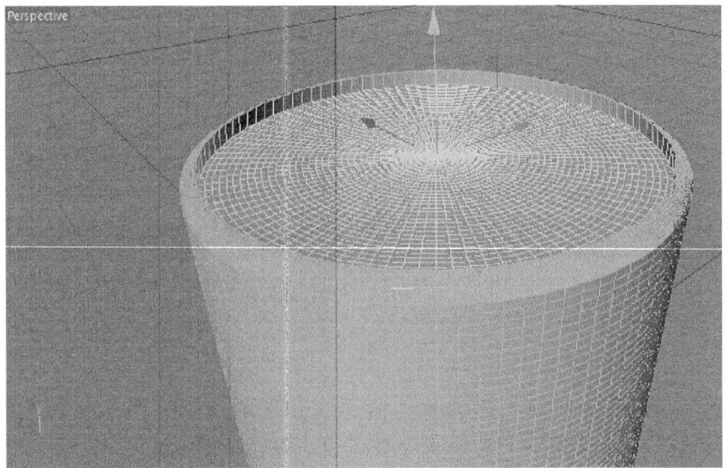

Figure 4-3 Moving the polygons of the Candle downward

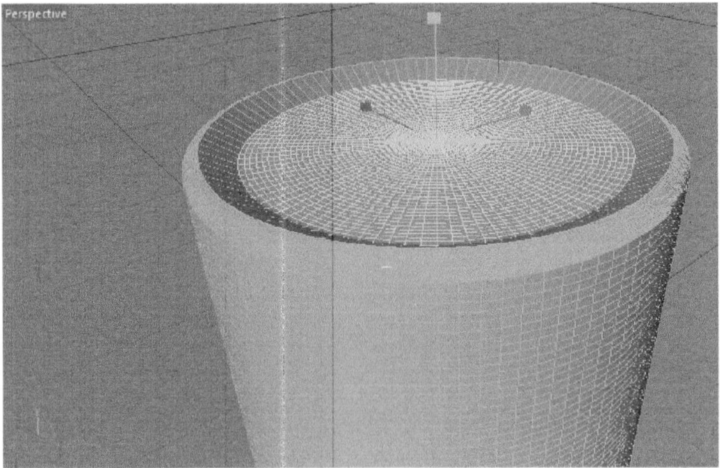

Figure 4-4 Scaling down the polygons of Candle

Sculpting the Candle

In this section, you will sculpt *Candle* using the sculpting brushes.

1. Select **Sculpt** from the **Layout** drop-down list located in the extreme right corner of the interface, as shown in Figure 4-5; the **Sculpt** layout is displayed with the **Sculpting** menu on the right of the viewport, refer to Figure 4-6.

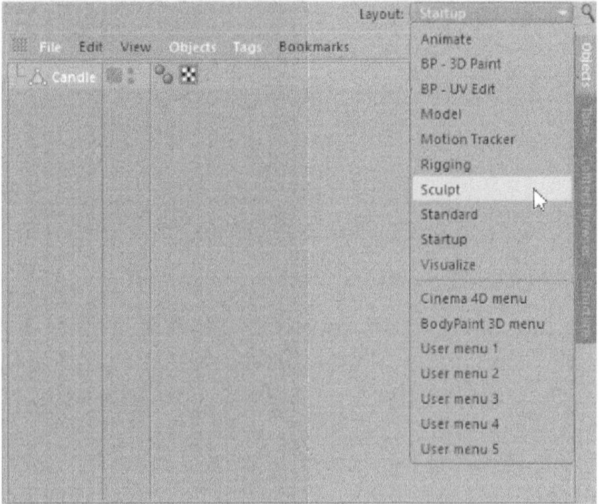

Figure 4-5 *Selecting **Sculpt** from the **Layout** drop-down list*

Figure 4-6 *The **Sculpt** layout*

2. Choose the **Model** tool from the Modes Palette. Next, choose the **Subdivide** tool from the **Sculpting** menu; the *Candle* is subdivided. Next, choose the **Objects** tab to display the Object Manager. In the Object Manager, you will notice that the **Sculpt Expression [Sculpt]** tag is added, as shown in Figure 4-7.

*Figure 4-7 The **Sculpt Expression [Sculpt]** tag added to the Object Manager*

The **Subdivide** tool is one of the most important tools in sculpting. It is used to create the points on the surface of the object to be sculpted using sculpting brushes. On increasing the subdivision level of an object, the file size is also increased.

The **Sculpt Expression [Sculpt]** tag is automatically created on choosing the **Subdivide** tool. It consists of all the sculpting information of the object to which it is assigned.

3. Choose **Display > Gouraud** from the Menu in editor view, if not already chosen; *Candle* is displayed in shading mode. Choose the **Pull** tool from the **Sculpting** menu. Next, press and hold the left mouse button and move the brush downward on *Candle* in the Perspective viewport to add strokes to the *Candle*, refer to Figure 4-8.

   The **Pull** tool is used to extrude the mesh toward the camera.

4. Make sure the **Pull** tool is chosen in the **Sculpting** menu. In the **Attributes** tab, select the **Invert** check box in the **Settings** area, as shown in Figure 4-9.

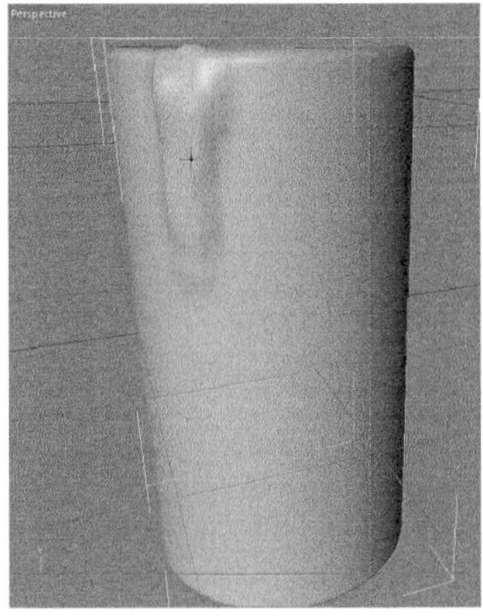

Figure 4-8 The strokes added

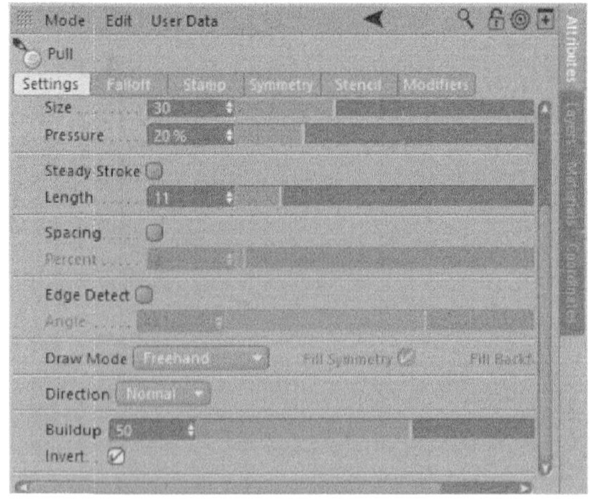

*Figure 4-9 The **Invert** check box selected in the **Settings** area in the Attribute Manager*

The **Invert** check box is used to reverse the effect of the brush. It pushes down the points of the surface.

5. Again, press and hold the left mouse button and move the brush downward on *Candle* in the Perspective viewport, refer to Figure 4-10.

6. Choose the **Wax** tool from the **Sculpting** menu. Next, press and hold the left mouse button and add strokes on the top of *Candle*, as shown in Figure 4-11.

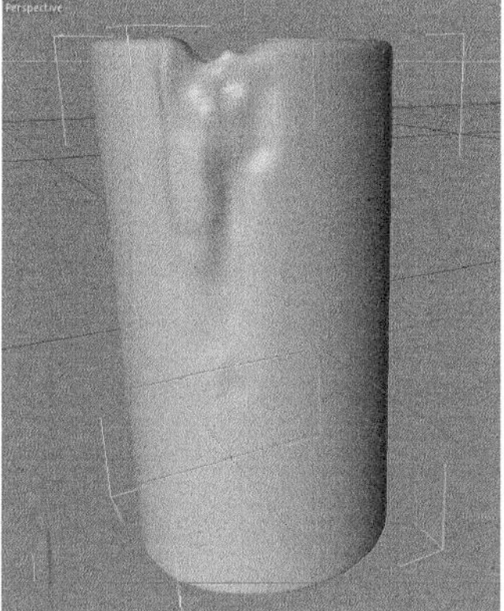

Figure 4-10 *Strokes added to the Candle*

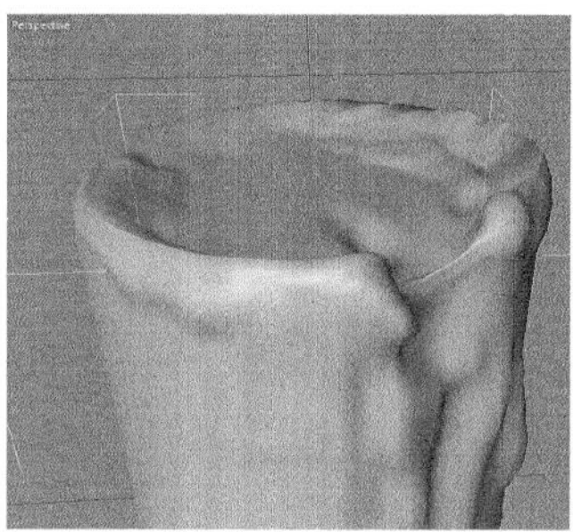

Figure 4-11 *Strokes added on the top of Candle*

The **Wax** tool is used to apply or remove the effect of material from the surface of the object. It can be compared to applying or removing clay or wax on a real-world object.

7. Choose the **Inflate** tool from the **Sculpting** menu. In the **Attributes** tab, select the **Steady Stroke** check box in the **Settings** area and enter **7** in the **Length** spinner. Next, press and hold the left mouse button and add strokes to the bottom of *Candle* in the Perspective viewport, refer to Figure 4-12.

   The **Inflate** tool is used to move the vertices of the surface along the direction of normals to create bumps on the surface. The **Steady Stroke** check box is used to attach a string that helps in making the brush straight. The **Length** spinner is used to define the length of the string.

8. Make sure the **Inflate** tool is chosen in the **Sculpting** menu. In the **Attributes** tab, set the parameters as follows:

   Size: **24** Pressure: **26.2**

   Next, press and hold the left mouse button and add strokes to the bottom of *Candle*, refer to Figure 4-13.

9. Choose the **Pull** tool from the **Sculpting** menu. In the **Attributes** tab, set the parameters as follows:

   Size: **25** Pressure: **30**

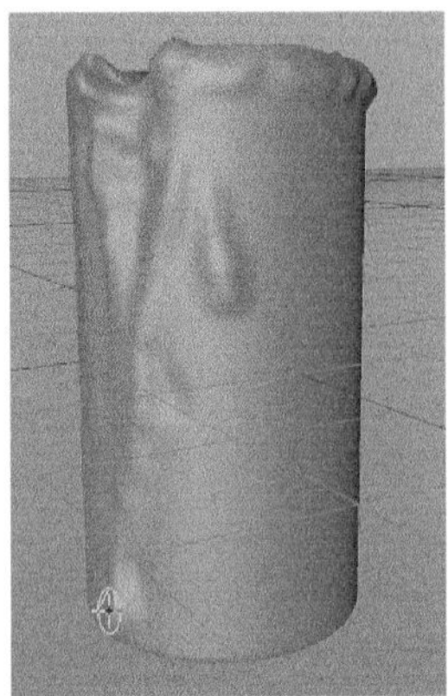

Figure 4-12 Adding strokes to the bottom of the Candle

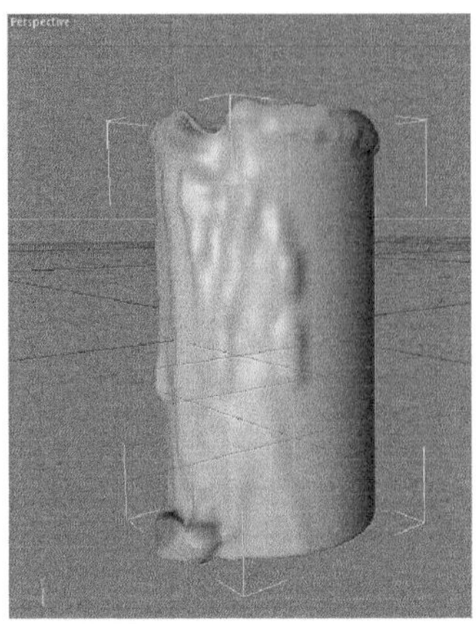

Figure 4-13 More strokes added to the bottom of the Candle

10. Press and hold the left mouse button and add strokes to the top of *Candle* in the Perspective viewport, as shown in Figure 4-14.

11. Choose the **Smooth** tool from the **Sculpting** menu. In the **Attributes** tab, set the parameters as follows:

    Size: **10** Pressure: **12**

12. Press and hold the left mouse button and add strokes to the top of *Candle* in the Perspective viewport to smoothen it, refer to Figure 4-15. Press SPACEBAR to deactivate the current tool.

    The **Smooth** tool is used to smoothen the surface of the object while sculpting.

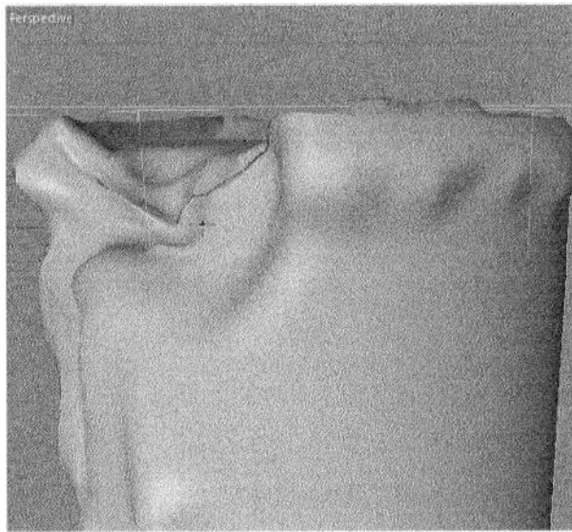

Figure 4-14 Adding strokes to the top of Candle

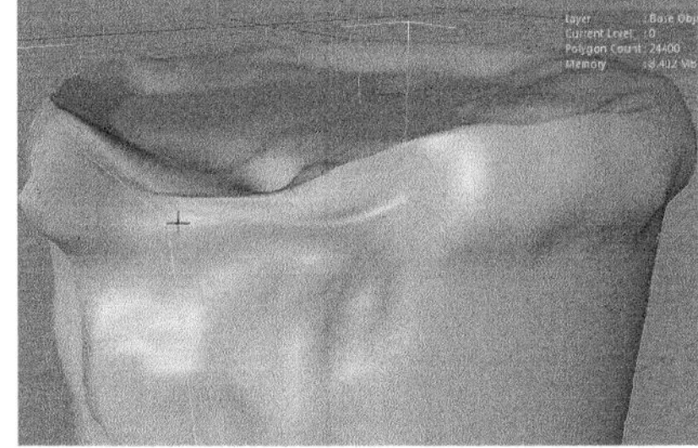

Figure 4-15 The smoothened surface of Candle

Creating the Wick of the Candle

In this section, you will create the wick of *Candle* using the **Cylinder** tool.

1. Select **Standard** from the **Layout** drop-down list located in the extreme right corner of the interface; the **Standard** layout is displayed. Choose **Create > Object** from the main menu; a cascading menu is displayed. Choose **Cylinder** from it; a cylinder is created in the Perspective viewport and the *Cylinder* object is added to the Object Manager.

2. Make sure *Cylinder* is selected in the Object Manager. In the Attribute Manager, choose the **Object** button; the **Object Properties** area is displayed. In this area, set the parameters as follows:

   Radius: **1** Height: **59** Height Segments: **25**

3. Choose the **Coord** button; the **Coordinates** area is displayed. In this area, enter **174.8** in the **P . Y** spinner.

4. In the Attribute Manager, choose the **Basic** button; the **Basic Properties** area is displayed. In this area, enter **Wick** in the **Name** text box; the cylinder is renamed as *Wick* in the Object Manager.

5. Make sure *Wick* is selected in the Object Manager and then choose the **Make Editable** tool from the Modes Palette; *Wick* is converted into a polygonal object.

6. Choose the **Bend** tool from the Command Palette; the *Bend* object is added to the Object Manager.

7. Make sure *Bend* is selected in the Object Manager. Press and hold the left mouse button on *Bend* and drag it to *Wick* in the Object Manager; the *Bend* object is connected to *Wick* in the Object Manager.

8. Make sure *Bend* object is selected in the Object Manager. In the Attribute Manager, choose the **Object** button; the **Object Properties** area is displayed. In this area, choose the **Fit to Parent** button and then set the other parameters as follows:

   Strength: **51** Angle: **-16**

   Figure 4-16 displays the *Bend* object applied to *Wick* in the Perspective viewport.

***Figure 4-16** The Wick of the Candle*

Changing the Background Color of the Scene

To change the background color of the scene to white in the final output, follow the steps given in Tutorial 1 of Chapter 2.

Saving and Rendering the Scene

In this section, you will save and render the scene. You can also view the final render of the scene by downloading the file *c04_cinema4d_r20_rndr.zip* from *www.cadsofttech.com*. The path of the file is mentioned at the beginning of the chapter.

1. Choose **File > Save** from the main menu; the **Save File** dialog box is displayed. In this dialog box, browse to the location *\Documents*.

2. Enter **c04tut1** in the **File name** text box and then choose the **Save** button.

3. Choose the **Render to Picture Viewer** tool from the Command Palette; the **Picture Viewer** window is displayed.

4. In the **Picture Viewer** window, choose **File > Save as**; the **Save** dialog box is displayed.

5. In the **Save** dialog box, select **JPEG** from the **Format** drop-down list and then choose the **OK** button; the **Save Dialog** dialog box is displayed. Next, browse to *\Documents\c4dR20\c04*. In the **File name** text box, enter **c04_tut1_rndr**. Next, choose the **Save** button; the rendered image is saved at the specified location.

   Figure 4-1 displays the final output.

EXERCISE

The rendered output of the model used in the exercise can be accessed by downloading the *c04_cinema4d_r20_exr.zip* file from *www.cadsofttech.com*. The path of the file is as follows: *Textbooks > Animation and Visual Effects > MAXON CINEMA 4D > MAXON CINEMA 4D R20 for Novices.*

Exercise 1

Using various sculpting tools, sculpt a barrel with cracks, as shown in Figure 4-17.

(Expected time: 10 min)

Figure 4-17 *A barrel with cracks*

Chapter 5

Texturing

Learning Objectives

After completing this chapter, you will be able to:

- *Work with the Material Manager*
- *Apply textures and colors to the objects*
- *Use node based materials*

INTRODUCTION

The appearance of the surface of an object in CINEMA 4D is defined by the material applied to it. The material describes how an object reflects or transmits light. When light hits an object, some of it gets absorbed and some is reflected. The smoother the surface, the shiner it will be. In this chapter, you will learn to assign various materials and textures to the objects in the scene to make them more realistic.

NODE BASED MATERIALS

In CINEMA 4D R20, uber, node, and some in-built node based materials are introduced, which can be used to create complex materials.

To create a uber material, choose **Create > New Uber Material** from the Material Manager; a material with the name **Uber** will be created in the Material Manager. Uber material is a generic material which is simple and very easy to use. You can edit this material in the Attribute Manager and in the **Material Editor** window. To edit node flow of this material, right-click on the material in the Material Manager and choose **Node Editor** from the shortcut menu displayed; the **Node Editor** window will be displayed with the **Uber Material.1** node. Right-click on this node and choose **Edit Asset** from the shortcut menu displayed; a node flow will be displayed in the **Node Editor** window. You can now edit this node flow as per the requirement.

To create a node material, choose **Create > New Node Material** from the Material Manager; a material with the name **Node** will be created and displayed in the Material Manager. Double-click on this material in the Material Manager; the **Node Editor** window will be displayed with default connected nodes, **Diffuse.1** and **Material.1**. In the **Node Editor** window, the **Assets** area contains variety of nodes under various categories to modify the node material. You can also add number of inputs to theses nodes, replace nodes, organize nodes, create asset, and so on in the **Node Editor** window. Besides, you can edit this node material in the Attribute Manager and in the **Material Editor** window also.

To use in-built node based materials such as car paint, ceramic, concrete, marble, and so on, choose **Create > Node Materials** from the Material Manager; a cascading menu will be displayed. Choose desired material from the cascading menu; the corresponding node material will be displayed in the Material Manager. This material can be modified in the Attribute Manager, in the **Node Editor** window, and in the **Material Editor** window.

TUTORIALS

All the files used in the tutorials can be downloaded from the CADSoft website (www.cadsofttech.com). These files are compressed in zip file format and are required to be extracted before using them in the tutorials. The path of the files is as follows: *Textbooks > Animation and Visual Effects > MAXON CINEMA 4D > MAXON CINEMA 4D R20 Studio for Novices*

Next, you need to browse to *\Documents\c4dR20* and create a new folder in it with the name *c05*. Next, extract the contents of the zip file in this folder.

Tutorial 1

In this tutorial, you will apply texture to the model of a dice. The final output of the textured model is shown in Figure 5-1. **(Expected time: 25 min)**

Figure 5-1 *The textured model of a dice*

The following steps are required to complete this tutorial:

a. Open the file.
b. Apply shader to the dice model.
c. Apply shader to the floor.
d. Change the background color of the scene.
e. Save and render the scene.

Opening the File

In this section, you will open the dice file.

1. Choose **File > Open** from the main menu; the **Open File** dialog box is displayed.

2. In the **Open File** dialog box, browse to *\Documents\c4dr20\c05\c05_tut1_start* and then choose the **Open** button; the *c05_tut1_start.c4d* file is displayed in the Perspective viewport, as shown in Figure 5-2.

Applying Shader to the Dice Model

In this section, you will apply shader to the dice model using the Material Manager.

1. Choose **Create > New Material** from the Material Manager menu, as shown in Figure 5-3; a new material slot is created in the Material Manager, refer to Figure 5-4. Alternatively, double-click in the empty area of the Material Manager; a new material with the name **Mat** is created in the Material Manager.

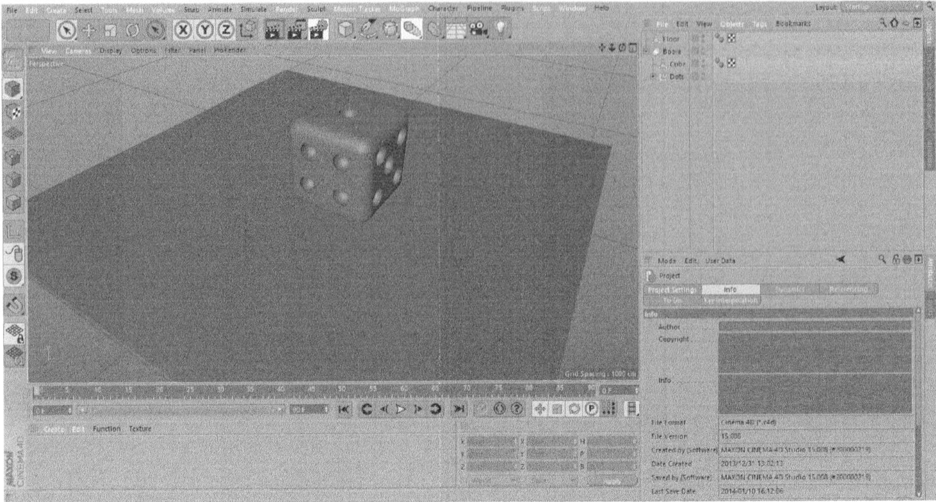

Figure 5-2 The c05_tut1_start.c4d file

The **New Material** option in the **Create** menu is used to create a new material. By default, the new material created is white in color and has specularity.

2. Make sure that the new material is selected in the Material Manager and then choose the **Basic** button from the Attribute Manager; the **Basic Properties** area is displayed. Enter **matDice** in the **Name** text box in the **Basic Properties** area; the new material is renamed as *matDice*.

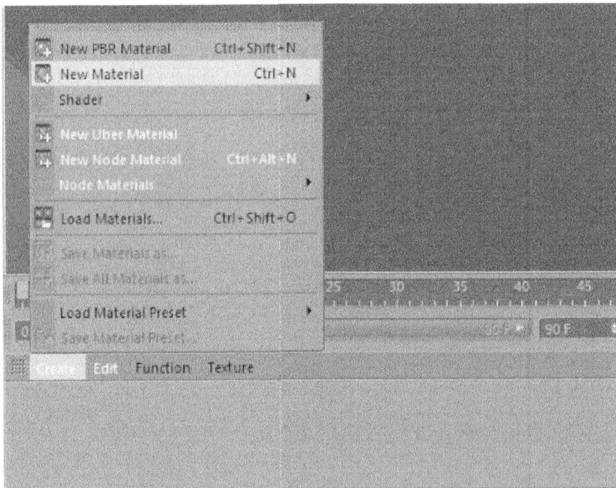

*Figure 5-3 Choosing **New Material** from the Material Manager menu*

Figure 5-4 Displaying the material slot in the Material Manager

Note

You can rename the material by right-clicking on the material slot; a shortcut menu is displayed. Choose **Rename** *from the shortcut menu; the* **Name** *dialog box is displayed. Enter a new name in the* **Name** *text box of this dialog box and choose the* **OK** *button. Alternatively, double-click on the material name in the Material Manager and enter a new name for it.*

3. In the **Basic Properties** area, make sure the **Reflectance** check box is selected; refer to Figure 5-5.

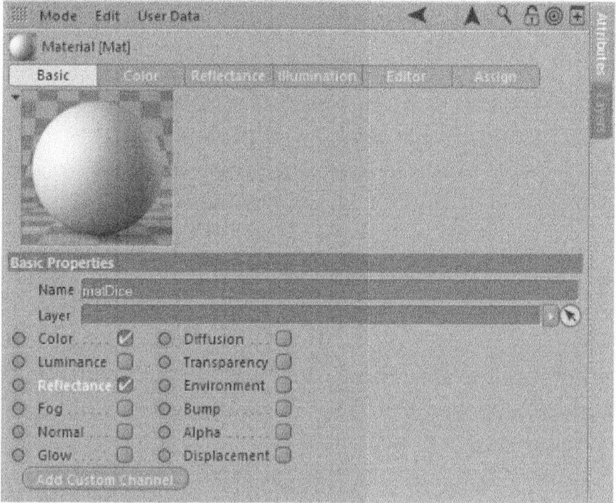

Figure 5-5 *The* ***Reflectance*** *check box selected*

4. In the Attribute Manager, choose the **Reflectance** button; the **Reflectance** area is displayed. In this area, choose the **Add** button; a flyout is displayed. Now, choose **Phong** from the flyout; a reflectance layer with the name **Layer 1** is added.

5. In the **Reflectance > Layer Color** area, click on the **Color** swatch to open the **Color Picker** dialog box. In this dialog box, choose the **RGB** button and then set the parameters as given below. Next, choose the **OK** button.

   R: **197** G: **145** B: **145**

   Enter **50** in the **Brightness** spinner.

   The **Color** option in the **Reflectance > Layer Color** area is used to set the color of the reflection. The **Brightness** option is used to adjust the brightness of the color reflected by the material.

Figure 5-6 *The matDice material applied to Cube*

6. Make sure *matDice* is selected in the Material Manager. In the Attribute Manager, choose the **Color** button; the **Color** area is displayed. In the **Color** area, choose the **RGB** button and then set the parameters as follows:

   R: **163** G: **216** B: **246**

The color of *matDice* changes to light blue.

The **Color** area is used to choose a color using the R, G, and B values.

7. Press and hold the left mouse button on *matDice* in the Material Manager and drag the cursor on *Cube* in the Object Manager; the *matDice* is applied to *Cube* in the Perspective viewport, refer to Figure 5-6.

   Next, you will apply the material to the dots of *Cube*.

8. Choose **Create > New Material** from the Material Manager menu; a new material slot with the name **Mat** is added to the Material Manager. Alternatively, double-click in the empty area of the Material Manager; a new material is added to it.

9. Make sure that the new material is selected in the Material Manager and double-click on the name **Mat**; a text box is displayed in the material slot. In this text box, enter **matDots**; the new material is renamed as *matDots*.

10. In the Attribute Manager, make sure the **Color** button is chosen; the **Color** area is displayed. In this area, set the parameters as follows:

    R: **0** G: **0** B: **0**

11. In the Attribute Manager, choose the **Reflectance** button; the **Reflectance** area is displayed. In this area, choose the **Add** button; a flyout is displayed. Now, choose **Phong** from the flyout; a reflectance layer with the name **Layer 1** is added.

12. In the **Layer Color** area, click on the **Color** swatch to open the **Color Picker** dialog box. In this dialog box, choose the **RGB** button and then set the parameters as given below. Next, choose the **OK** button:

    R: **68** G: **62** B: **62**

    Enter **34** in the **Brightness** spinner.

13. Press and hold the left mouse button on *matDots* in the Material Manager and drag the cursor on *Dots* in the Object Manager; the *matDots* is applied to all the dots in the Perspective viewport, as shown in Figure 5-7.

Applying Shader to the Floor

In this section, you will apply shader to the floor.

1. Double-click in the empty area of the Material Manager; a new material slot is created in the Material Manager.

2. Make sure that the new material is selected in the Material Manager and double-click on the name **Mat**; a text box is displayed. In this text box, enter **matFloor**; the new material is renamed as *matFloor*.

Figure 5-7 The Dot material applied to dots of the Cube

3. In the Attribute Manager, make sure the **Reflectance** button is chosen; the **Reflectance** area is displayed. In this area, choose the **Add** button; a flyout is displayed. Now, choose **Phong** from the flyout; a reflectance layer with the name **Layer 1** is added.

4. In the Attribute Manager, choose the **Color** button; the **Color** area is displayed. In this area, choose the browse button located next to the **Texture** parameter, as shown in Figure 5-8; the **Open File** dialog box is displayed.

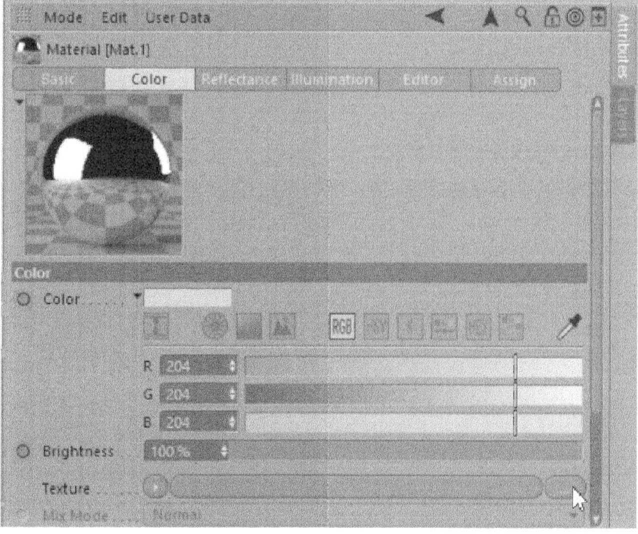

Figure 5-8 Choosing the browse button

5. In this dialog box, browse to *\Documents\c4dr20\c05\Wood_Texture.jpg*. Next, choose the **Open** button; the texture is applied to the material slot in the **Color** area of the Attribute Manager.

6. In the Attribute Manager, choose the **Reflectance** button; the **Reflection** area is displayed. In the **Layer Color** area, enter **10** in the **Brightness** spinner.

7. Press and hold the left mouse button on *matFloor* in the Material Manager and drag the cursor to *Floor* in the Object Manager; the *matFloor* is applied to *Floor* in the Perspective viewport, as shown in Figure 5-9.

Figure 5-9 *The matFloor applied to Floor*

Changing the Background Color of the Scene

To change the background color of the scene to white in the final output, follow the steps given in Tutorial 1 of Chapter 2.

Saving and Rendering the Scene

In this section, you will save and render the scene. You can also view the final render of the composition by downloading the file *c05_cinema4d_r20_rndr.zip* from *www.cadsofttech.com*. The path of the file is mentioned at the beginning of the chapter.

1. Choose **File > Save** from the main menu; the **Save File** dialog box is displayed. In this dialog box, browse to the location *\Documents\c4dr20\c05*.

2. Enter **c05tut1** in the **File name** text box and then choose the **Save** button.

3. In the Perspective viewport, set the camera angle using the Viewport Navigation Tools located at the top right of the Perspective viewport. Next, choose the **Render to Picture Viewer** tool from the Command Palette. Alternatively, press SHIFT+R; the **Picture Viewer** window is displayed.

4. In the **Picture Viewer** window, choose **File > Save as**; the **Save** dialog box is displayed.

5. In the **Save** dialog box, select **JPEG** from the **Format** drop-down list and then choose the **OK** button; the **Save Dialog** dialog box is displayed. Next, browse to *\Documents\c4dr20\c05*. In the **File name** text box, type **c05_tut1_rndr**. Next, choose the **Save** button; the rendered image is saved at the desired location.

   Figure 5-1 displays the final output.

Tutorial 2

In this tutorial, you will apply material to the exterior scene that you downloaded earlier using Node Editor. The final output of the scene with the materials applied is shown in Figure 5-10.

(Expected time: 25 min)

Figure 5-10 *The exterior scene with the materials applied*

The following steps are required to complete this tutorial:

a. Open the file.
b. Create and apply material to floor.
c. Create and apply material to wall.
d. Modify and apply material to table.
e. Modify and apply material to cup.
f. Modify and apply material to glass.
g. Save and render the scene.

Opening the File

In this section, you will open the scene.

1. Choose **File > Open** from the main menu; the **Open File** dialog box is displayed.

2. In the **Open File** dialog box, browse to *\Documents\c4dr20\c05\c05_tut2_start* and then choose the **Open** button; the *c05_tut2_start.c4d* file is displayed in the Perspective viewport, as shown in Figure 5-11.

Figure 5-11 *The c05_tut2_start.c4d file*

Creating and Applying Material to Floor

In this section, you will create and apply new node material to floor using Node Editor.

1. Choose **Create > New Node Material** from the Material Manager menu, as shown in Figure 5-12. Alternatively, press CTRL+ALT+N in the empty area of the Material Manager; a new node material with the name **Node** is created in the Material Manager, refer to Figure 5-13.

2. Double-click on the name **Node** in the Material Manager; a text box is displayed. In this text box, enter **matfloor**; the new material is renamed as *matfloor*.

3. Double click on *matfloor* in the Material Manager; the **Node Editor (1) [matfloor]** window is displayed, as shown in Figure 5-14.

   You will notice that two nodes, **Diffuse.1** and **Material.1** are available in the **Node Editor (1) [matfloor]** window.

4. Right-click on the **Color** input of the **Diffuse.1** node; a shortcut menu is displayed. Choose **Load Texture** from the shortcut menu, as shown in Figure 5-15; the **Choose an image to load** dialog box is displayed.

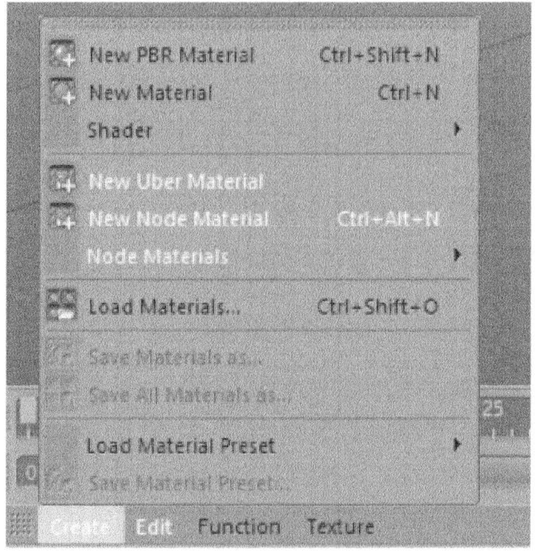

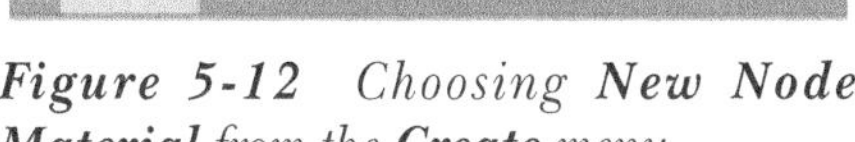

Figure 5-12 *Choosing* ***New Node Material*** *from the* ***Create*** *menu*

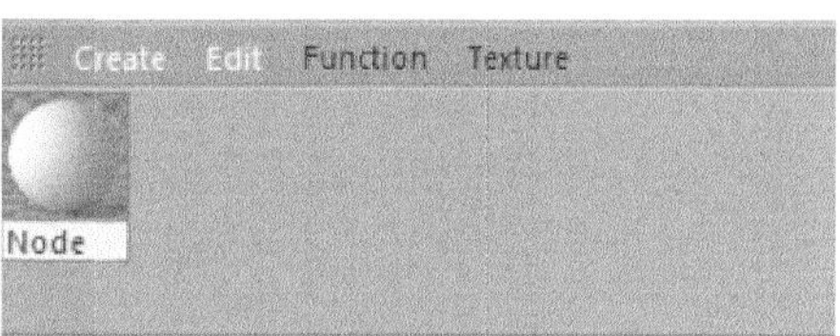

Figure 5-13 *New node material created in the Material Manager*

Figure 5-14 *The* ***Node Editor (1) [matfloor]*** *window*

5. In this dialog box, browse to *\Documents\c4dr20\c05\floor texture.jpg*. Next, choose the **Open** button; the **floor texture.jpg** node is added to the **Color** input of the **Diffuse.1** node, as shown in Figure 5-16.

6. Press and hold the left mouse button on the *matfloor* material in the Material Manager and drag the cursor to *floor* in the Object Manager; the *matfloor* material is applied to *floor* in the Perspective viewport.

7. Select the **Texture Tag "matfloor"** texture tag in the Object Manager. Make sure that the **Tag** button is chosen in the Attribute Manager. Also, make sure that the **Tile** check box is selected.

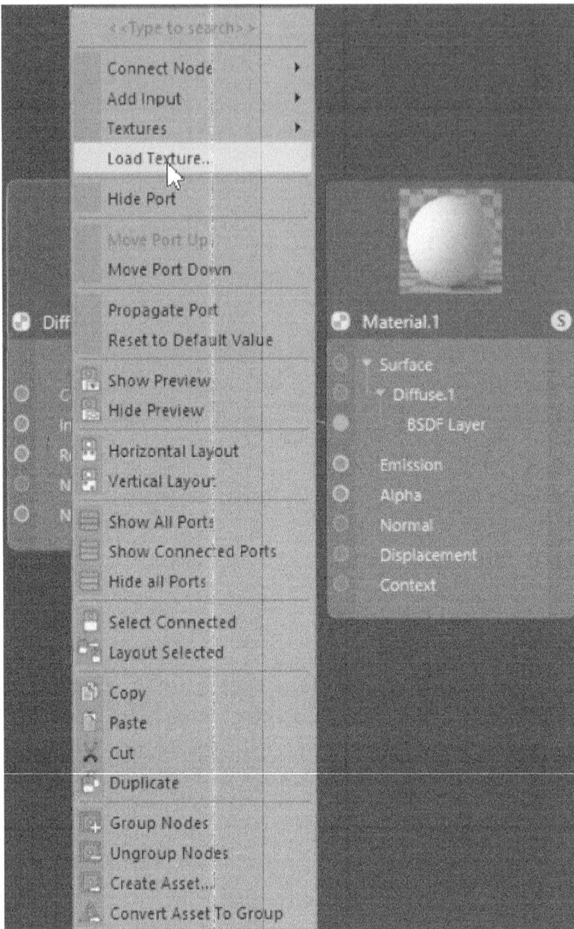

*Figure 5-15 Choosing **Load Texture** from the shortcut menu*

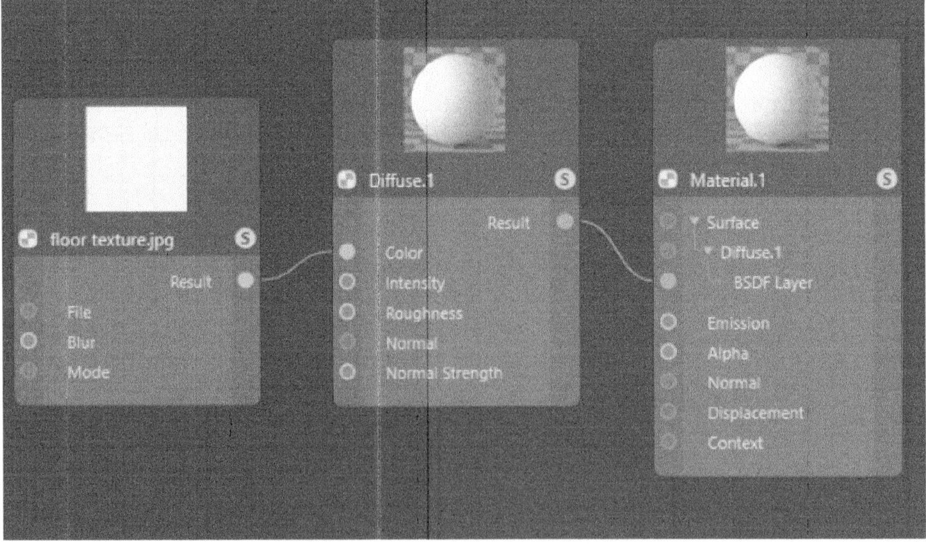

*Figure 5-16 The **floor texture.jpg** node added to the **Color** input of the **Diffuse.1** node*

8. In the **Tag Properties** area, select **UVW mapping** from the **Projection** drop-down list. Next, select the **Tile** check box and set the parameters as follows:

   Tiles U: **8** Tiles V: **8**

9. Choose the **Render to Picture Viewer** tool from the Command Palette. Alternatively, press SHIFT+R; the **Picture Viewer** window that shows floor material is displayed, refer to Figure 5-17.

Figure 5-17 *The floor material displayed*

Creating and Applying Material to Wall

In this section, you will create and apply new node material to wall using Node Editor.

1. Choose **Create > New Node Material** from the Material Manager menu. Alternatively, press CTRL+ALT+N in the empty area of the Material Manager; a new node material with the name **Node** is created in the Material Manager.

2. Double-click on the name **Node** in the Material Manager; a text box is displayed. In this text box, enter **matwall** in the **Name** text box; the new material is renamed as *matwall*.

3. Double click on *matwall* in the Material Manager; the **Node Editor (1) [matwall]** window is displayed.

4. Right-click on the **Color** input of the **Diffuse.1** node; a shortcut menu is displayed. Choose **Load Texture** from the shortcut menu, as shown in Figure 5-15; the **Choose an image to load** dialog box is displayed.

5. In this dialog box, browse to *\Documents\c4dr20\c05\wall texture.jpg*. Next, choose the **Open** button; the **wall texture.jpg** node is added to the **Color** input of the **Diffuse.1** node. Close the **Node Editor (1) [matwall]** window.

6. Press and hold the left mouse button on the *matwall* material in the Material Manager and drag the cursor to *wall* in the Object Manager; the *matfloor* material is applied to *wall* in the Perspective viewport.

7. Select the **Texture Tag "matwall"** texture tag in the Object Manager. Make sure that the **Tag** button is chosen in the Attribute Manager. Also, make sure that the **Tile** check box is selected.

8. In the **Tag Properties** area, select **Cubic** from the **Projection** drop-down list and set the parameters as follows:

   Tiles U: **24** Tiles V: **24**

9. Choose the **Render to Picture Viewer** tool from the Command Palette. Alternatively, press SHIFT+R; the **Picture Viewer** window is displayed that shows the render view of wall material, refer to Figure 5-18. Close the **Picture Viewer** window.

Figure 5-18 *The wall material displayed*

Modifying and Applying Material to Table

In this section, you will modify the existing wood node material.

1. Choose **Create > Node Materials** from the Material Manager menu; a cascading menu is displayed, as shown in Figure 5-19. Choose **Wood** from the cascading menu; a node material with the name **Wood** is created in the Material Manager.

2. Double-click on the name **Wood** in the Material Manager; a text box is displayed. In this text box, enter **mattable** in the **Name** text box; the new material is renamed as *mattable*.

3. Press and hold the left mouse button on the *mattable* material in the Material Manager and drag the cursor to *table* in the Object Manager; the *mattable* material is applied to *table* in the Perspective viewport.

4. Make sure that the *mattable* material is selected in the Material Manager and then choose the **Base** button from the Attribute Manager; the **Base** area is displayed. Enter **33** in the **Grains** edit box.

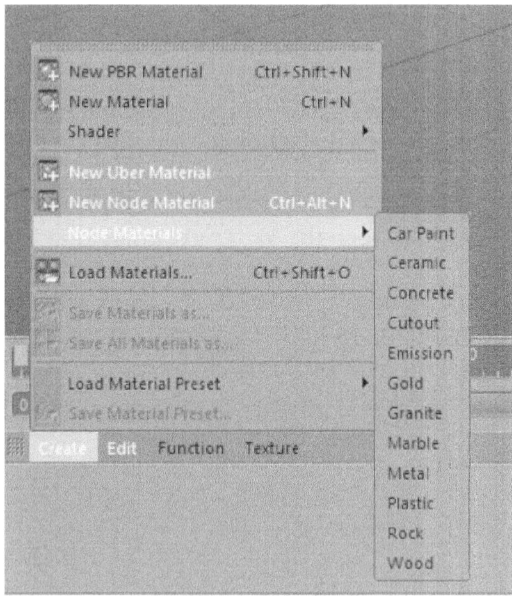

Figure 5-19 *The cascading menu displayed*

5. Choose the **Veins Deformation** button from the Attribute Manager; the **Veins Deformation** area is displayed. Enter **60** in the **Deformation** edit box.

6. Choose the **Render to Picture Viewer** tool from the Command Palette. Alternatively, press SHIFT+R; the **Picture Viewer** window is displayed that shows table material, refer to Figure 5-20. Close the **Picture Viewer** window.

Figure 5-20 *The mattable material displayed*

Modifying and Applying Material to Cup

In this section, you will modify the existing ceramic node material.

1. Choose **Create > Node Materials** from the Material Manager menu; a cascading menu is displayed, refer to Figure 5-42. Choose **Ceramic** from the cascading menu; a node material with the name **Ceramic** is created in the Material Manager.

2. Double-click on the name **Ceramic** in the Material Manager; a text box is displayed. In this text box, enter **matcup**; the new material is renamed as *matcup*.

3. Press and hold the left mouse button on the *matcup* material in the Material Manager and drag the cursor to *cup1* and *cup2* in the Object Manager; the *matcup* material is applied to cups in the Perspective viewport.

4. Double-click on the **matcup** material in the Material Manager; the **Material Editor** window is displayed. Choose the **Node Editor** button from this window; the **Node Editor (1) - matcup** window is displayed.

5. Right-click on the **Color** input of the **Ceramic Material** node; a shortcut menu is displayed. Choose **Load Texture** from the shortcut menu; the **Choose an image to load** dialog box is displayed.

6. In this dialog box, browse to *\Documents\c4dr20\c05\ceramic texture.jpg*. Next, choose the **Open** button; the **ceramic texture.jpg** node is added to the **Color** input of the **Ceramic Material** node. Next, close the **Node Editor (1) - matcup** and **Material Editor** windows.

7. Select the **Texture Tag "matcup"** texture tag corresponding to *cup1* in the Object Manager. Make sure that the **Tag** button is chosen in the Attribute Manager.

8. Make sure that the **Tile** check box is selected. Also, select the **Seamless** check box; the **matcup** material is displayed properly on *cup1*.

9. Select the **Texture Tag "matcup"** texture tag corresponding to *cup2* in the Object Manager. Make sure that the **Tag** button is chosen in the Attribute Manager.

10. Make sure that the **Tile** check box is selected. Also, select the **Seamless** check box; the **matcup** material is displayed properly on *cup2*, refer to Figure 5-21.

Modifying and Applying Material to Glass

In this section, you will modify the existing plastic node material.

1. Choose **Create > Node Materials** from the Material Manager menu; a cascading menu is displayed. Choose **Plastic** from the cascading menu; a node material with the name **Plastic** is created in the Material Manager.

2. Double-click on the name **Plastic** in the Material Manager; a text box is displayed. In this text box, enter **matglass**; the new material is renamed as *matglass*.

Figure 5-21 *The matcup material displayed*

3. Press and hold the left mouse button on the *matglass* material in the Material Manager and drag the cursor to *glass1* and *glass2* in the Object Manager; the *matglass* material is applied to glasses in the Perspective viewport.

4. Make sure the **matglass** material is selected in the Material Manager. Also, make sure that the **Base** button is chosen in the Attribute Manager.

5. In the **Base** area, choose the **RGB** button and then set the parameters as follows:

   R: **140** G: **12** B: **54**

   Figure 5-22 shows *matglass* material applied to glasses.

Saving and Rendering the Scene

In this section, you will save and render the scene. You can also view the final render of the scene by downloading the file *c05_cinema4d_r20_rndr.zip* from *www.cadsofttech.com*. The path of the file is mentioned at the beginning of the chapter.

1. Choose **File > Save** from the main menu; the **Save File** dialog box is displayed. In this dialog box, browse to the location *\Documents\c4dr20\c05*.

2. Enter **c05tut2** in the **File name** text box and then choose the **Save** button.

3. In the Perspective viewport, set the camera angle using the Viewport Navigation Tools located at the top right of the Perspective viewport. Next, you will render the scene. For rendering, refer to Tutorial 1.

Figure 5-10 displays the final output.

Figure 5-22 *The matglass material displayed*

EXERCISE

The rendered output of the model used in the exercise can be accessed by downloading the *c05_cinema4d_r20_exr.zip* file from *www.cadsofttech.com*. The path of the file is as follows: *Textbooks > Animation and Visual Effects > MAXON CINEMA 4D > MAXON CINEMA 4D R20 Studio for Novices*

Exercise 1

Download the file *c05_cinema4d_r20_exr.zip* containing the camera model shown in Figure 5-23 from *www.cadsofttech.com*. Next, extract the contents of the file and then texture the camera model using various textures and shaders. Render the scene to get the final output, as shown in Figure 5-24. **(Expected time: 30 min)**

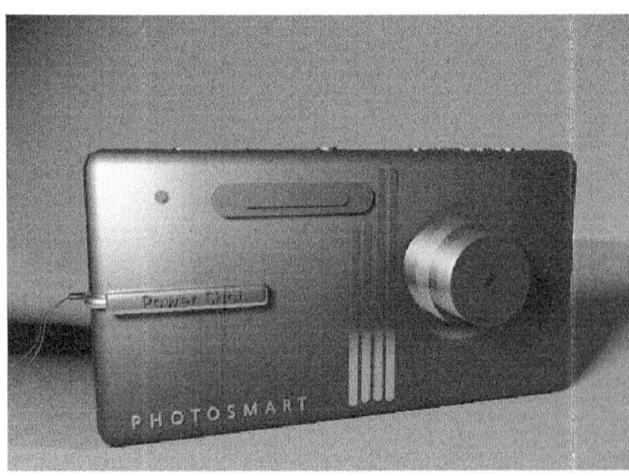

Figure 5-23 *The final output*

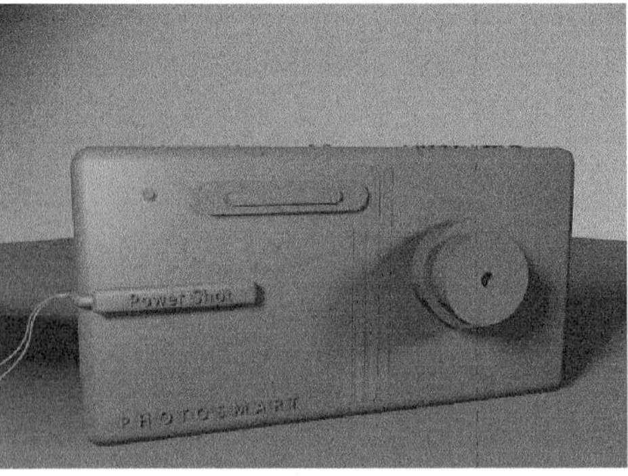

Figure 5-24 *The camera model*

Chapter 6

Lighting

Learning Objectives

After completing this chapter, you will be able to:

- *Add lights to a scene*
- *Illuminate a scene*

INTRODUCTION

In computer graphics, lighting plays a vital role in defining the look of a scene. Lighting is primarily used to produce the effect of light and shadows. Also, you can add depth to the scene by using advanced lighting techniques. There are seven types of lights available in CINEMA 4D. All the lights are treated as objects, and can be transformed, deleted, and duplicated.

TUTORIALS

All the files used in the tutorials can be downloaded from the CADSoft website (*www.cadsofttech.com*). These files are compressed in zip file format and are required to be extracted before using them in the tutorials. The path of the files is as follows: *Textbooks > Animation and Visual Effects > MAXON CINEMA 4D > MAXON CINEMA 4D R20 Studio for Novices*

Next, you need to browse to *\Documents\c4dR20* and create a new folder in it with the name *c06*. Next, extract the contents of the zip file in this folder.

Tutorial 1

In this tutorial, you will illuminate a scene using the torch light, as shown in Figure 6-1.

(Expected time: 15 min)

Figure 6-1 *The torchlight*

The following steps are required to complete this tutorial:

a. Open the file.
b. Add lights to the scene.
c. Save and render the scene.

Opening the File

In this section, you will open the file.

1. Choose **File > Open** from the main menu; the **Open File** dialog box is displayed.

2. In the **Open File** dialog box, browse to *\Documents\c06_c4dr20__tut\c06_tut1_start.c4d* and then choose the **Open** button; the *c06_tut1_start.c4d* file is opened, as shown in Figure 6-2.

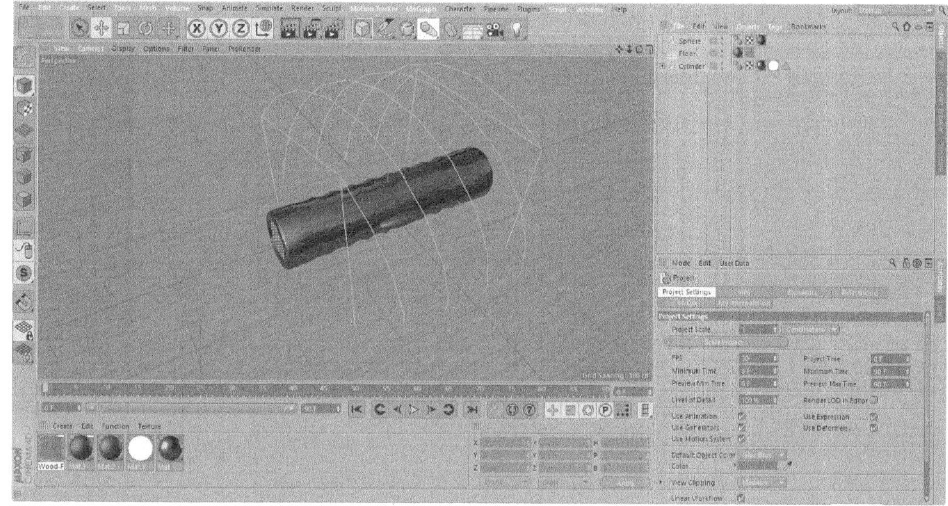

Figure 6-2 *The c06_tut1_start.c4d file*

Adding Lights to the Scene

In this section, you will add lights to the scene.

1. Press and hold the left mouse button on the **Light** tool in the Command Palette; a flyout with various tools is displayed, as shown in Figure 6-3. Choose the **Spot Light** tool from it; the *Light* object is added to the Object Manager.

   The **Spot Light** tool is used to cast a beam of light in a conical shape.

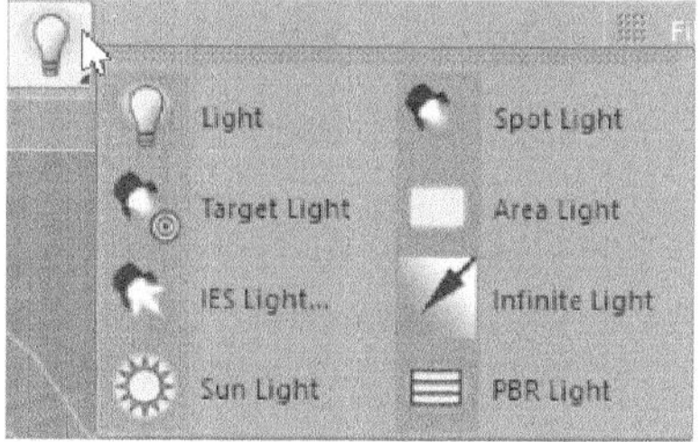

Figure 6-3 *The flyout displayed with various tools*

2. In the Attribute Manager, choose the **Coord** button; the **Coordinates** area is displayed. In this area, set the parameters as follows:

   P . X: **53** P . Y: **6** R . H: **90**

3. Choose the **Details** button; the **Details** area is displayed. In this area, make sure the **Aspect Ratio** is set to 1 and then set the parameters as follows:

   Inner Angle: **12** Outer Angle:**16** Contrast: **31**

4. In the Attribute Manager, choose the **General** button; the **General** area is displayed. In this area, enter **180** in the **Intensity** spinner and select the **Shadow Maps (Soft)** option from the **Shadow** drop-down list. Next, select **Inverse Volumetric** from the **Visible Light** drop-down list.

The value in the **Intensity** spinner is used to set the brightness of the light. More the value of intensity, brighter will be the light.

The options in the **Shadow** drop-down list are used to enable shadows in the scene. The **Shadows Maps (Soft)** option in the drop-down list is used to enable a smooth transition from lighting to shadow effect in the scene.

The **Inner Angle** spinner is used to adjust the inner angle of the standard spotlight. The **Outer Angle** spinner is used to adjust the illumination of the light in total. The **Aspect Ratio** spinner is used to adjust the shape of the cone of the spot light. The **Contrast** spinner is used to adjust the transition between the softness and the hardness of the lit surface.

5. Choose the **Visibility** button; the **Visibility** area is displayed. In this area, set the parameters as follows:

   Edge Falloff: **60** Inner Distance: **227** Outer Distance: **538**
   Sample Distance: **65**

   The value of the **Edge Falloff** spinner specifies the speed at which the density of light decreases when it moves towards the cone of the spotlight.

   After entering these values, you need to render the scene in the Perspective viewport to get the result, as shown in Figure 6-4.

Figure 6-4 *The rendered view of the Perspective viewport*

Next, you will illuminate the scene.

6. Press and hold the left mouse button on the **Light** tool in the Command Palette; a flyout with various tools is displayed, refer to Figure 6-3. Choose the **Light** tool from it; the *Light.1* object is added to the Object Manager.

7. Make sure *Light.1* is selected in the Object Manager. In the Attribute Manager, choose the **General** button; the **General** area is displayed. In this area, enter **50** in the **Intensity** spinner and select **Square Spot** from the **Type** drop-down list. Next, select **Shadow Maps (Soft)** from the **Shadow** drop-down list.

   The options in the **Type** drop-down list are used to define the types of lights to be used in a scene. The **Square Spot** option is best suited to cast a square-shaped light ray on the surface.

8. In the Attribute Manager, choose the **Coord** button; the **Coordinates** area is displayed. In this area, set the parameters as follows:

P . X: **-500**	P . Y: **500**	P . Z: **-500**
R . H: **-45**	R . P: **-35**	

9. Choose the **Details** button; the **Details** area is displayed. In this area, enter **105** in the **Outer Angle** spinner.

   Figure 6-5 displays *Light.1* in the Perspective viewport.

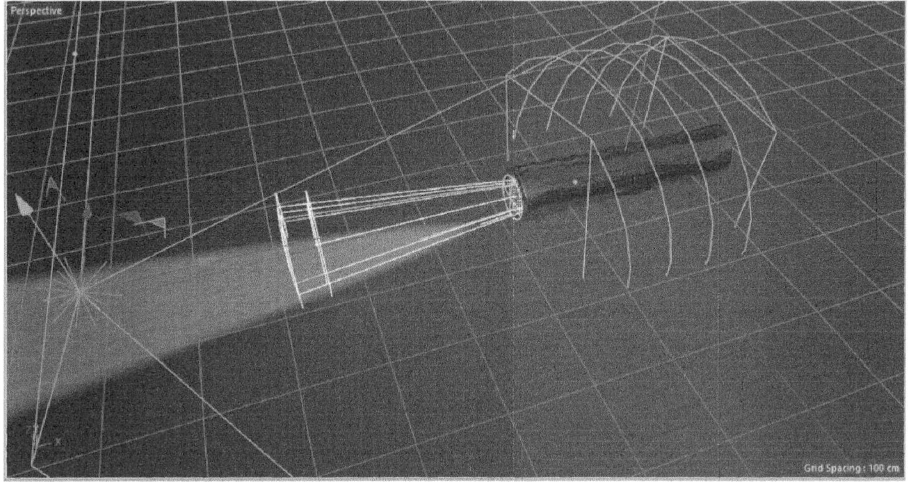

Figure 6-5 *Light.1 displayed in the Perspective viewport*

Saving and Rendering the Scene

In this section, you will save and render the file. You can also view the final render of the scene by downloading the file *c06_cinema4d_r20_rndr.zip* from *www.cadsofttech.com*. The path of the file is mentioned at the beginning of the chapter.

1. Choose **File > Save** from the main menu; the **Save File** dialog box is displayed. In this dialog box, browse to the location *\Documents\c4dr20\c06*.

2. Enter **c06tut1** in the **File name** text box and then choose the **Save** button.

3. In the Perspective viewport, set the camera angle using the Viewport Navigation Tools located at the top right of the Perspective viewport. Next, you will render the scene. For rendering, refer to Tutorial 1 of Chapter 2.

   The output of the scene is shown in Figure 6-1.

Tutorial 2

In this section, you will illuminate a night scene, as shown in Figure 6-6.

(Expected time: 25 min)

Figure 6-6 *The illuminated night scene*

The following steps are required to complete this tutorial:

a. Open the file.
b. Illuminate the street lights.
c. Save and render the scene.

Opening the File

In this section, you will open the file.

1. Choose **File > Open** from the main menu; the **Open File** dialog box is displayed. In the **Open File** dialog box, browse to *\Documents\c4dr20\c06\c06_tut2_start.c4d* and then choose the **Open** button; the *c06_tut2_start* file is opened, as shown in Figure 6-7.

Illuminating the Street Lights

In this section, you will illuminate the street lights using the **Spot Light** tool.

1. Press and hold the left mouse button on the **Light** tool in the Command Palette; a flyout is displayed. Choose the **Spot Light** tool from it; *Light* is added to the Object Manager.

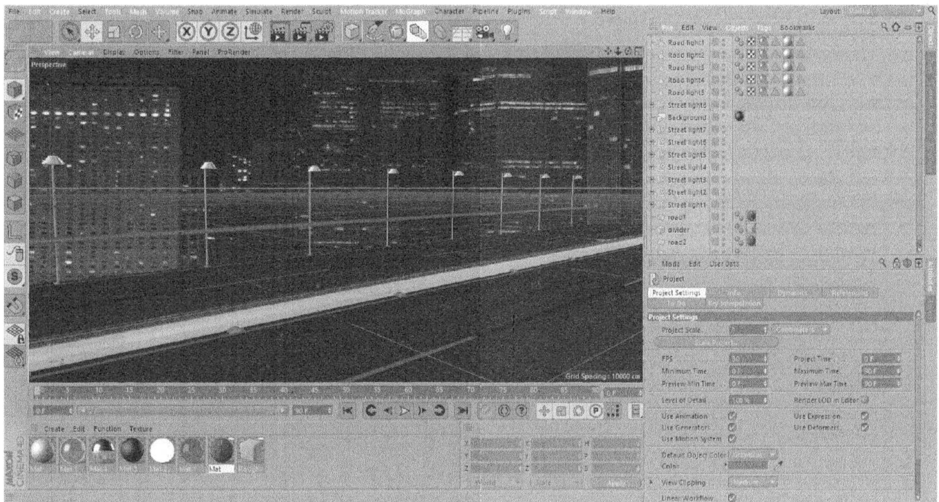

Figure 6-7 The c06_tut2_start.c4d file

2. In the Attribute Manager, choose the **General** button; the **General** area is displayed. In this area, select **Shadow Maps (Soft)** from the **Shadow** drop-down list and **Volumetric** from the **Visible Light** drop-down list. Also, choose the **RGB** button and then set the parameters corresponding to the **Color** option as follows:

   R: **252** G: **222** B: **204**

   The options in the **Visible Light** drop-down list are used to define the volumetric effects of the light. The **Visible Light** drop-down list is available only when the **Omni** and **Spot** lights are used. Selecting **Volumetric** from the **Visible Light** drop-down list ensures that the light emitted from the object will cast shadow. However, on selecting this option, rendering time will increase.

3. In the Attribute Manager, choose the **Coord** button; the **Coordinates** area is displayed. In this area, set the parameters as follows:

   P . X: **-25160.40** P . Y: **10997** P . Z: **-34089.09**
   R . P: **-90**

4. Choose the **Details** button; the **Details** area is displayed. In this area, enter **65** in the **Outer Angle** spinner.

5. In the Attribute Manager, choose the **Visibility** button; the **Visibility** area is displayed. In this area, enter **15000** in the **Outer Distance** spinner.

   After entering the values, the spot light is positioned in the scene in the Perspective viewport, as shown in Figure 6-8.

Figure 6-8 *Light positioned in the scene*

6. Select *Light* in the Object Manager and create a copy of *Light* using the CTRL key; a copy of *Light* is created with the name *Light.1*.

7. Make sure *Light.1* is selected in the Object Manager. In the Attribute Manager, choose the **Coord** button; the **Coordinates** area is displayed. In this area, enter **-20323.77** in the **P . Z** spinner.

   After entering the values, *Light.1* is positioned in the scene in the Perspective viewport, as shown in Figure 6-9.

8. Create 6 more copies of *Light.1* and enter corresponding value in the **P . Z** spinner for the copied lights, as shown in Table 6-1.

Table 6-1 *Values to be entered in the **P . Z** spinner*

Light to be selected	Value to be entered in the P . Z spinner
Light.2	-6768.247
Light.3	6827.229
Light.4	21833.845
Light.5	35865.109
Light.6	49681.329
Light.7	64076.595

After entering the values, all the lights are positioned in the Perspective viewport, as shown in Figure 6-10.

Figure 6-9 *Light.1 positioned in the scene*

Figure 6-10 *Lights positioned in the Perspective viewport*

Next, you will create a light to illuminate the other side of the road.

9. Press F2; the Top viewport is activated. In the Top viewport, press and hold the left mouse button on the **Light** tool in the Command Palette; a flyout is displayed. Choose the **Light** tool from it; *Light.8* is created in the Top viewport and added to the Object Manager, as shown in Figure 6-11.

10. Make sure *Light.8* is selected in the Object Manager. In the Attribute Manager, choose the **General** button; the **General** area is displayed. In this area, set the value of the **Intensity** spinner to **45**. Next, select the **Raytraced (Hard)** option from the **Shadow** drop-down list and the **Inverse Volumetric** option from the **Visible Light** drop-down list.

The **Raytraced (Hard)** option in the **Shadow** drop-down list is used to cast hard shadows for any type of light settings.

11. Choose the **Coord** button; the **Coordinates** area is displayed. In this area, set the parameters as follows:

    P . X: **13044** P . Y: **15504**

12. Choose the **Visibility** button; the **Visibility** area is displayed. In this area, enter **12416** in the **Outer Distance** spinner.

    Press F1; the Perspective viewport is maximized. After entering the values, *Light.8* is positioned in the scene, as shown in Figure 6-12.

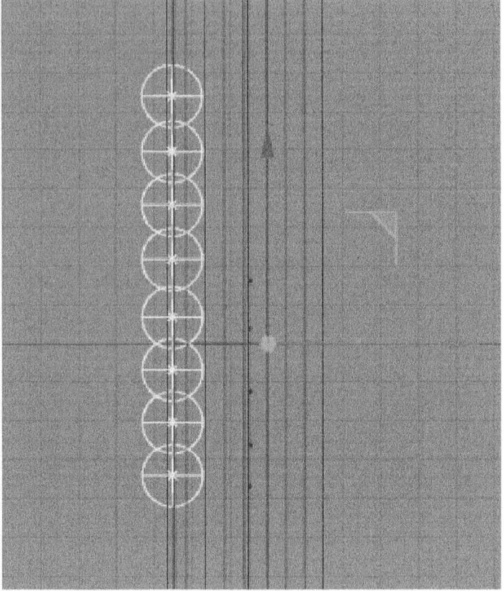

Figure 6-11 *Light.8 created in the Top viewport*

Figure 6-12 *Light.8 positioned in the scene*

Saving and Rendering the Scene

In this section, you will save the scene. You can also view the final rendered scene by downloading the file *c06_cinema4d_r20_rndr.zip* from *www.cadsofttech.com*. The path of the file is mentioned at the beginning of the chapter.

1. Choose **File > Save** from the main menu; the **Save File** dialog box is displayed. In this dialog box, browse to the following location *\Documents\c4dr20\c06*. Enter **c06tut2** in the **File name** text box and then choose the **Save** button.

2. In the Perspective viewport, set the camera angle using the Viewport Navigation Tools located on the top right of the Perspective viewport. Next, you need to render the scene. For rendering, refer to Tutorial 1 of Chapter 2.

EXERCISE

The rendered output of the model used in the following exercise can be accessed by downloading the *c06_cinema4d_r20_exr.zip* file from *www.cadsofttech.com*. The path of the file is as follows: *Textbooks > Animation and Visual Effects > MAXON CINEMA 4D > MAXON CINEMA 4D R20 Studio for Novices*

Exercise 1

Extract the contents of the *c06_cinema4d_r20_exr.zip* file and then open *c06_exr01_start.c4d*, as shown in Figure 6-13. Add lights to the scene to get the output shown in Figure 6-14.

(Expected time: 30 min)

Figure 6-13 *The living room scene*

Figure 6-14 *The scene after adding lights to it*

Chapter 7

Rigging

Learning Objectives

After completing this chapter, you will be able to:

- *Understand the concept of rigging*
- *Apply constraints*

INTRODUCTION

Rigging is the process of preparing an object or a character for animation. To rig an object, you need to add bones and controls to it. In this chapter, you will learn to create a functional rig for a human hand and a table lamp by adding bones to it and later skinning it. You will also learn the concept of forward and inverse kinematics and apply constraints.

TUTORIAL

All the files used in the tutorialscan be downloaded from the CADSoft website (*www.cadsofttech.com*). These files are compressed in zip file format and are required to be extracted before using them in the tutorials. The path of the files is as follows: *Textbooks > Animation and Visual Effects > MAXON CINEMA 4D > MAXON CINEMA 4D R20 Studio for Novices*

Next, you need to browse to *\Documents\c4dR20* and create a new folder in it with the name *c07*. Next, extract the contents of the zip file in this folder.

Tutorial 1

In this tutorial, you will rig a hand, as shown in Figure 7-1. **(Expected time: 25 min)**

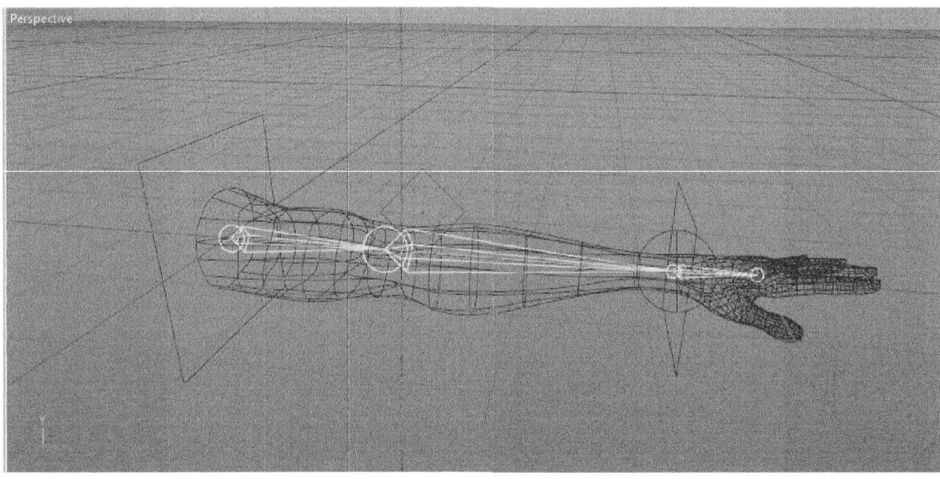

Figure 7-1 *The rig of the hand*

The following steps are required to complete this tutorial:

a. Open the file.
b. Create bone structure for the hand.
c. Create IK chain of the bone structure.
d. Create controllers for the hand.
e. Add constraint to the bones and controllers.
f. Bind the rig.
g. Save the scene.

Opening the File

In this section, you will open the file.

1. Choose **File > Open** from the main menu; the **Open File** dialog box is displayed.

2. In the **Open File** dialog box, browse to *\Documents\c4dr20\c07\c07_tut1_start.c4d* and then choose the **Open** button; the *c07_tut1_start* file is opened, as shown in Figure 7-2.

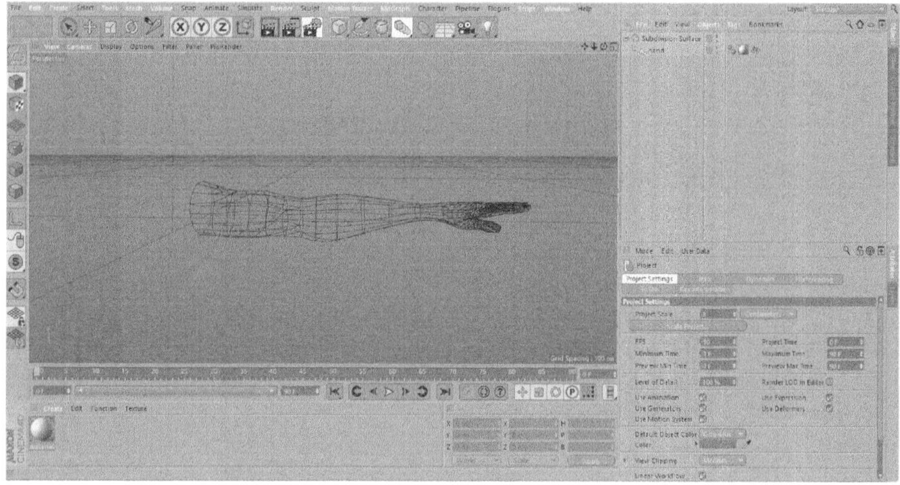

Figure 7-2 *The c07_tut1_start file*

Creating Bone Structure for Hand

In this section, you will create bone structure for hand using **Joint Tool**.

1. Press F2; the Top viewport is activated. Choose **Character > Joint Tool** from the main menu.

   The **Joint Tool** is used to create bones in the mesh of the object or character.

2. Select *hand* in the Object Manager. In the Top viewport, press and hold the CTRL key and click on the shoulder joint of the hand, as shown in Figure 7-3. Next, click on the elbow part, on the wrist part, and then on the palm; a bone structure is created in the viewport, as shown in Figure 7-4.

3. In the Object Manager, expand *hand*. You will notice that hierarchy of joints is also created in the Object Manager.

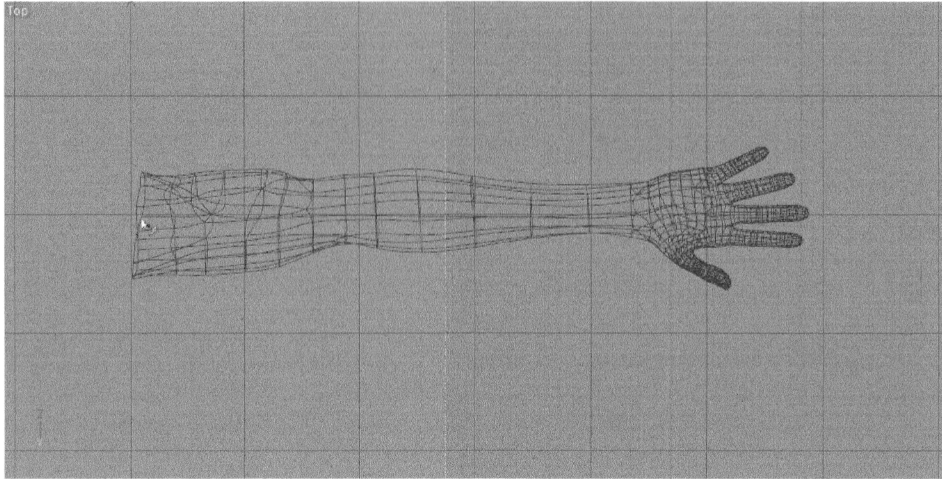

Figure 7-3 *Clicking on the shoulder joint of the hand*

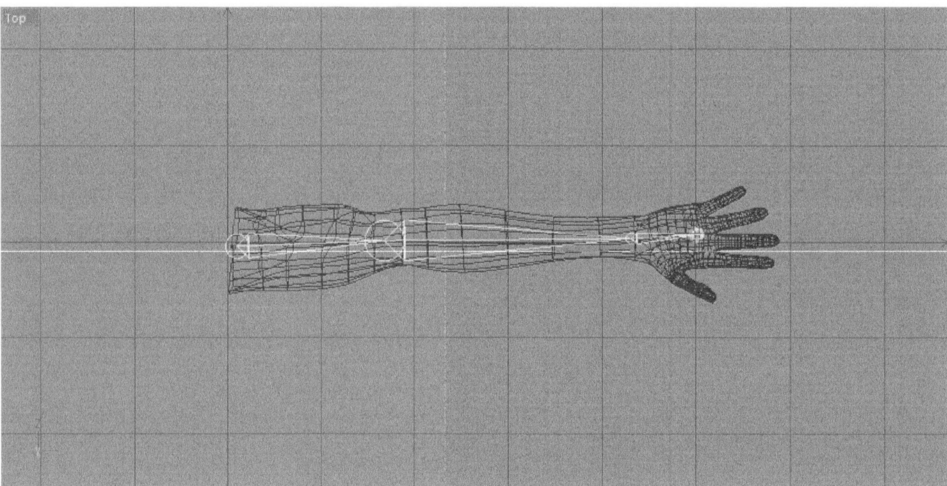

Figure 7-4 *Bone structure created*

4. Press F4 to maximize the Front viewport. Next, align the joints in the Front viewport, as shown in Figure 7-5.

5. In the Object Manager, rename *Joint.1* as *shoulder_joint*, *Joint.2* as *elbow_joint*, *Joint.3* as *wrist_joint*, and *Joint.4* as *end_joint*.

Creating IK Chain of the Bone Structure

In this section, you will create IK chain of the bone structure.

1. Select *shoulder_joint* and *wrist_joint* using the CTRL key in the Object Manager. Next, choose **Character > Commands > Create IK Chain** from the main menu, as shown in Figure 7-6; an IK Chain is created and *wrist_joint.Goal* is added to the Object Manager. Press F1; the

Perspective viewport is maximized. Figure 7-7 shows the IK chain created in the Perspective viewport.

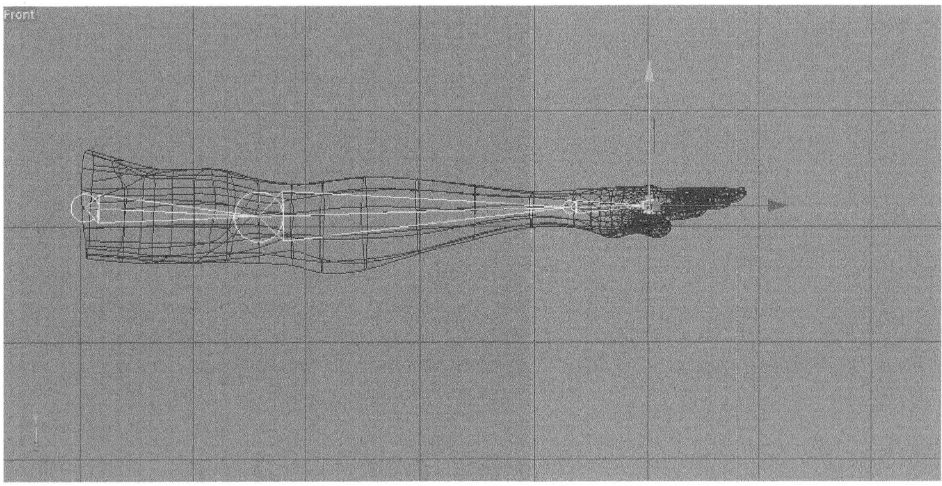

***Figure 7-5** All joints aligned in the Front viewport*

The **Create IK Chain** tool is used to create a complete IK chain for the selected joint objects in a hierarchy.

Next, you will change the icon of *wrist_joint.Goal* to make it clearly visible. You can use the O key to zoom.

2. Make sure *wrist_joint.Goal* is selected in the Object Manager. In the Attribute Manager, choose the **Object** button; the **Object Properties** area is displayed. In this area, select **Sphere** from the **Display** drop-down list; the icon of *wrist_joint.Goal* gets modified. Next, enter **40** in the **Radius** spinner. Figure 7-8 shows the changed icon of *wrist_joint. Goal*.

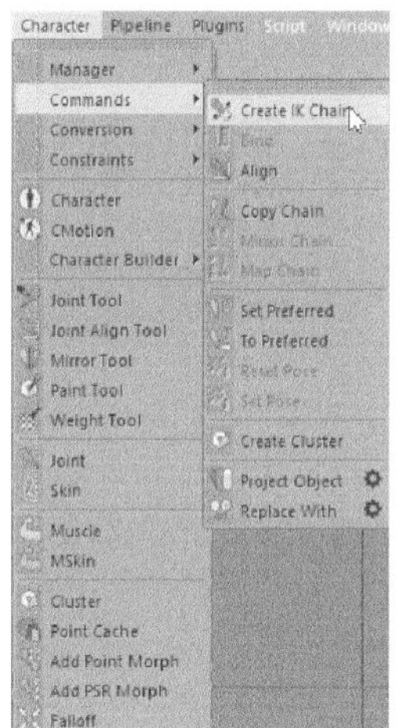

***Figure 7-6** Choosing the **Create IK Chain** from the main menu*

Creating Controllers for the Hand

In this section, you will create controllers for the hand using splines.

1. Press F3; the Right viewport is maximized. Choose **Create > Spline > Rectangle** from the main menu; a rectangle is created in the Right viewport and is added to the Object Manager.

2. Make sure that *Rectangle* is selected in the Object Manager and the **Object** button is chosen in the Attribute Manager. In the **Object Properties** area, enter **200** in both the **Width** and **Height** spinners.

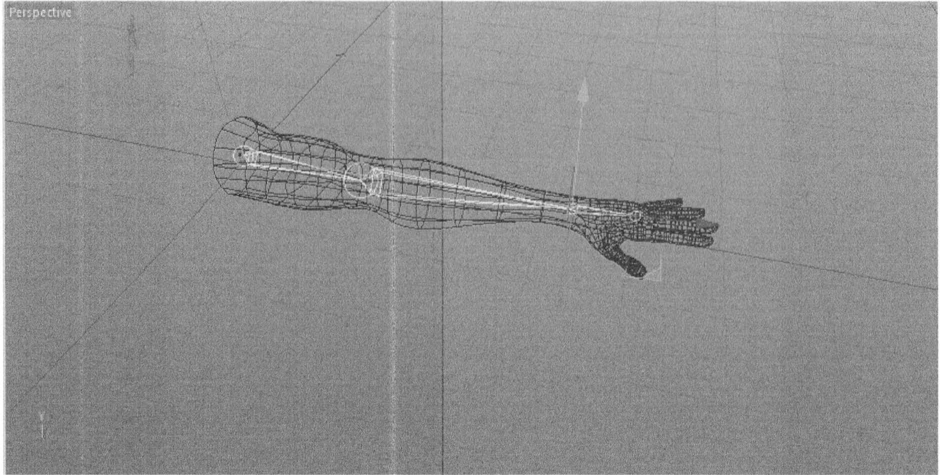

Figure 7-7 *The IK chain created in the Perspective viewport*

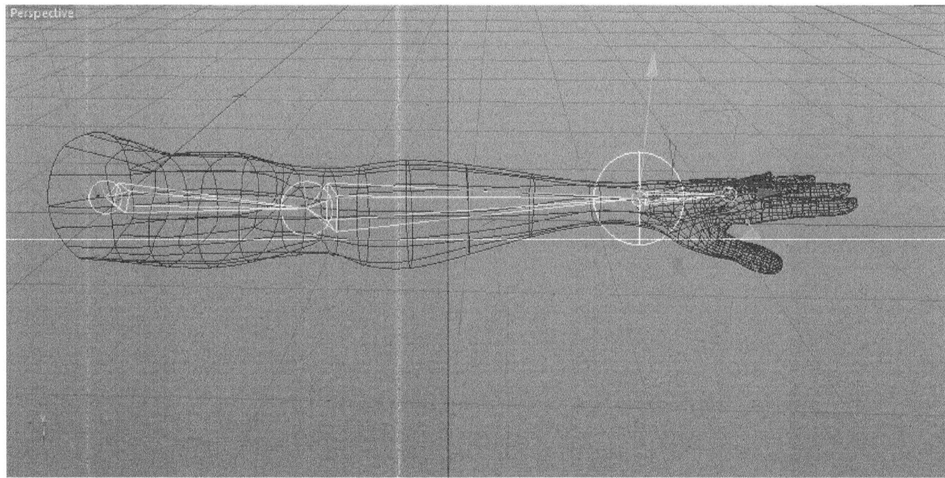

Figure 7-8 *The changed icon of wrist_joint.Goal*

3. Choose the **Basic** button; the **Basic Properties** area is displayed. In this area, enter **shoulder control** in the **Name** text box; *Rectangle* is renamed as *shoulder control*. Next, press F1; the Perspective viewport is maximized. Figure 7-9 shows *shoulder control* in the Perspective viewport.

   Next, you will create a wrist control.

4. In the Object Manager, make sure *shoulder control* is selected. Next, press and hold the left mouse button along with the CTRL key and drag the cursor above *shoulder control*. Next, release the left mouse button and the CTRL key; a copy of *shoulder control* is created with the name *shoulder control.1*. Rename it as *wrist control*.

5. In the Attribute Manager, choose the **Object** button; the **Object Properties** area is displayed. In this area, enter **125** in both the **Width** and **Height** spinners.

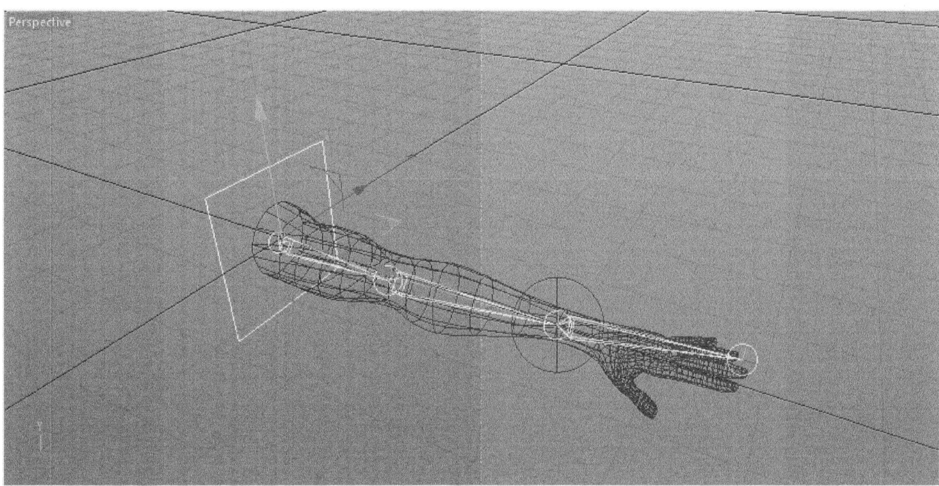

Figure 7-9 *The shoulder control in the Perspective viewport*

6. Choose the **Coord** button in the Attribute Manager; the **Coordinates** area is displayed. In this area, enter **431.053** in the **P . X** spinner; *wrist control* is aligned with the wrist.

   Figure 7-10 displays *wrist control* in the Perspective viewport.

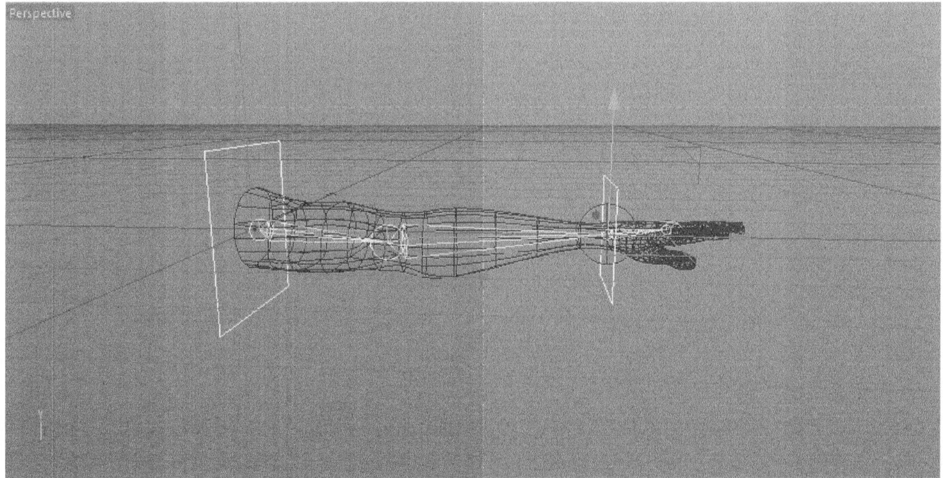

Figure 7-10 *Displaying the controllers of hand*

Next, you will create pole control for rotational movement of hand.

7. In the Object Manager, select **IK Expression (IK)** tag of *shoulder_joint*. 

8. In the Attribute Manager, make sure the **Tag** button is chosen. In the **Pole Vector** area, choose the **Add Pole** button; *shoulder_joint.Pole* is displayed in the **Object** edit box located on the left of the **Add Pole** button and *shoulder_joint.Pole* is added to the Object Manager.

9. Select *shoulder_joint.Pole* in the Object Manager. In the Attribute Manager, choose the **Object** button; the **Object Properties** area is displayed. In this area, select **Diamond** from the **Display** drop-down list. Next, enter **50** in the **Radius** spinner.

Figure 7-11 shows the changed icon of *shoulder_joint.Pole* in the Perspective viewport.

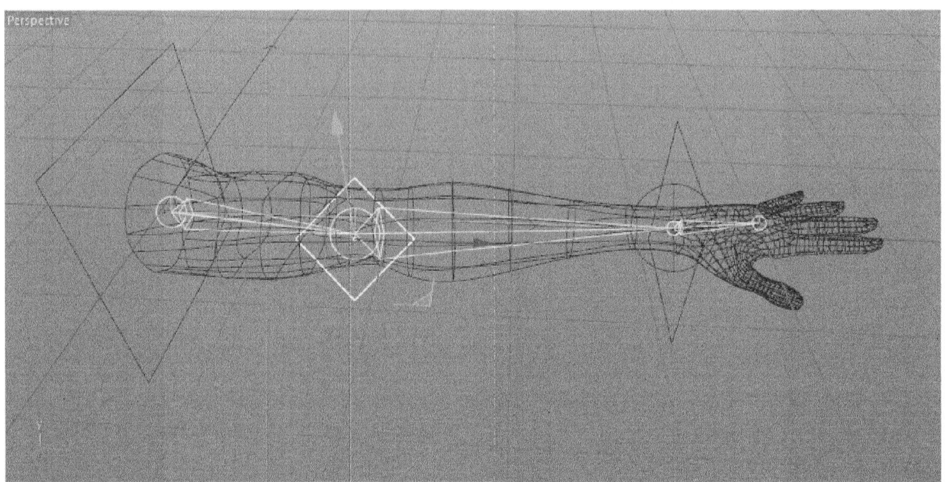

Figure 7-11 *The changed icon of shoulder_joint.Pole*

Next, you will create hierarchy for controls.

10. In the Object Manager, select *wrist control* and press and hold the left mouse button. Next, drag and drop it on *wrist_joint.Goal*; *wrist control* is connected with *wrist_joint.Goal.*

11. Select *wrist_joint.Goal* and press and hold the left mouse button. Next, drag and drop it on *shoulder control*; *wrist_joint.Goal* is connected with *shoulder control.*

Figure 7-12 shows hierarchy for controls in the Object Manager.

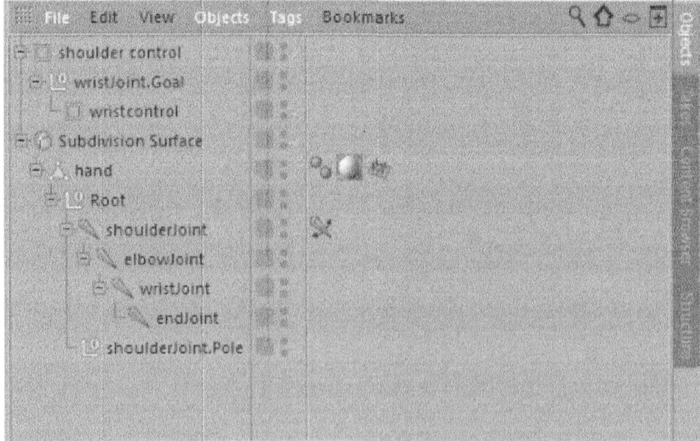

Figure 7-12 *Hierarchy for controls in the Object Manager*

Adding Constraints to the Bones and Controllers

In this section, you will add constraints to the joints.

1. In the Object Manager, select *Root* and right-click on it; a shortcut menu is displayed. In this shortcut menu, choose **Character Tags > Constraint**, refer to Figure 7-13. The constraint is applied to *Root* and the **Constraint Expression [Constraint]** tag is added to the Object Manager.

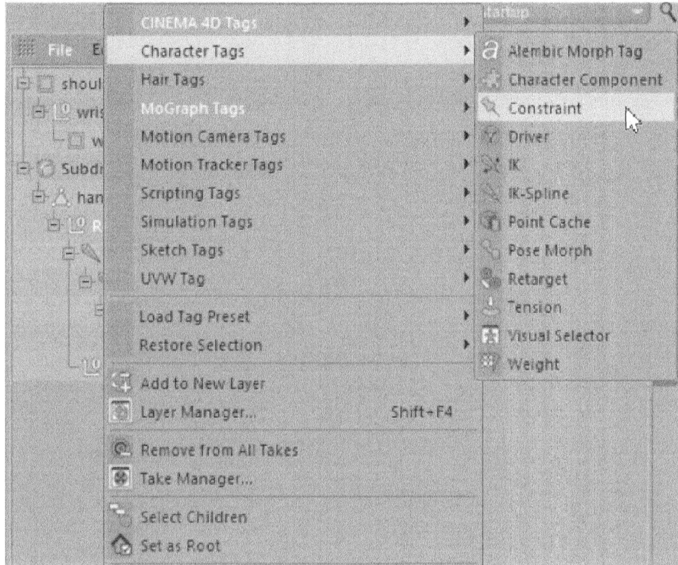

***Figure 7-13** Choosing **Constraint** from the shortcut menu*

2. In the **Constraints** area, select the **PSR** check box from the Attribute Manager. Next, choose the **PSR** button; the **PSR** area is displayed. In the **PSR** area, choose the arrow button on the right of the **Target** edit box and select *shoulder control* in the Object Manager; *shoulder control* is displayed in the **Target** edit box.

   The PSR constraint is used to move, rotate, and scale an object along with the target object.

3. In the Object Manager, select *shoulder control* and rotate it; all joints and controls also rotate along with *shoulder control*, refer to Figure 7-14. Next, press CTRL+ Z to undo the rotation.

4. In the Object Manager, select *wrist_joint* and right-click on it; a shortcut menu is displayed. In this shortcut menu, choose **Character Tags > Constraint**. The constraint is applied to *wrist_joint* and added to the Object Manager.

5. In the **Constraints** area, select the **Parent** check box from the Attribute Manager. Next, choose the **Parent** button; the **Parent** area is displayed. In the **Parent** area, choose the arrow button on the right of the **Target** edit box and select *wrist control* in the Object Manager; *wrist control* is displayed in the **Target** edit box.

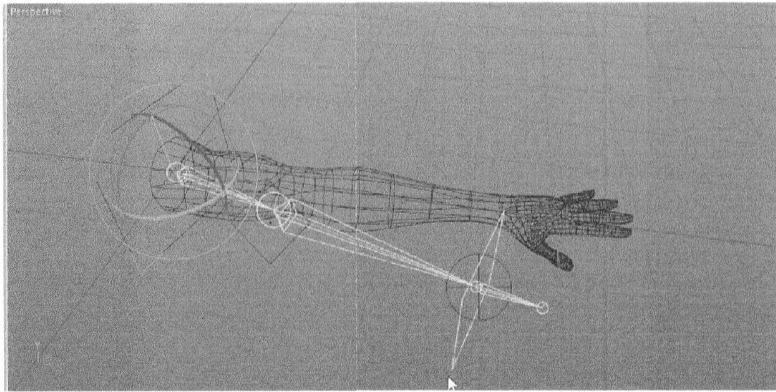

Figure 7-14 *All joints and controls rotating along with shoulder control in the Perspective viewport*

6. In the Object Manager, select *wrist control* and rotate it; *wrist_joint* and *end_joint* also rotate along with it, refer to Figure 7-15. Next, press CTRL+ Z to undo the rotation.

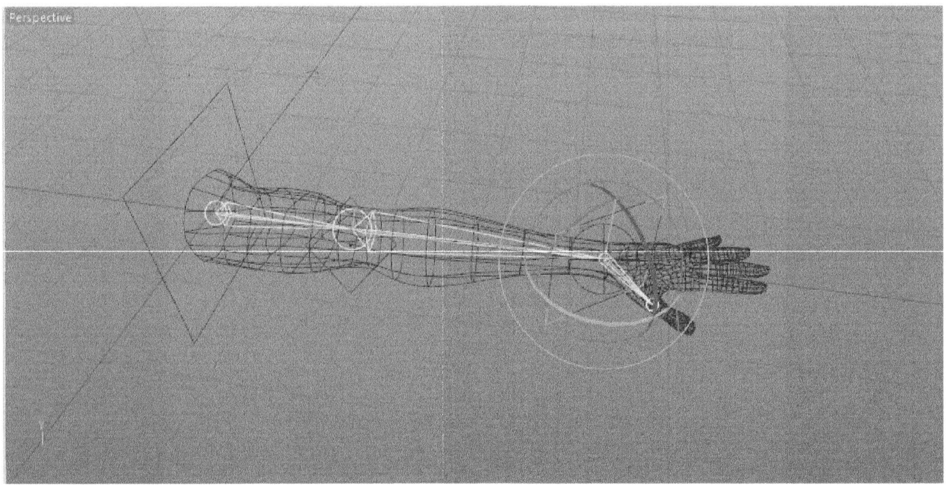

Figure 7-15 *The wrist_joint and end_joint rotating along with wrist control*

7. In the Object Manager, select *shoulder_joint.Pole* and move it in the Perspective viewport to change its position, as shown in Figure 7-16.

8. In the Object Manager, select *wrist_joint.Goal* and move it in the Perspective viewport, as shown in Figure 7-17. You will notice that elbow movement is controlled by *wrist_joint.Goal,* refer to Figure 7-17. Next, press CTRL+ Z to undo the rotation.

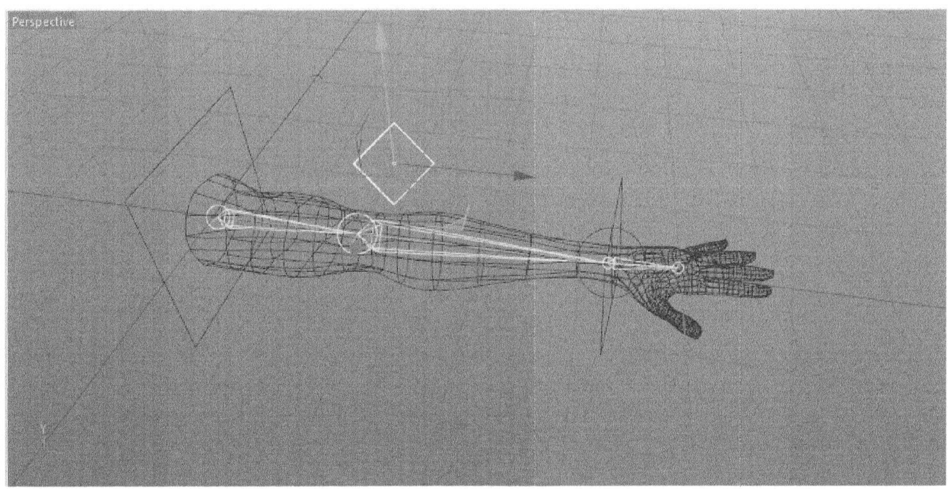

Figure 7-16 *Position of shoulder_joint.Pole changed*

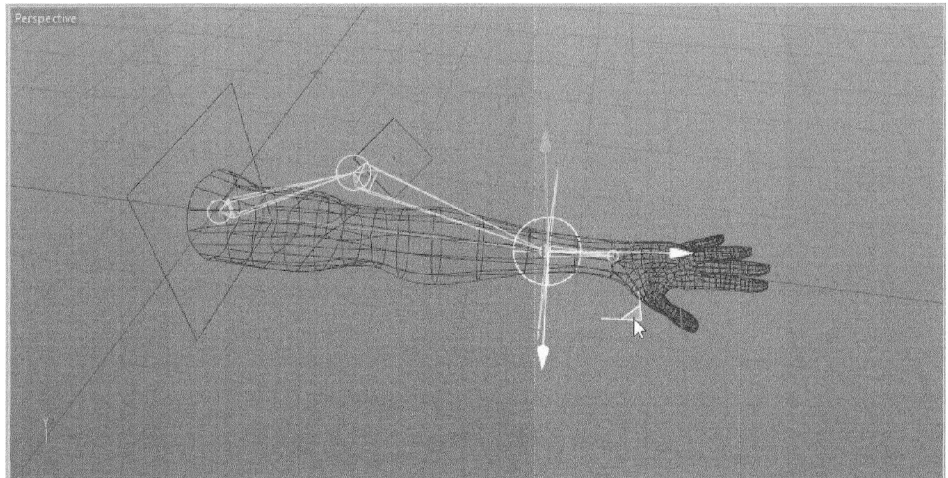

Figure 7-17 *Elbow movement controlled by wrist_joint.Goal*

9. In the Object Manager, select *shoulder_joint.Pole* and move it in the Perspective viewport, refer to Figure 7-18. You will notice that elbow rotation is controlled with *shoulder_joint.Pole*. Next, press CTRL+ Z to undo the rotation.

Binding the Rig

In this section, you will bind the rig using the **Bind** tool.

1. Select *hand, Root, shoulder_joint, elbow_joint, wrist_joint,* and *end_joint* in the Object Manager using the CTRL key.

2. Choose **Character > Commands > Bind** from the main menu; *Skin* is added to the Object Manager, as shown in Figure 7-19.

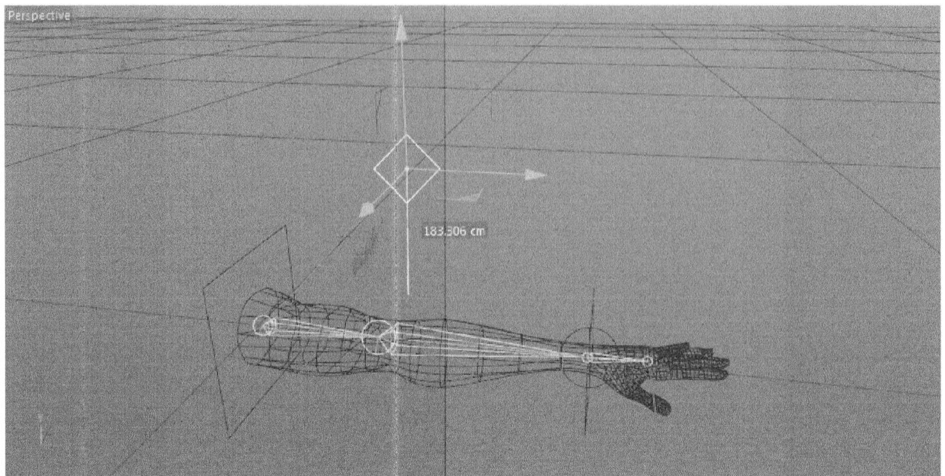

Figure 7-18 *Elbow rotation controlled by shoulder_joint.Pole*

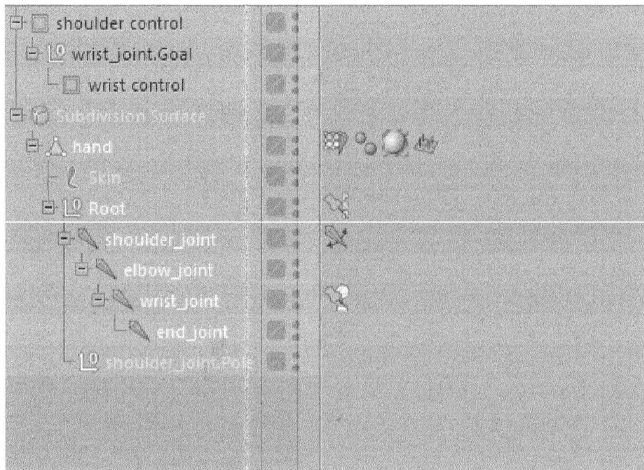

Figure 7-19 *Skin added to the Object Manager*

Now, rotate *shoulder control*; full arm rotates along with it. Also, move *wrist_joint.Goal*; the elbow moves along with it. Similarly, rotate *wrist control* to rotate wrist. Finally move *shoulder_joint. pole* to rotate the arm.

Saving the Scene

After completing the tutorial, you will save the file using the steps given next.

1. Choose **File > Save As** from the main menu; the **Save File** dialog box is displayed. In this dialog box, browse to the location *\Documents\c4dr20\c07*.

2. Enter **c07tut1** in the **File name** edit box and then choose the **Save** button.

EXERCISE

The rendered output of the model used in the following exercise can be accessed by downloading the *c07_cinema4d_r20_exr.zip* from *www.cadsofttech.com*. The path of the file is as follows: *Textbooks > Animation and Visual Effects > MAXON CINEMA 4D > MAXON CINEMA 4D R20 Studio for Novices*

Exercise 1

Extract the contents of the *c07_cinema4d_r20_exr.zip* file of a human leg from *www.cadsofttech.com* and then create a rig for the leg, as shown in Figure 7-20. **(Expected time: 30 min)**

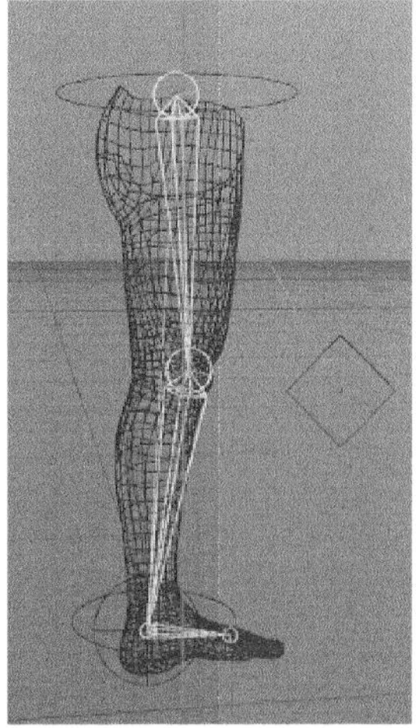

Figure 7-20 *Rig for a human leg*

Chapter 8

Animation

Learning Objectives

After completing this chapter, you will be able to:

- *Create key animation*
- *Create path animation*
- *Work with the Timeline panel*

INTRODUCTION

Animation is an act of giving life to a 3D object or character. To animate an object, you need to define different positions, rotations, and scaling of an object at different frames in the time slider. On playing an animation, all frames are displayed one after the other in quick succession to create an illusion of movement. In this chapter, you will learn about the playback control buttons available in the Animation toolbar. You will also learn to use the Timeline panel.

TUTORIALS

All the files used in the tutorials can be downloaded from the CADSoft website (*www.cadsofttech.com*). These files are compressed in zip file format and are required to be extracted before using them in the tutorials. The path of the files is as follows: *Textbooks > Animation and Visual Effects > MAXON CINEMA 4D > MAXON CINEMA 4D R20 Studio for Novices*

Next, you need to browse to *\Documents\c4dr20* and create a new folder in it with the name *c08*. Next, extract the contents of the zip file in this folder.

Tutorial 1

In this tutorial, you will create a basket ball animation, as shown in Figure 8-1.

(Expected time: 35 min)

Figure 8-1 *The basket ball at frame 66*

The following steps are required to complete this tutorial:

a. Open the file.
b. Animate the basketball.
c. Fine-tune the animation.
d. Save and render the animation.

Opening the File

In this section, you will open the file.

1. Choose **File > Open** from the main menu; the **Open File** dialog box is displayed.

2. In the **Open File** dialog box, browse to *\Documents\c4dr20\c08\c08_tut1_start.c4d* and then choose the **Open** button; the *c08_tut1_start.c4d* file is opened, as shown in Figure 8-2.

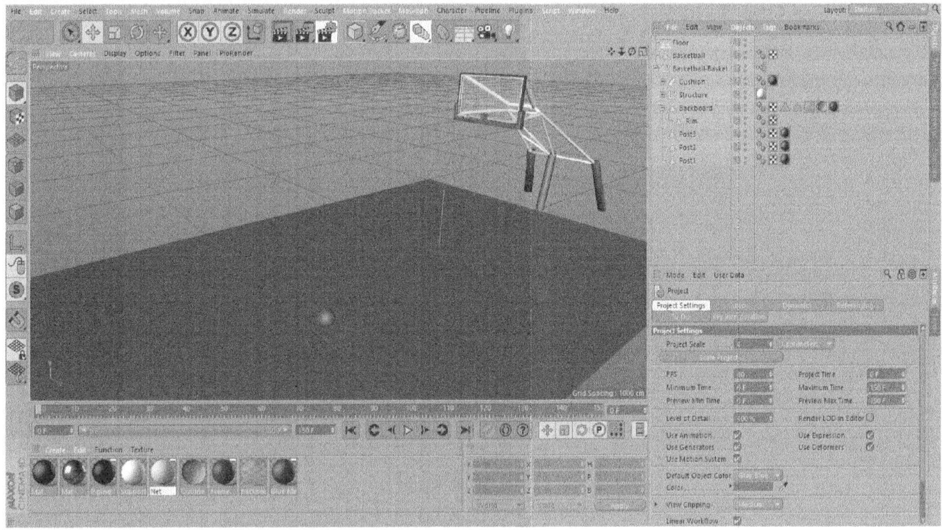

Figure 8-2 *The c08_tut1_start.c4d file*

Animating the Basketball

In this section, you will animate the *basketball* by adding the keyframes.

1. Press F3; the Right viewport is maximized. In the Animation toolbar, choose the **Autokeying** button and make sure that the timeslider is set to frame 0.

2. Select *basketball* in the Object Manager and then choose the **Coord** button in the Attribute Manager, if not already chosen; the **Coordinates** area is displayed. In the **Coordinates** area, right-click on the circle located on the left of the **P . X** spinner; a shortcut menu is displayed. Choose **Animation > Add Keyframe** from the shortcut menu; the circle located on the left of **P . X**, **P . Y**, and **P . Z** turns red.

3. In the **Coordinates** area, set the parameters as follows:

   P . X: **-40.84** P . Y: **464.471** P . Z: **-815.996**

   Figure 8-3 displays *basketball* at frame 0.

4. In the Animation toolbar, move the timeslider to frame 10. Alternatively, enter **10** in the **Current Time** spinner; the timeslider is set to frame 10.

5. Make sure *basketball* is selected in the Object Manager. In the **Coordinates** area, set the parameters as follows:

   P . Y: **796.753** P . Z: **-455.277**

   Figure 8-4 displays *basketball* at frame 10.

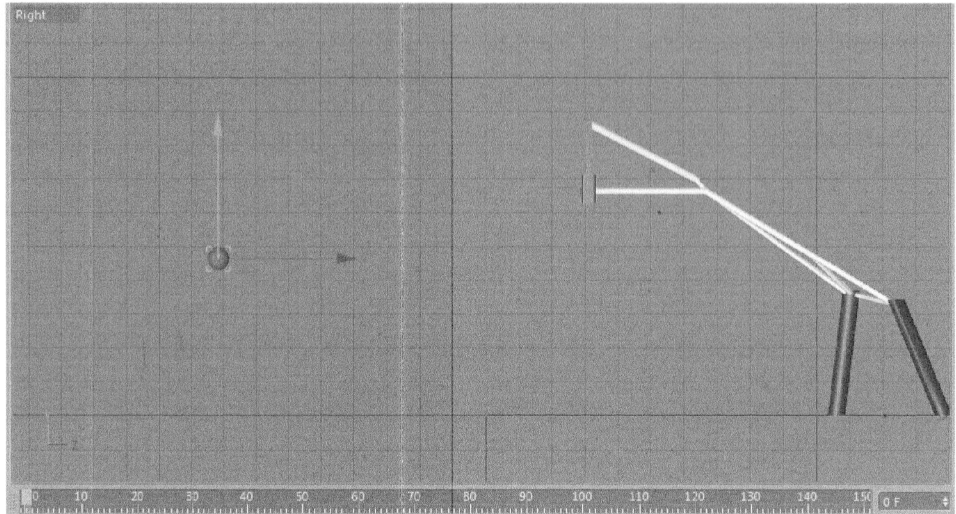

Figure 8-3 *The basketball at frame 0*

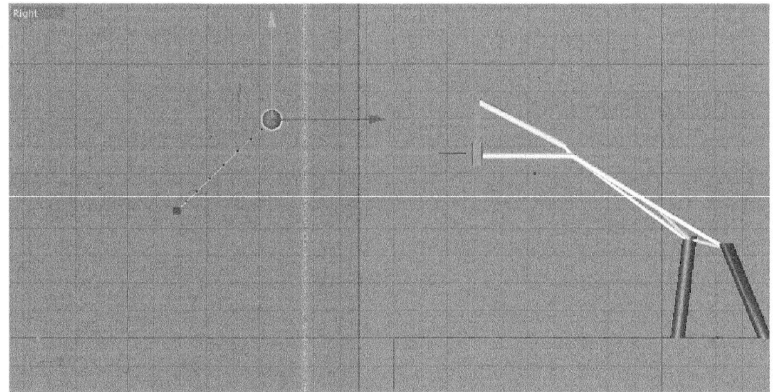

Figure 8-4 *The basketball at frame 10*

6. In the Animation toolbar, move the timeslider to frame 20.

7. Make sure *basketball* is selected in the Object Manager. In the **Coordinates** area, set the parameters as follows:

   P . Y: **954.44** P . Z: **28.102**

   Figure 8-5 displays *basketball* at frame 20.

8. In the Animation toolbar, move the timeslider to frame 30.

9. Make sure *basketball* is selected in the Object Manager. In the **Coordinates** area, set the parameters as follows:

   P . Y: **739.71** P . Z: **248.523**

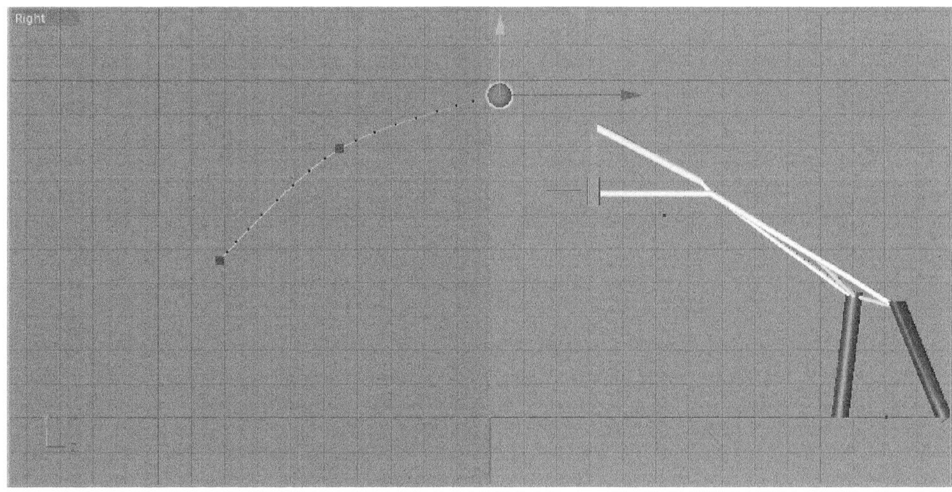

Figure 8-5 *The basketball at frame 20*

Figure 8-6 displays *basketball* at frame 30.

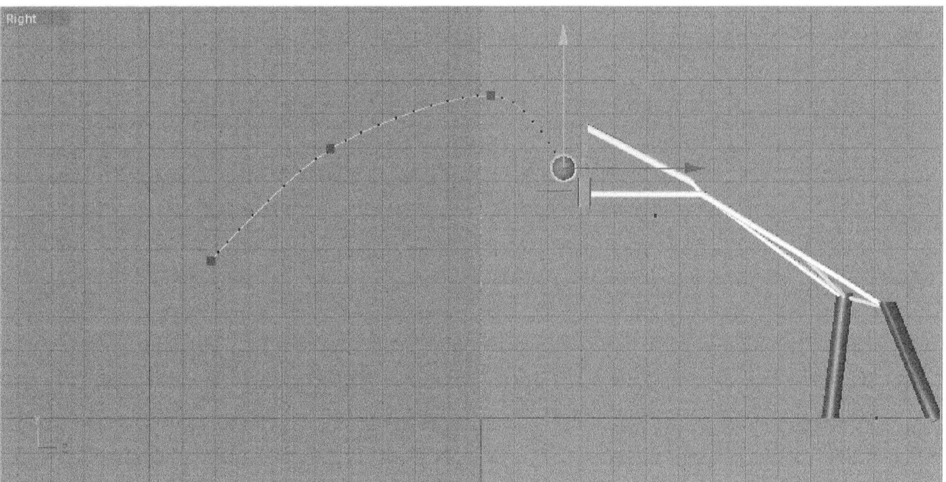

Figure 8-6 *The basketball at frame 30*

10. In the Animation toolbar, move the timeslider to frame 34.

11. Make sure *basketball* is selected in the Object Manager. In the **Coordinates** area, set the parameters as follows:

    P . Y: **567.025** P . Z: **235.442**

    Figure 8-7 displays *basketball* at frame 34.

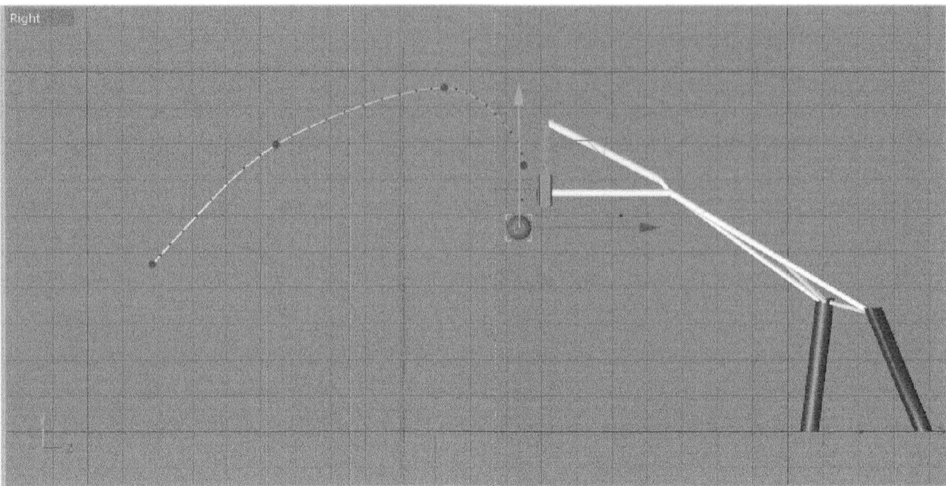

Figure 8-7 *The basketball at frame 34*

12. Similarly, move the timeslider to frames and set the values in the Attribute Manager as given in Table 8-1.

Table 8-1 *The transformation values of basketball*

Frame to be selected	P . Y	P . Z
40	29.429	18.251
50	332.391	-95.207
64	30.581	-229.294
73	227.576	-322.123
84	31.041	-435.581
91	141.612	-507.782
100	32.92	-609.611
150	32.92	-1061.761

Figure 8-8 displays *basketball* at frame 150.

13. Choose the **Play Forwards** button from the Animation toolbar to view the animation of *basketball*.

    Next, you will rotate *basketball.*

14. Make sure *basketball* is selected in the Object Manager. Next, move the timeslider to frame 0. In the **Coordinates** area, right-click on the circle located on the left of the **R . H** spinner; a shortcut menu is displayed. From this shortcut menu, choose **Animation > Add Keyframe**; the circle located at the left of the **R . H**, **R . P**, and **R . B** spinners turn red.

15. Move the timeslider to frames and set the values in the Attribute Manager as given in Table 8-2.

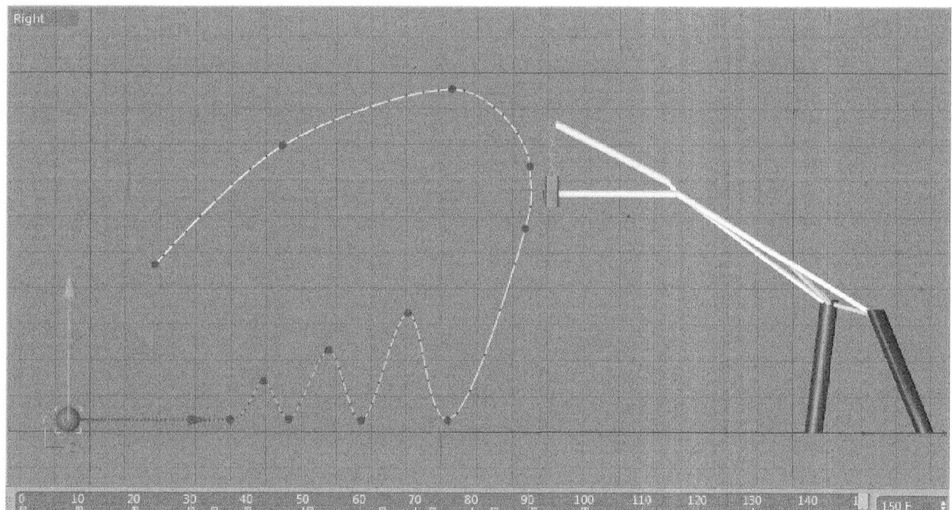

Figure 8-8 The basketball at frame 150

Table 8-2 The rotation values of basketball

Frame to be selected	R . P
40	90
64	180
84	270
100	360
150	520

Next, you will create the squash and stretch effect on *basketball* when it touches *Floor*.

16. Move the timeslider to frame 39. In the **Coordinates** area, right-click on the circle located on the left of the **S . X** spinner; a shortcut menu is displayed. From this shortcut menu, choose **Animation > Add Keyframe**; the circle located at the left of the **S . X**, **S . Y**, and **S . Z** spinners turns red.

    Next, you need to copy the keyframe created at frame 39 to other frames.

17. Make sure *basketball* is selected in the Object Manager and right-click on it; a shortcut menu is displayed. Choose **Show FCurves** from the shortcut menu, refer to Figure 8-8; the **Timeline** window is displayed.

18. Select **Scale . X**, **Scale . Y**, and **Scale . Z**, from the list displayed on the left pane of the **Timeline** window. Next, select the keyframe at frame 39 by using the rectangular marquee selection, as shown in Figure 8-9. Next, press CTRL+C. Now, move the timeslider to frame 43 and press CTRL+V; the selected keyframe is copied to frame 43.

*Figure 8-9 Selecting the keyframe from the **Timeline** window*

Note

*Choose **F-Curve > Show All Tracks** from the **Timeline** window menu bar to display only the selected curves in the window.*

19. Similarly copy the selected keyframe at frames 67 and 87. Next, minimize the **Timeline** window.

20. Move the timeslider to frame 40. Select *basketball* in the Object Manager again. In the **Coordinates** area, enter the value **0.87** in the **S . Z** spinner; *basketball* is squashed and a keyframe is created at this frame, refer to Figure 8-10.

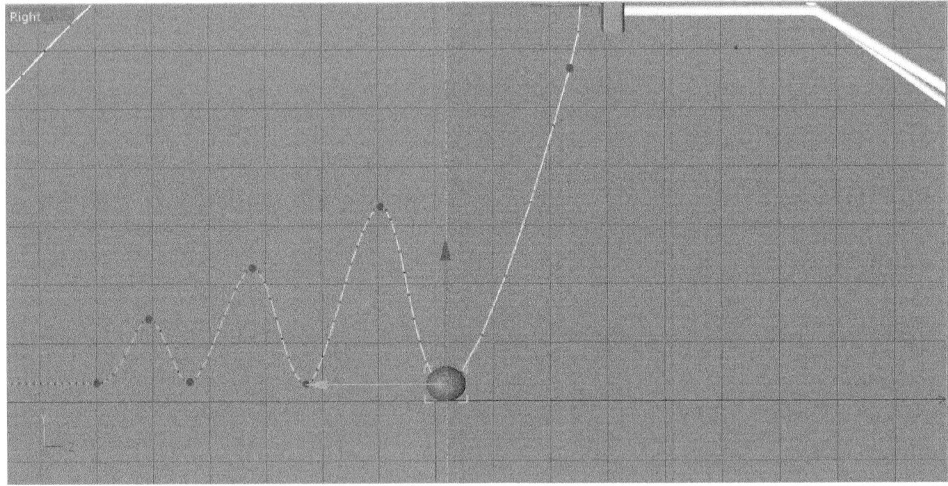

Figure 8-10 Squashed basketball at frame 40

21. Move the timeslider to frame 64. In the **Coordinates** area, enter the value **0.87** in the **S . Y** spinner; basketball is squashed and a keyframe is created at this frame.

22. Move the timeslider to frame 84. In the **Coordinates** area, enter the value **0.87** in the **S . X** spinner; basketball is squashed and a keyframe is created at this frame.

23. Choose the **Play Forwards** button from the Animation toolbar to view the animation of *basketball*.

Fine-Tuning the Animation

In this section, you will fine-tune the animation using the **Timeline** window.

1. In the Animation toolbar, move the timeslider to frame 40. Next, maximize the **Timeline** window. Select **Position Y** from the list displayed on the left pane of the **Timeline** window. Select the keyframe at frame 40 by using the rectangular marquee selection, refer to Figure 8-11.

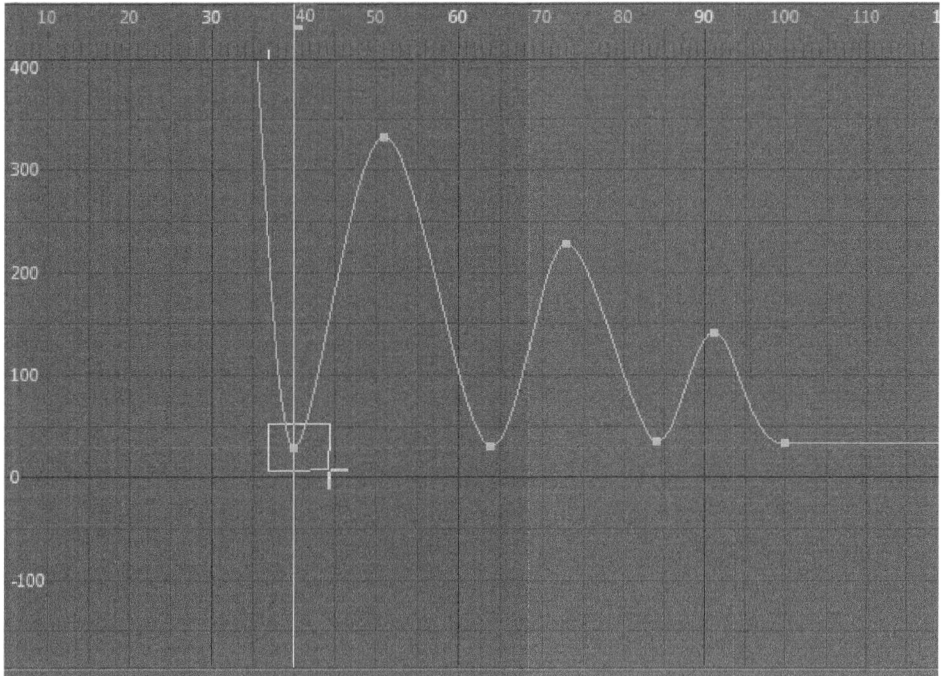

***Figure 8-11** Selecting the keyframe from the **Timeline** window*

2. Choose the **Break Tangents** button from the **Timeline** window and then move the tangents using the **Move** tool to add weight to *basketball* when it touches *Floor*, refer to Figure 8-12.

3. Similarly, select the keyframes at frame 64, 84, and 100, one by one, by using the rectangular marquee selection and then move their tangents, as shown in Figure 8-13 as done in previous steps.

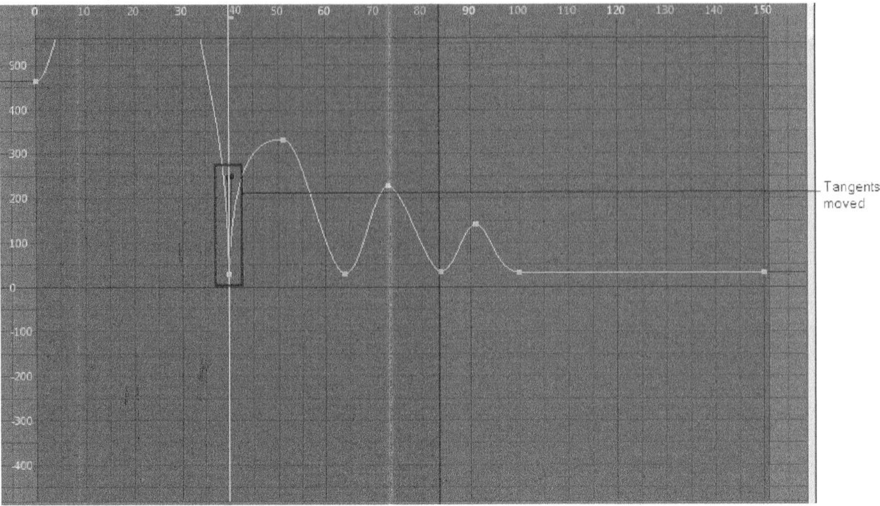

*Figure 8-12 Moving the tangents in the **Timeline** window*

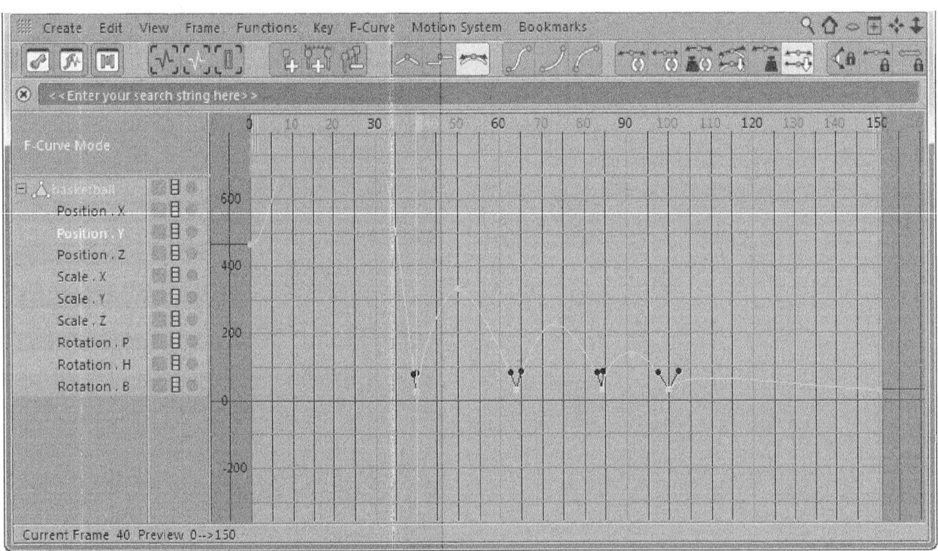

Figure 8-13 Moving the tangents at other frames

4. Select the keyframes at frames 50, 73, and 91 one by one from the **Timeline** window and then choose the **Ease Ease** button.

5. Choose the **Play Forwards** button from the Animation toolbar to view the animation of *basketball.*

Saving and Rendering the Animation

In this section, you will save and render the animation. You can also view the final render sequence by downloading the file *c08_cinema4d_r20_rndr.zip* from *www.cadsofttech.com*. The path of the file is mentioned at the beginning of the chapter.

1. Choose the **Edit Render Settings** tool from the Command Palette; the **Render Settings** window is displayed. In this window, choose the **Output** button; the **Output** area is displayed. In this area, enter **150** in the **To** spinner; the **Frames** option gets updated to **151** (from 0 to 150).

2. Choose the **Save** button from the list displayed on the left in the **Render Settings** window; the **Regular Image** area is displayed. In this area, make sure that the **Save** check box is selected. Next, choose the browse button located next to the **File** text box; the **Save File** dialog box is displayed.

3. In the **Save File** dialog box, browse to the location *\Documents\c4dr20\c08* and enter **c08tut1** in the **File name** text box. Next, choose the **Save** button.

4. Select the **AVI Movie** option from the **Format** drop-down list. Next, close the **Render Settings** window.

5. Choose the **Render to Picture Viewer** tool from the Command Palette; the **Picture Viewer** window is displayed and the rendering begins. The file is automatically saved at the specified location.

Tutorial 2

In this tutorial, you will animate the cart using the path animation and key animation, refer to Figure 8-14. **(Expected time: 25 min)**

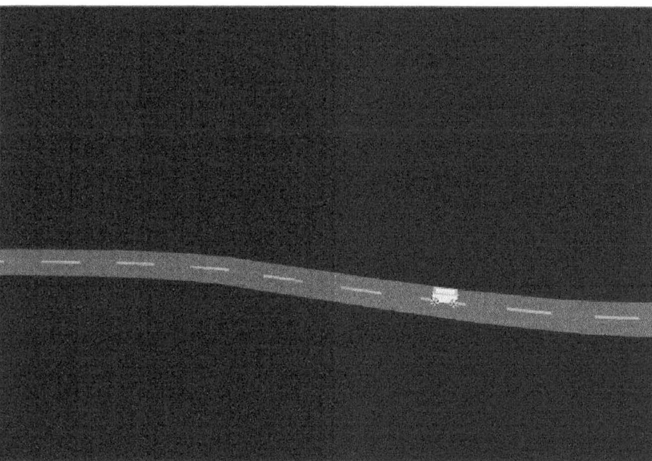

Figure 8-14 *Moving cart at frame 45*

The following steps are required to complete this tutorial:

a. Open the file.
b. Align the cart along a spline path.
c. Move the cart.
d. Rotate the wheels of the cart.
e. Save and render the scene.

Opening the File

In this section, you will open the file.

1. Choose **File > Open** from the main menu; the **Open File** dialog box is displayed.

2. In the **Open File** dialog box, browse to *\Documents\ c4dr20\c08\c08_tut2_start.c4d* and then choose the **Open** button; the *c08_tut2_start* file is opened, as shown in Figure 8-15.

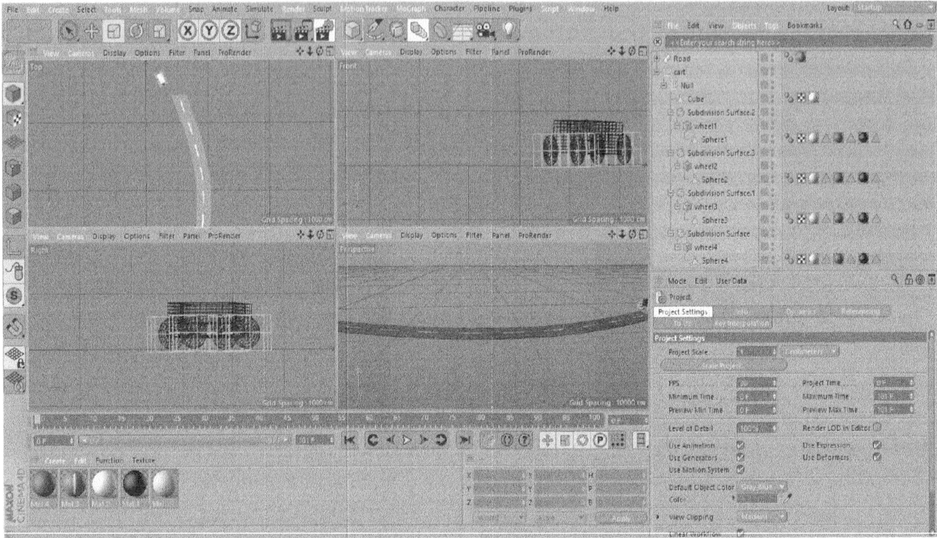

Figure 8-15 The c08_tut2_start file

Aligning the Cart along a Spline Path

In this section, you will align the cart along a spline path using a CINEMA 4D tag.

1. Select *cart* in the Object Manager. Next, right-click on it; a shortcut menu is displayed. Choose **CINEMA 4D Tags > Align to Spline** from the shortcut menu, as shown in Figure 8-16; the **Align to Spline Expression [Align to Spline]** tag is added to the Object Manager, as shown in Figure 8-17.

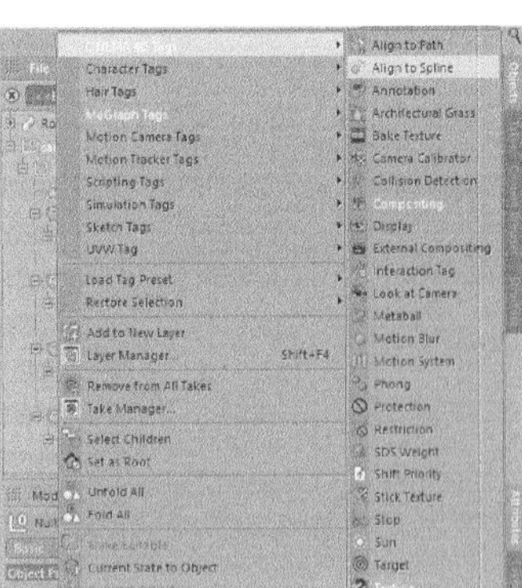

Figure 8-16 Choosing ***Align to Spline*** *from the shortcut menu*

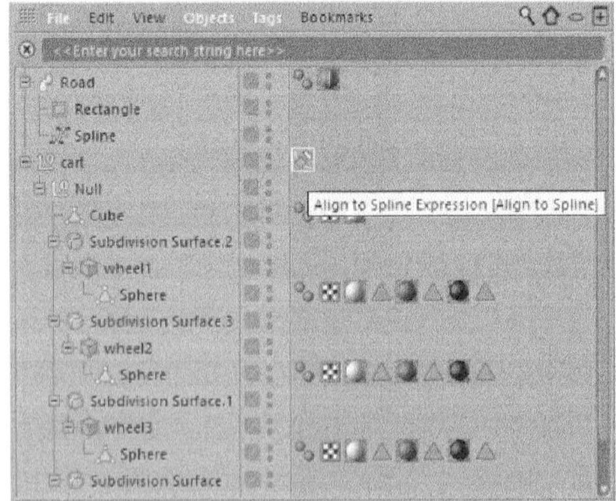

Figure 8-17 The ***Align to Spline Expression [Align to Spline]*** *tag in the Object Manager*

2. Expand *Road* in the Object Manager. Also, make sure the **Align to Spline Expression [Align to Spline]** tag is selected in the Object Manager.

3. In the Attribute Manager, make sure the **Tag** button is chosen. Next, choose the Arrow button located next to the **Spline Path** option in the **Tag Properties** area; the shape of the cursor is changed. Next, select *Spline* from the Object Manager; *Spline* is displayed in the **Spline Path** edit box in the Attribute Manager, refer to Figure 8-18. Maximize the Perspective viewport. You will notice that *cart* is aligned with *Road* in the Perspective viewport, as shown in Figure 8-19.

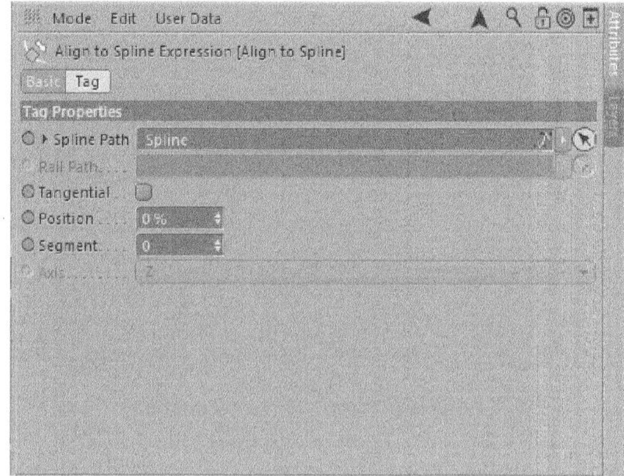

Figure 8-18 *Spline displayed in the **Spline Path** edit box*

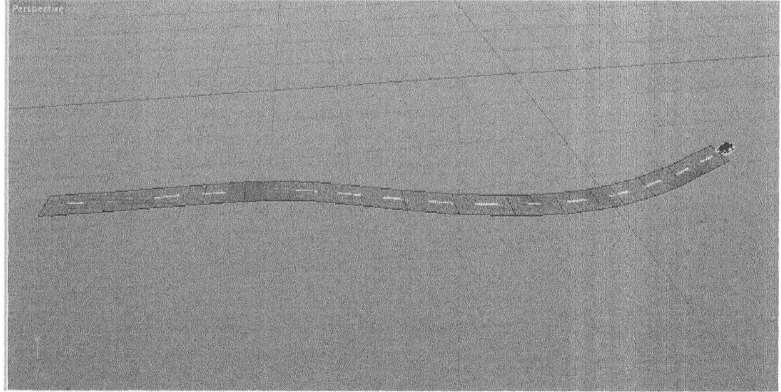

Figure 8-19 *cart aligned with Road*

Moving the Cart

In this section, you will move *cart* by setting the keyframe for the **Position** spinner of the **Align to Spline Expression [Align to Spline]** tag.

1. Make sure the timeslider is at frame 0. In the Attribute Manager, right-click on the circle located at the left of the **Position** spinner in the **Tag Properties** area; a shortcut menu is displayed. Choose **Animation > Add Keyframe** from it; the circle turns red and a keyframe is added at frame 0.

2. Move the time slider to frame 101. Next, in the Attribute Manager, enter **100** in the **Position** spinner.

3. Right-click on the circle located at the left of the **Position** spinner; a shortcut menu is displayed. Choose **Animation > Add Keyframe** from it; the circle turns red and a keyframe is added at frame 101. Also, *cart* is moved to the end of *Road*.

4. Choose the **Play Forwards** button from the Animation toolbar. You will notice that *cart* is not moving exactly along *Road* on its curved stretch, refer to Figure 8-20. To overcome it, select the **Tangential** check box located above the **Position** spinner in the Attribute Manager.

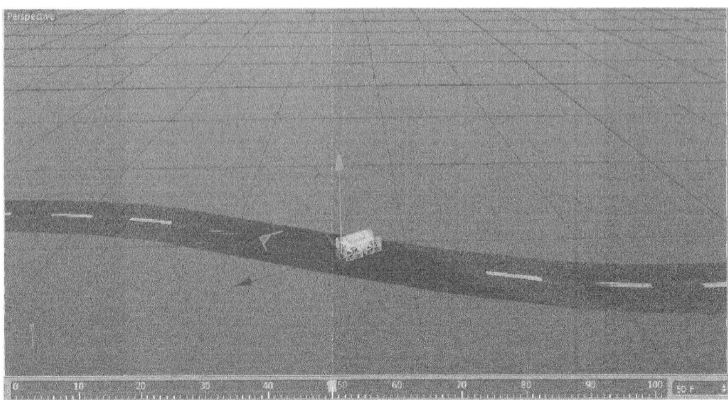

Figure 8-20 *cart at frame 50*

5. Choose the **Play Forwards** button from the Animation toolbar again. Now, you will notice that *cart* is moving exactly along *Road*.

Rotating the Wheels of the Cart

In this section, you will rotate the wheels of *cart* by setting keyframes at different frames to get a realistic look. You will also use the Timeline panel in the **Animation** layout to copy and paste the repetitive keyframes.

1. In the Object Manager, select *Sphere1*. In the Animation toolbar, choose the **Autokeying** button and make sure that the timeslider is set to frame 0.

2. In the Attribute Manager, choose the **Coord** button; the **Coordinates** area is displayed. Next, right-click on the circle located at the left of the **R . H** spinner and choose **Animation > Add Keyframe** from the shortcut menu displayed; a keyframe is added for *Sphere1* at frame 0.

3. Similarly, move the timeslider to the frames mentioned in Table 8-3 and add keyframes by setting the rotation values in the Attribute Manager as given in Table 8-3.

Table 8-3 *Rotation values for Sphere1*

Frame to be selected	R . H
5	-90
10	-180
15	-270
20	-360
21	0

You will notice that one round of rotation of *wheel1* is completed by setting the keyframes mentioned above.

Next, you need to copy these keyframes to repeat the rotation of *wheel1*. To copy the keyframes, you will use the Timeline panel in the **Animate** layout.

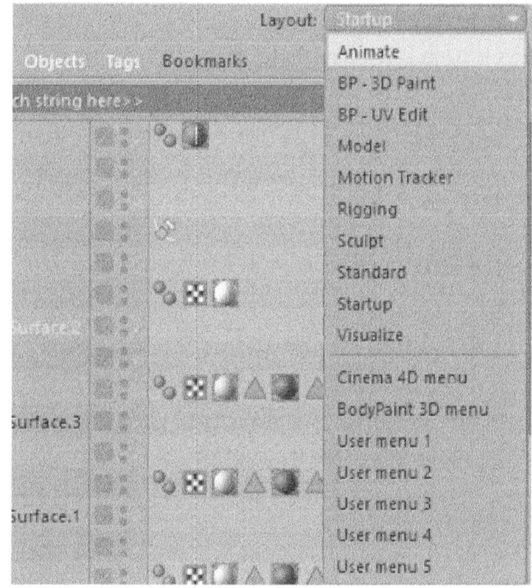

Figure 8-21 *Selecting **Animate** from the **Layout** drop-down list*

4. Select **Animate** from the **Layout** drop-down list located at the top right corner of the interface, as shown in Figure 8-21; the Animation layout is displayed, as shown in Figure 8-22.

5. In the **Animate** layout, enlarge the Timeline panel and zoom in the newly keyframes created using the navigation tools in it, refer to Figure 8-23. Figure 8-23 shows the modified size of the Timeline panel.

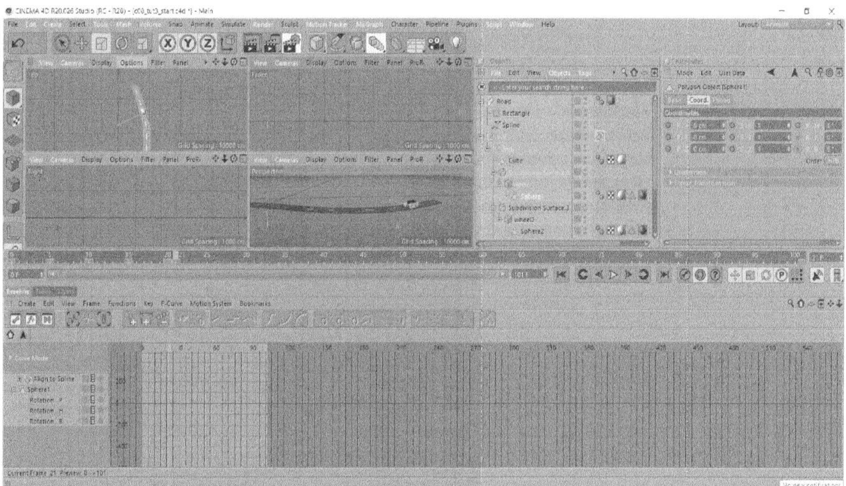

Figure 8-22 *The **Animate** layout displayed*

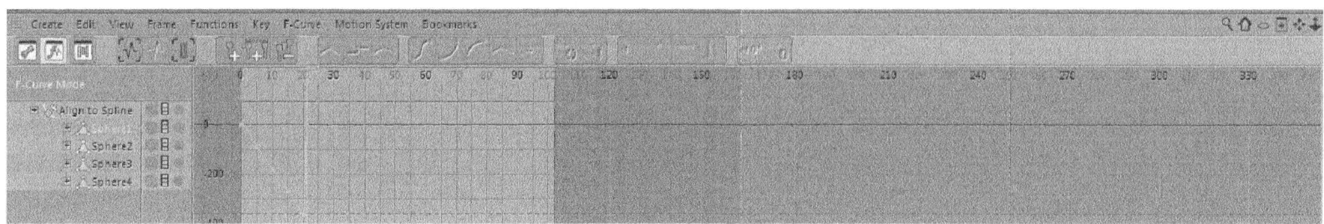

Figure 8-23 *The modified size of the Timeline panel*

6. Select five keyframes (excluding the keyframe at frame 0) in the Timeline panel by using the rectangular marquee selection, as shown in Figure 8-24.

7. Choose **Edit > Copy** from the Timeline menu, as shown in Figure 8-25.

8. Move the timeslider to frame 25. Next, choose **Edit > Paste** from the Timeline menu; the keyframes are copied, refer to Figure 8-26.

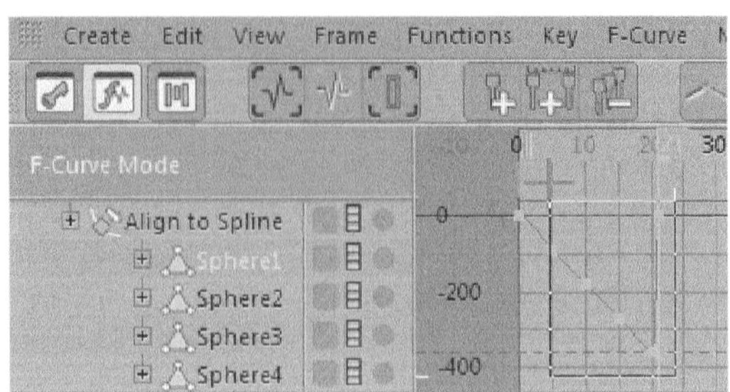

Figure 8-24 *Selecting all keyframes*

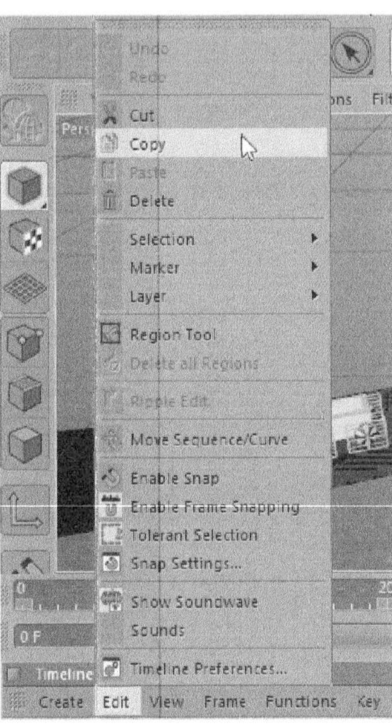

Figure 8-25 *Choosing **Copy** from the **Edit** menu*

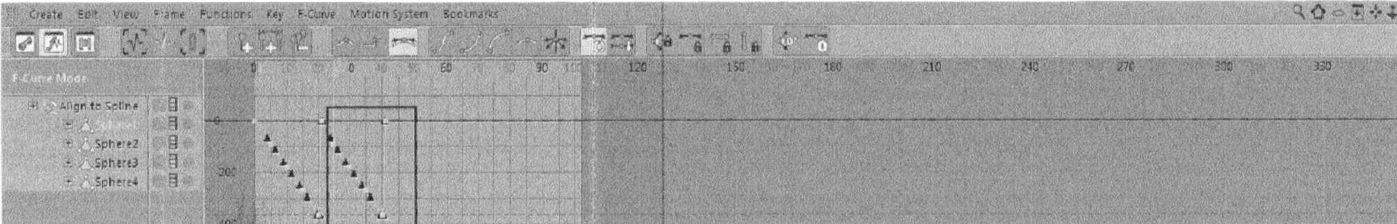

Figure 8-26 *Copied keyframes*

9. Move the timeslider to frame 45. Next, choose **Edit > Paste** from the Timeline menu; the keyframes are copied.

10. Move the timeslider to frame 65. Next, choose **Edit > Paste** from the Timeline menu; the keyframes are copied.

11. Move the timeslider to frame 85. Next, choose **Edit > Paste** from the Timeline menu; the keyframes are copied. Figure 8-27 shows all keyframes for *Sphere1*.

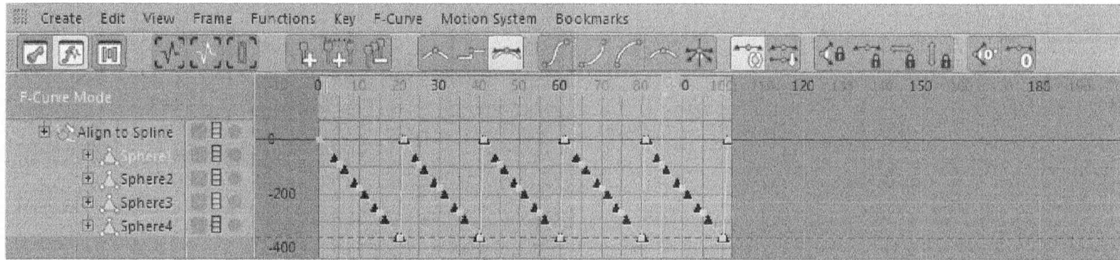

Figure 8-27 All keyframes for Sphere1

12. Move the timeslider to frame 0. In the Object Manager, select *Sphere2*.

13. In the Attribute Manager, choose the **Coord** button; the **Coordinates** area is displayed. Next, right-click on the circle located at the left of the **R . H** spinner and choose **Animation > Add Keyframe** from the shortcut menu displayed; a keyframe is added for *Sphere2* at frame 0.

14. Choose the **Dope Sheet** button and then select *Sphere1*. Next, select all keyframes from the Timeline panel using the rectangular marquee selection.

15. Choose **Edit > Copy** from the Timeline menu. Next, select *Sphere2* and make sure the timeslider is at frame 0. Now, choose **Edit > Paste** from the Timeline menu; all keyframes of *Sphere1* are copied to *Sphere2*.

16. Repeat the steps 13 through 15 for *Sphere3* and *Sphere4* in the Object Manager to set keyframes for them.

Saving and Rendering the Animation

In this section, you will save and render the animation. You can also view the final render sequence by downloading the file *c08_cinema4d_r20rndr.zip* from *www.cadsofttech.com*. The path of the file is mentioned at the beginning of the chapter.

1. Choose the **Edit Render Settings** tool from the Command Palette; the **Render Settings** window is displayed. In this window, choose the **Output** button; the **Output** area is displayed. In this area, enter **101** in the **To** spinner; the **Frames** option gets updated to **102** (from 0 to 101).

2. Choose the **Save** button from the list displayed on the left in the **Render Settings** window; the **Regular Image** area is displayed. In this area, make sure that the **Save** check box is selected. Next, choose the browse button located next to the **File** text box; the **Save File** dialog box is displayed.

3. In the **Save File** dialog box, browse to the location *\Documents\c4dr20\c08* and enter **c08tut2** in the **File name** text box. Next, choose the **Save** button. Select the **AVI Movie** option from the **Format** drop-down list. Next, close the **Render Settings** window.

EXERCISE

The rendered video sequence of the animation in the exercise can be accessed by downloading the *c08_cinema4d_r20_exr.zip* file from *www.cadsofttech.com*. The path of the file is as follows: *Textbooks > Animation and Visual Effects > MAXON CINEMA 4D > MAXON CINEMA 4D R20 Studio for Novices*

Exercise 1

Open the model shown in Figure 8-28 and then animate the keys falling from the table. Also, fine-tune the animation. **(Expected time: 35 min)**

Figure 8-28 *The c08_exr01_start file*

Chapter 9

Introduction to UV Mapping

Learning Objectives

After completing this chapter, you will be able to:

- *Work in different UV layouts*
- *Paint texture on 3D models*

INTRODUCTION

UV mapping is a process to project texture maps onto a 3D object. UVs are two dimensional texture coordinates that define a two dimensional coordinate system called UV texture space. The letters U and V in UV indicate the axes in the coordinate space. You can use the UV texture space to place image maps on a 3D surface in CINEMA 4D. UV mapping is a method used to provide a connection between a 3D model and the image or the texture map to be mapped on it. In CINEMA 4D, you need to UV map the model to apply a texture on it.

The BodyPaint 3D layout in CINEMA 4D is used to create and edit UV maps. In this chapter, you will learn to paint textures on the models using the Body Paint 3D.

TUTORIAL

All the files used in the tutorials can be downloaded from the CADSoft website (*www.cadsofttech.com*). These files are compressed in zip file format and are required to be extracted before using them in the tutorials. The path of the files is as follows: *Textbooks > Animation and Visual Effects > MAXON CINEMA 4D > MAXON CINEMA 4D R20 Studio for Novices*

Next, you need to browse to *\Documents\c4dr20* and create a new folder in it with the name *c09*. Next, extract the contents of the zip file in this folder.

Tutorial 1

In this tutorial, you will paint texture on a 3D model using the **BodyPaint 3D** tool. The final output is shown in Figure 9-1. **(Expected time: 30 min)**

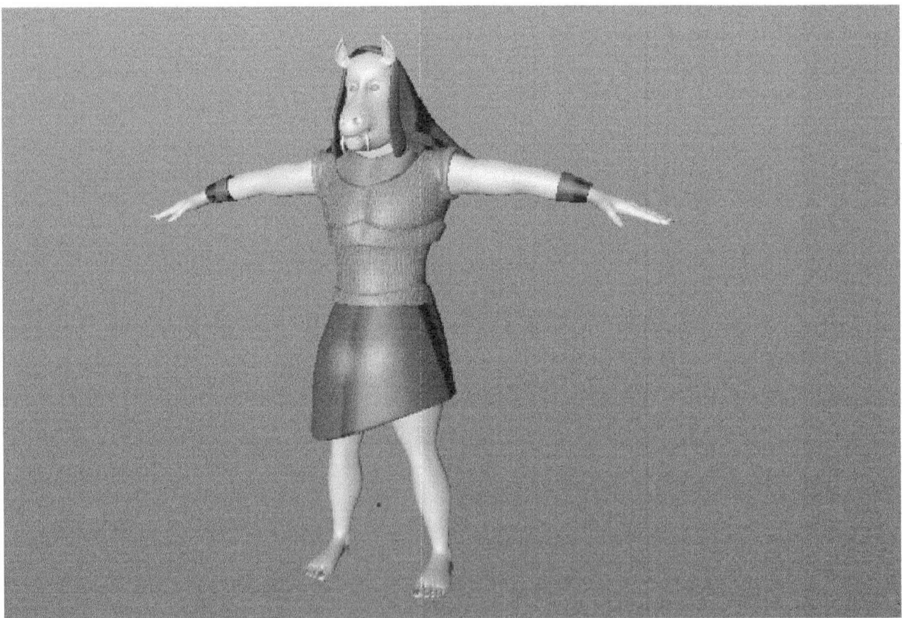

Figure 9-1 *The 3D model after applying body paint*

The following steps are required to complete this tutorial:

a. Open the file.
b. Unwrap the body of the model.
c. Paint the body of the model.
d. Paint clothes of the model.
e. Save and render the scene.

Opening the File

In this section, you will open the file.

1. Choose **File > Open** from the main menu; the **Open File** dialog box is displayed.

2. In the **Open File** dialog box, browse to *\Documents\c4dr20\c09\c09_tut1_start* and then choose the **Open** button; the *c09_tut1_start.c4d* file is opened, as shown in Figure 9-2.

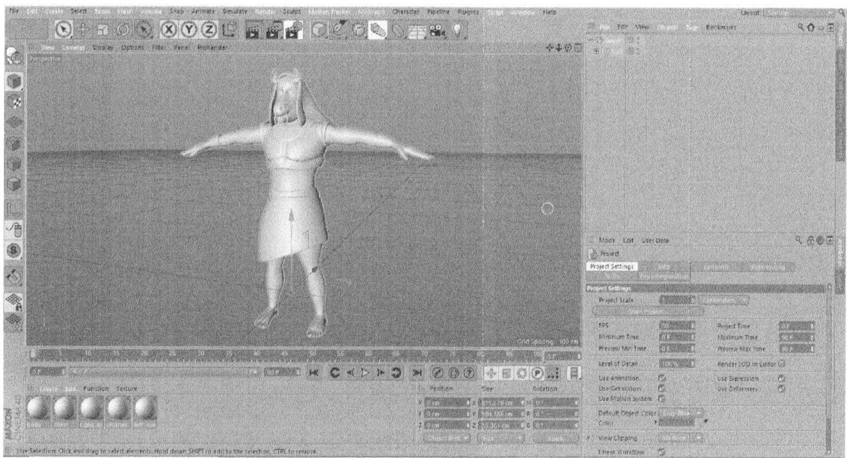

Figure 9-2 *The c09_tut1_start.c4d file*

Unwrapping the Body of the Model

In this section, you will unwrap the body of the model.

1. Make sure that the **BP UV Edit** option is selected from the **Layout** drop-down list.

2. Make sure *beast* is selected in the Object Manager and choose the **Paint Setup Wizard** tool from the Command Palette; the **BodyPaint 3D Setup Wizard** dialog box is displayed.

3. In the **BodyPaint 3D Setup Wizard** dialog box, make sure that the **Objects** radio button is selected. Next, choose the **Next>>** button; the **UV Setup** area is displayed in the **BodyPaint 3D Setup Wizard** dialog box, refer to Figure 9-8.

4. In the **BodyPaint 3D Setup Wizard** dialog box, choose the **Next>>** button; the **Material Options** area is displayed. Now, choose the **Finish >>** button and the **Close** button to close the dialog box.

Painting the Body of the Model

In this section, you will paint the body of the model.

1. Make sure that the **BP UV Edit** option is selected from the **Layout** drop-down list.

2. In the Object Manager, expand *Beast* and then expand *Null*. Now, select *Body* from the list of objects displayed.

3. Choose the **Colors** tab; the **Color** area is displayed, refer to Figure 9-3. Also, choose the **RGB** button. In the **Color** area, set the parameters as follows:

   R: **239** G: **200** B: **159**

*Figure 9-3 The **Color** area displayed*

4. Choose **Tools > Paint Tools > Fill Bitmap** from the main menu, as shown in Figure 9-4.

*Figure 9-4 Choosing **Paint Tools > Fill Bitmap** tool from the **Tools** menu*

The **Fill Bitmap** tool is used to fill the adjoining pixels with the selected color on a single click.

5. Using the **Fill Bitmap** tool, click on *Body* of the model in the Perspective viewport; *Body* is filled with the selected color, as shown in Figure 9-5.

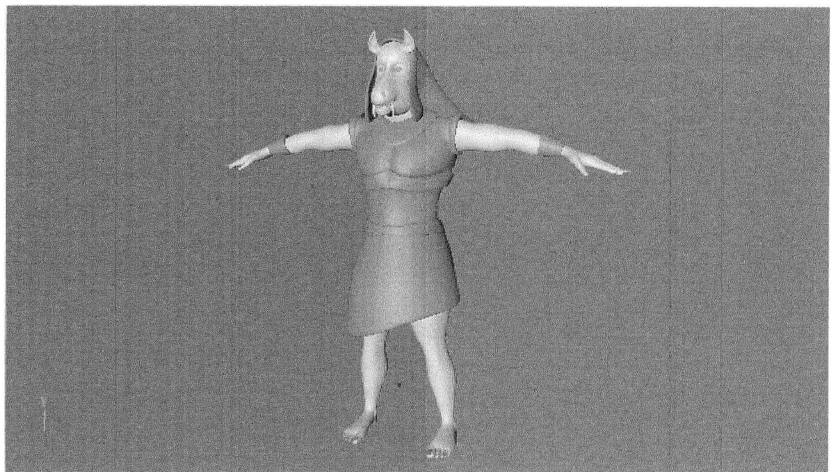

Figure 9-5 *The model filled with the selected color in the Perspective viewport*

Next, you will paint *chest* of the model.

6. In the **BP UV Edit** layout, choose the **Objects** tab; the Object Manager is displayed.

7. Select *chest* from the Object Manager. Now, choose the **Colors** tab; the **Color** area is displayed. In this area, select the **Texture Pain**t radio button.

8. Choose the arrow button located below the **Texture Paint** radio button; a flyout is displayed. Choose the **Load from Disc** option from the flyout; the **Select a Pattern** dialogue box is displayed. Now, select the **Armour.jpg** file from the list.

9. Move the cursor on *chest* and click; the texture gets applied on *chest*, as shown in Figure 9-6.

Painting the Clothes of the Model

In this section, you will paint the clothes of the model.

1. Make sure that the **BP UV Edit** option is selected from the **Layout** drop-down list.

2. Choose the **Objects** tab; the Object Manager is displayed. Select *Clothes* from the Object Manager.

3. Choose the **Colors** tab; the **Color** area is displayed. In this area, select the **Solid Color** radio button. Next, choose the **RGB** button and set the values for the parameters as follows:

   R: **106** G: **68** B: **29**

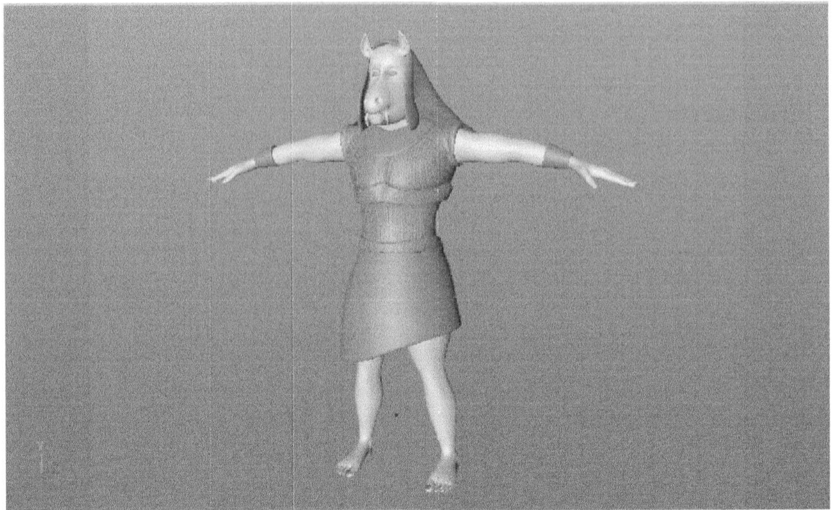

Figure 9-6 The color filled on chest

4. Choose **Tools > Paint Tools > Fill Bitmap** from the main menu. Next, click on *Clothes*; *Clothes* is filled with the selected color.

5. Choose the **Colors** tab; the **Color** area is displayed. In this area, enter **3** in the **Brightness** spinner.

6. Choose the **Brushes** tab from the bottom right side of the **BP UV Edit** layout. Next, expand **Default Presets> BodyPaint Presets> Brushes**: the list of brushes is displayed.

7. Expand the **Standard Tools** group of brushes by clicking on the triangle located on the left side. Next, select the **Airbrush** brush.

8. Choose the **Brush** tool from the Modes Palette and paint the clothes of the model, refer to Figure 9-7.

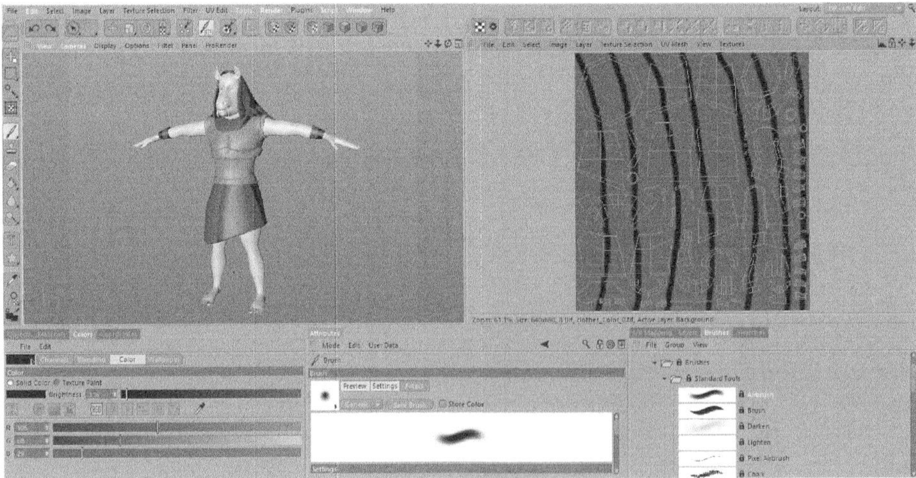

*Figure 9-7 The clothes painted using the **Brush** tool*

9. Make sure the **Brushes** tab is chosen on the bottom right side of the **BP UV Edit** layout. Next, expand **Multibrushes > Dosch Texture Brushes** and select the **Bark** brush.

10. Choose the **Settings** button in the **Attributes** tab; the **Settings** area is displayed. In this area, enter **2** in the **Hardness** spinner.

11. Choose the **Brush** tool from the Modes Palett and paint on the clothes of the model, as shown in Figure 9-8.

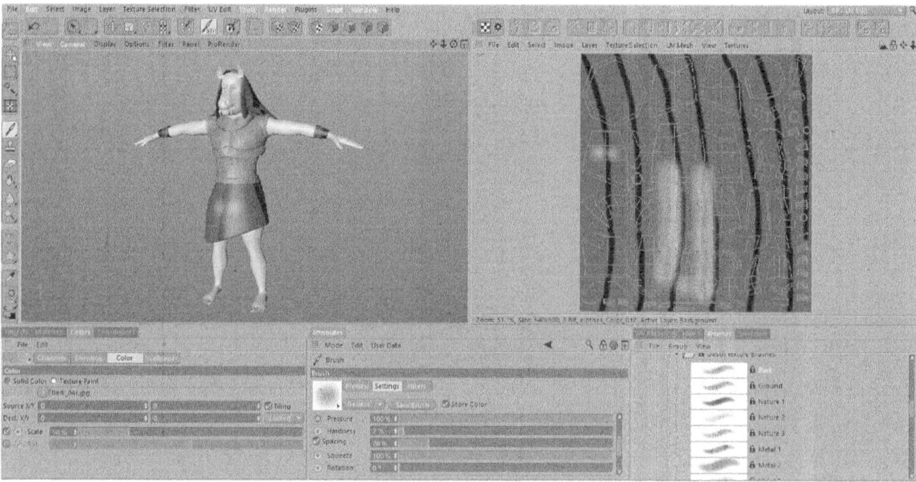

Figure 9-8 *The clothes painted using the **Brush** tool in the Texture View*

Saving and Rendering the Scene

In this section, you will save and render the scene. You can also view the final render of the model by downloading the file *c09_cinema4d_r20_rndr.zip* from *www.cadsofttech.com*. The path of the file is mentioned at the beginning of the chapter.

1. Choose **File > Save As** from the main menu; the **Save File** dialog box is displayed. In this dialog box, browse to the location *\Documents\c4dr20\c09*.

2. Enter **c09tut1** in the **File name** text box and then choose the **Save** button.

3. In the Perspective viewport, set the camera angle using the Viewport Navigation Tools located on the top right of the Perspective viewport. Next, you need to render the scene. For rendering, refer to Tutorial 1 of Chapter 2.

   The output of the model is shown in Figure 9-1.

EXERCISE

The rendered output of the model used in the exercise can be accessed by downloading the *c09_cinema4d_r20_exr.zip* from *www.cadsofttech.com*. The path of the file is as follows: *Textbooks > Animation and Visual Effects > MAXON CINEMA 4D > MAXON CINEMA 4D R20 Studio for Novices*

Exercise 1

Extract the contents of the *c09_cinema4d_r20_exr.zip* file. Open the model of a T-shirt and then paint it using the paint tools available in the **BP 3D Paint** layout, refer to Figure 9-9.

(Expected time: 30 min)

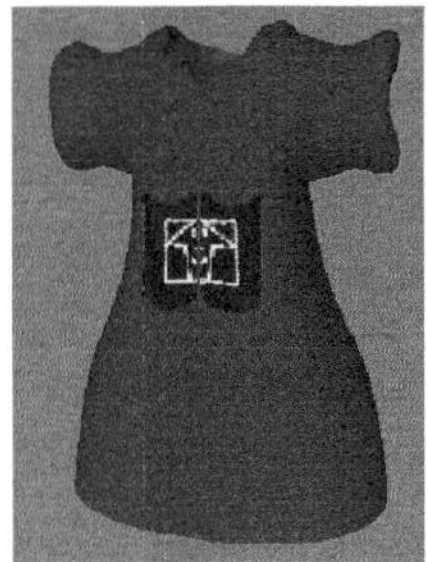

Figure 9-9 *The final output*

Chapter 10

Rendering

Learning Objectives

After completing this chapter, you will be able to:
- *Understand Global Illumination*
- *Create render passes*
- *Create the caustic patterns*

INTRODUCTION

The term render is derived from a French word which means to give back or yield. The process of rendering translates the created scene into a finalized 2D image. In this process, all textures and lighting in the scene are combined together to create a single flat image.

TUTORIAL

All the files used in the tutorials can be downloaded from the CADSoft website (*www.cadsofttech.com*). These files are compressed in zip file format and are required to be extracted before using them in the tutorials. The path of the files is as follows: *Textbooks > Animation and Visual Effects > MAXON CINEMA 4D > MAXON CINEMA 4D R20 Studio for Novices*

Next, you need to browse to *\Documents\c4dr20* and create a new folder in it with the name *c10*. Next, extract the contents of the zip file in this folder.

Tutorial 1

In this tutorial, you will render a table clock, as shown in Figure 10-1, and create render passes. **(Expected time: 25 min)**

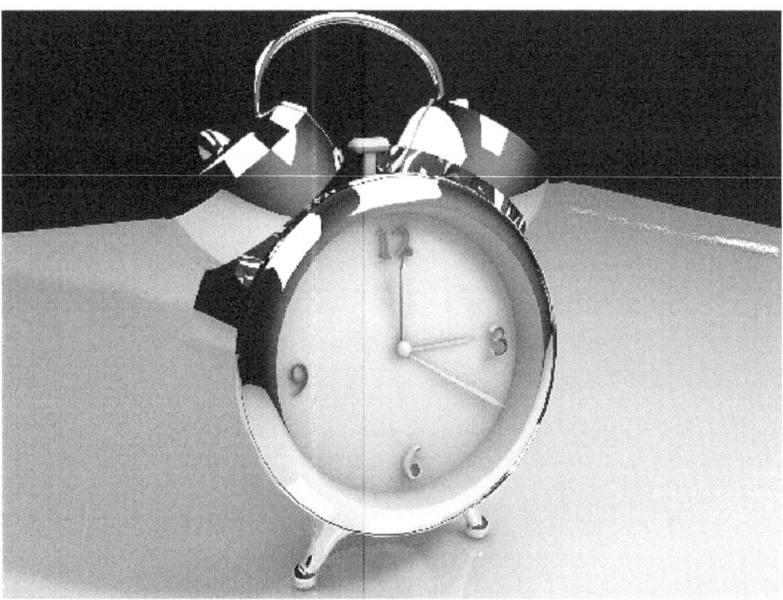

Figure 10-1 *The final rendered table clock*

The following steps are required to complete this tutorial:

a. Open the file.
b. Set lights in the scene.
c. Set global illumination and ambient occlusion attributes.
d. Create render passes.
e. Save and render the scene.

Opening the File

In this section, you will open the file.

1. Choose **File > Open** from the main menu; the **Open File** dialog box is displayed.

2. In the **Open File** dialog box, browse to *\Documents\c4dr20\c10\c10_tut1_start* and then choose the **Open** button; the *c10_tut1_start.c4d* file is opened, as shown in Figure 10-2.

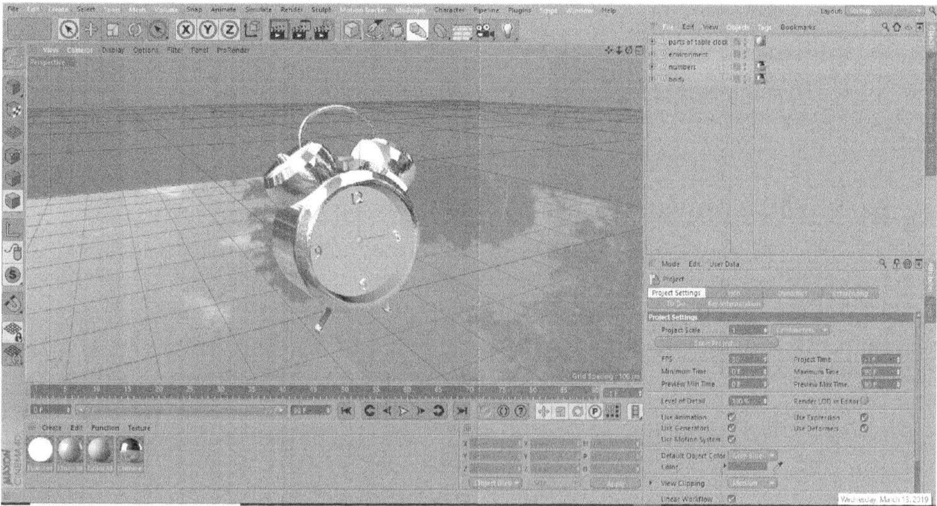

***Figure 10-2** The c10_tut1_start.c4d file*

Setting Lights in the Scene

In this section, you will illuminate the scene using the Light object.

1. Choose the **Light** tool from the Command Palette; the *Light* object is added to the Object Manager.

2. In the Attribute Manager, make sure the **General** button is chosen. In the **General** area, select **Shadow Maps (Soft)** from the **Shadow** drop-down list.

3. Choose the **Coord.** button; the **Coordinates** area is displayed. In this area, set the parameters as follows:

   P . X: **298.829** P . Y: **361.2** P . Z: **124.33**

4. Choose the **Shadow** button in the Attribute Manager; the **Shadow** area is displayed. In this area, enter **72** in the **Density** spinner.

   After entering these values, press CTRL+R; the rendered output is displayed in the viewport, as shown in Figure 10-3.

Figure 10-3 Displaying the rendered view

Setting Global Illumination and Ambient Occlusion Attributes

In this section, you will set global illumination and ambient occlusion attributes.

1. Choose the **Edit Render Settings** tool from the Command Palette; the **Render Settings** window is displayed. In this window, choose the **Effect** button; a flyout is displayed, as shown in Figure 10-4.

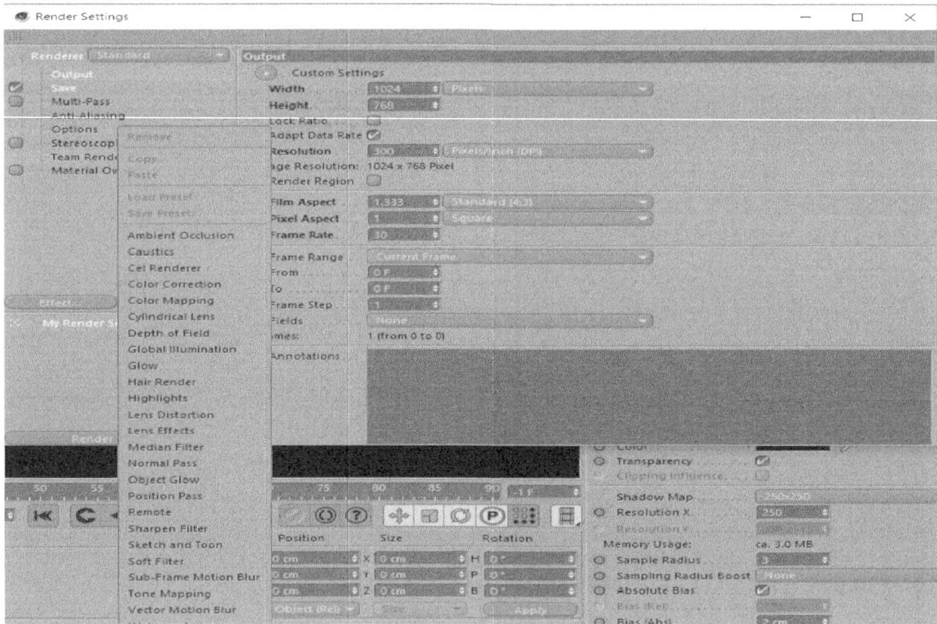

*Figure 10-4 The flyout displayed on choosing the **Effect** button*

The options available in the flyout displayed on choosing the **Effect** button are used to add effects such as Global Illumination, Glow, and so on while rendering a scene in CINEMA 4D.

2. In this flyout, choose **Global Illumination**; the **Global Illumination** area is displayed. In the **General** area, set the options, as shown in Figure 10-5.

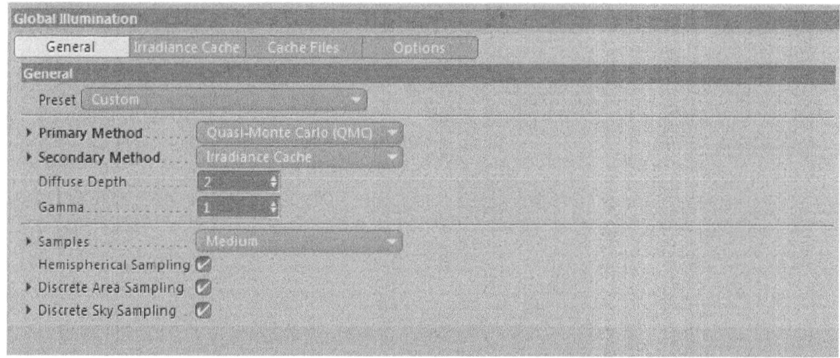

***Figure 10-5** The **Global Illumination** area*

3. In the **Global Illumination** area, choose the **Irradiance Cache** button; the **Irradiance Cache** area is displayed. In this area, enter **60** in the **Smoothing** spinner. Next, minimize the **Render Settings** window.

4. Press CTRL+R; the rendered clock is displayed in the viewport, as shown in Figure 10-6. Notice that the render now looks better.

***Figure 10-6** The rendered clock*

5. Maximize the **Render Settings** window. In this window, choose the **Effect** button; a flyout is displayed. In this flyout, choose **Ambient Occlusion**; the **Ambient Occlusion** area is displayed. Next, minimize the **Render Settings** window.

6. Press CTRL+R; the rendered clock is displayed in the viewport, as shown in Figure 10-7. You will notice that contact shadows are now prominent in the render.

Creating Render Passes

The Multi-pass rendering in CINEMA 4D allows you to post-edit your renders in a compositing package such as Nuke or Fusion. In this section, you will create ambient occlusion, shadow, diffuse, reflection, refraction, global illumination, and illumination passes.

1. Maximize the **Render Settings** window. In this window, choose the **Multi-Pass** button; a flyout is displayed, as shown in Figure 10-8.

Figure 10-7 The rendered clock

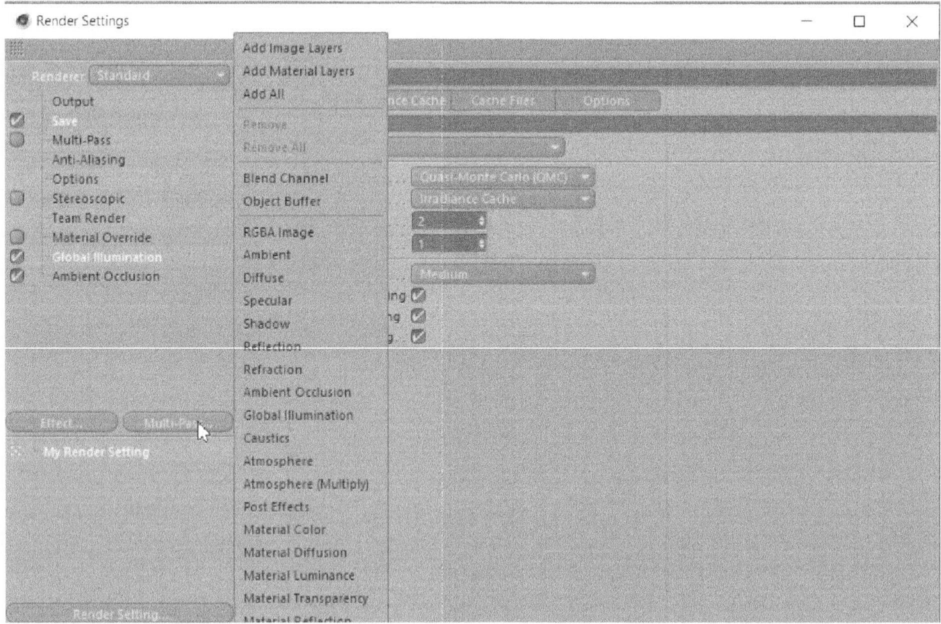

***Figure 10-8** The flyout displayed on choosing the **Multi-Pass** button*

The options in this flyout are used to create render passes such as shadow, reflection, specular, and so on.

2. In the flyout, choose **Ambient Occlusion**; the **Ambient Occlusion** pass is added to the **Render Settings** window.

   The **Ambient Occlusion** pass shows how the regions of the image illuminated by the ambient light are affected by the Environment object. This pass simulates the soft shadows that appear in the crevices of the objects when lit by indirect light.

3. Choose the **Multi-Pass** button; a flyout is displayed. In this flyout, choose **Reflection**; the **Reflection** pass is added to the **Render Settings** window.

The **Reflection** pass is used to display the reflective surfaces of an image.

4. Similarly, choose **Refraction**, **Shadow**, **Diffuse**, **Global Illumination**, and **Illumination** from the flyout; the chosen passes are added to the **Render Settings** window.

   The **Refraction** pass is used to display the refractive surface of the image. The **Shadow** pass is used to display the shaded areas of the image. The **Diffuse** pass is used to render diffuse lighting of the scene.

   In the world of computer graphics, Global Illumination is the process of interchanging the lights between different objects of a scene. Although it increases the rendering time, but it illuminates the entire scene uniformly.

5. Select the **Multi-Pass** check box in the **Render Settings** window.

6. Choose the **Save** option from the list displayed on the left in the **Render Settings** window; the **Regular Image** area is displayed. In this area, select the **Alpha Channel** check box, as shown in Figure 10-9.

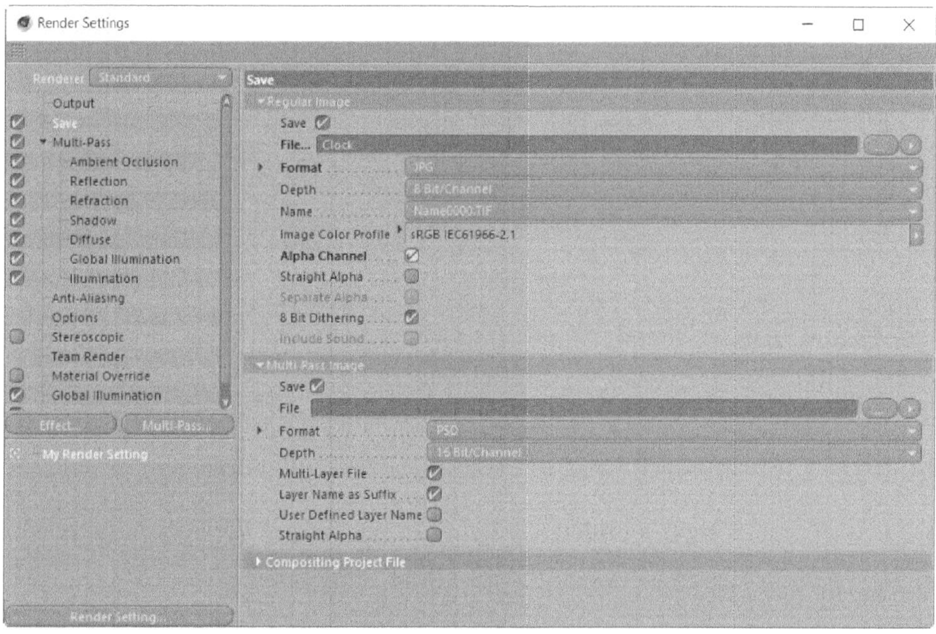

*Figure 10-9 Selecting the **Alpha Channel** check box in the **Render Settings** window*

The **Alpha Channel** check box is used to calculate a pre-multiplied alpha channel on rendering. The pixels in the alpha channel are either black or white. The black pixels indicate that there is no object present in the scene, whereas the white pixels indicate the presence of objects in the scene.

7. In the **Render Settings** window, choose the **Output** option; the **Output** area is displayed. In this area, set the parameters as follows:

   Width: **1920** Height: **1200**

Now, close the **Render Settings** window.

The **Width** and **Height** spinners are used to set the width and height of the rendered image, respectively.

8. Choose the **Render to Picture Viewer** tool from the Command Palette; the rendering begins in the **Picture Viewer** window, refer to Figure 10-10. You can adjust the zoom level of the rendered image by using the middle mouse button.

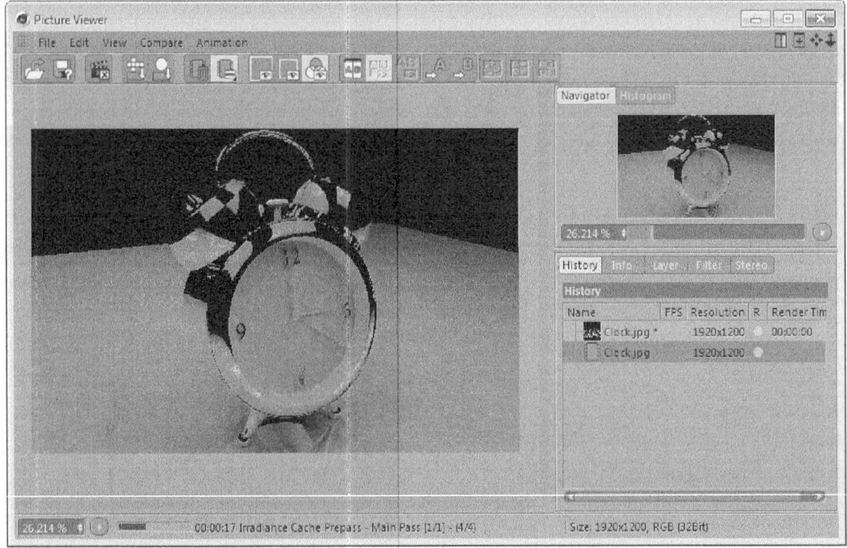

*Figure 10-10 The rendering process in the **Picture Viewer** window*

9. In the **Picture Viewer** window, choose the **Layer** button; the **Layer** area is displayed. In this area, select the **Multi-Pass** radio button, refer to Figure 10-11; all the render passes are displayed in the **Layer** area.

   Next, you will display the render passes one by one in the **Picture Viewer** window.

10. Make sure the rendering is completed and then in the **Picture Viewer** window, click on the icon corresponding to the **Alpha** pass in the **Layer** area; the **Alpha** channel is displayed, as shown in Figure 10-12.

11. Click on the eye icons of all the passes one by one excluding that of the **Ambient Occlusion** pass; the **Ambient Occlusion** pass is displayed, as shown in Figure 10-13.

12. Similarly, you can view all the desired passes by clicking on the display tags of the undesired passes in the **Picture Viewer** window. Figures 10-14 through 10-17 display different render passes.

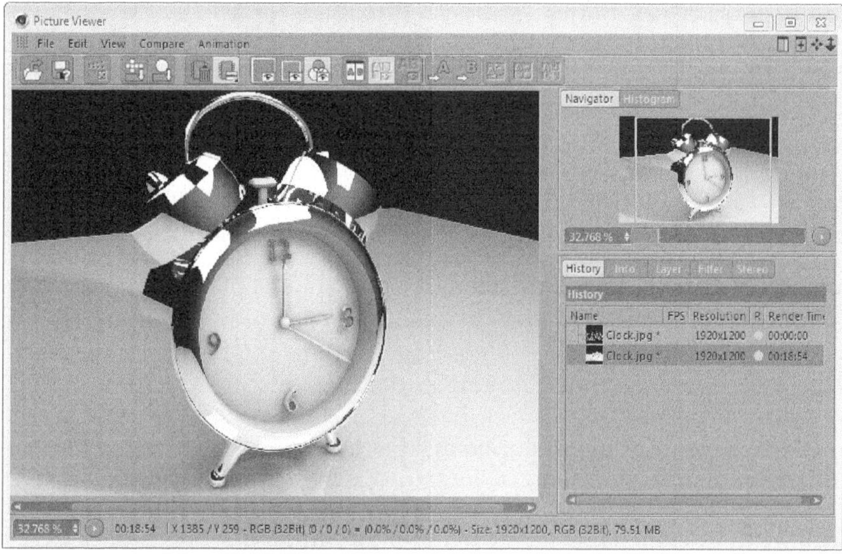

Figure 10-11 *The render passes displayed in the* ***Picture Viewer*** *window*

Figure 10-12 *Displaying the* ***Alpha*** *pass in the* ***Picture Viewer*** *window*

Figure 10-13 *The* ***Ambient Occlusion*** *pass displayed in the* ***Picture Viewer*** *window*

Figure 10-14 *The* ***Reflection*** *pass displayed in the* ***Picture Viewer*** *window*

Figure 10-15 *The* ***Global Illumination*** *pass displayed in the* ***Picture Viewer*** *window*

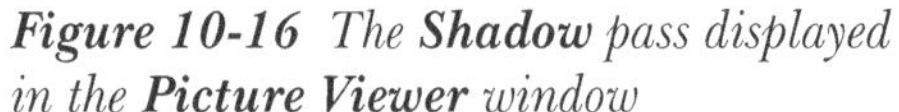

*Figure 10-16 The **Shadow** pass displayed in the **Picture Viewer** window*

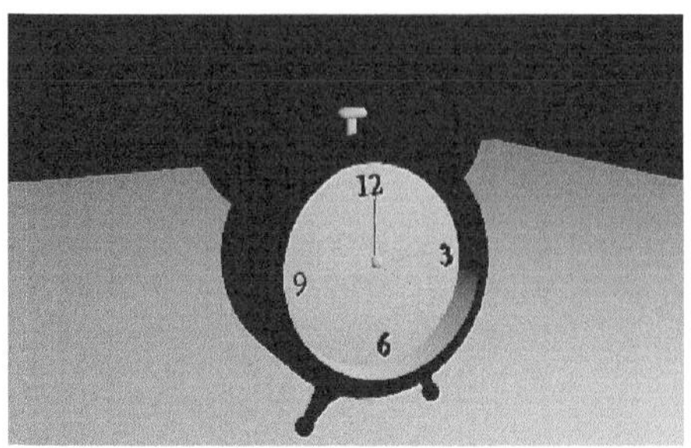

*Figure 10-17 The **Diffuse** pass displayed in the **Picture Viewer** window*

Saving and Rendering the Scene

In this section, you will save and render the scene. You can also view the final render of the composition by downloading the file *c10_cinema4d_r20_rndr.zip* from *www.cadsofttech.com*. The path of the file is mentioned at the beginning of the chapter.

1. Choose **File > Save** from the main menu; the **Save File** dialog box is displayed. In this dialog box, browse to the location *\Documents\c4dr20\c10*.

2. Enter **c10tut1** in the **File name** text box and then choose the **Save** button.

3. In the Perspective viewport, set the camera angle using the Viewport Navigation Tools located on the top right of the Perspective viewport. Next, you need to render the scene. For rendering, refer to Tutorial 1 of Chapter 2.

   Figure 10-1 displays the final output.

EXERCISE

The rendered output of the model used in the exercise can be accessed by downloading the *c10_cinema4d_r20_exr.zip* file from *www.cadsofttech.com*. The path of the file is as follows: *Textbooks > Animation and Visual Effects > MAXON CINEMA 4D > MAXON CINEMA 4D R20 Studio for Novices*

Exercise 1

Open the model that you textured in Tutorial 2 of Chapter 5. Next, render it with Global Illumination and Ambient Occlusion effects, as shown in Figure 10-18.

(Expected time: 25 min)

Figure 10-18 Scene after rendering

This page is intentionally left blank

Chapter 11

MoGraph

Learning Objectives

After completing this chapter, you will be able to:

- *Create clones*
- *Add MoGraph effectors*

INTRODUCTION

MoGraph is a huge advancement in the field of motion graphics. It is a toolset in CINEMA 4D which helps you to create spectacular visual effects, logos, and text.

MoGraph is a collection of objects, shaders, and scripts that can be combined to create models and animations. In this chapter, you will learn about some of the tools and effectors available in MoGraph toolset of CINEMA 4D.

TUTORIALS

All the files used in the tutorials can be downloaded from the CADSoft website (*www.cadsofttech.com*). These files are compressed in zip file format and are required to be extracted before using them in the tutorials. The path of the files is as follows: *Textbooks > Animation and Visual Effects > MAXON CINEMA 4D > MAXON CINEMA 4D R20 Studio for Novices*

Next, you need to browse to *\Documents\c4dr20* and create a new folder in it with the name *c11*. Next, extract the contents of the zip file in this folder.

Tutorial 1

In this tutorial, you will create an abstract model, shown in Figure 11-1 by using the MoGraph toolset. **(Expected time: 20 min)**

Figure 11-1 *The abstract model to be created*

The following steps are required to complete this tutorial:

a. Create the objects.
b. Create the clones of the object.
c. Change the background color of the scene.
d. Save and render the scene.

Creating the Objects

In this section, you will create a sphere and a cube object.

1. Choose **Create > Object** from the main menu; a cascading menu is displayed. Now, choose **Sphere** from it; a sphere is created in the Perspective Viewport and *Sphere* is added to the Object Manager.

2. Make sure *Sphere* is selected in the Object Manager. In the Attribute Manager, make sure the **Object** button is chosen; the **Object Properties** area is displayed. In this area, enter **300** in the **Radius** spinner.

3. Choose **Create > Object** from the main menu; a cascading menu is displayed. Now, choose **Cube** from it; a cube is created in the Perspective Viewport and *Cube* is added to the Object Manager.

4. Make sure *Cube* is selected in the Object Manager. In the Attribute Manager, make sure the **Object** button is chosen; the **Object Properties** area is displayed. In this area, set the parameters as follows:

   Size . Y: **60** Size . Z: **191**

   Select the **Fillet** check box and enter **10** in the **Fillet Radius** spinner.

5. In the Attribute Manager, choose the **Coord** button; the **Coordinates** area is displayed. In this area, set the parameters as follows:

   P . X: **-182.39** P . Y: **239.04**

   Figure 11-2 displays *Cube* positioned in the Perspective viewport.

Creating the Clones of the Object

In this section, you will create clones of the object using the **Cloner** object.

1. Choose **MoGraph > Cloner** from the main menu; the **Cloner** object is added to the Object Manager.

   The **Cloner** tool is a commonly used tool in MoGraph. It is used to create duplicates of the objects.

2. In the Object Manager, select *Cube* and then drag it to *Cloner*; the *Cube* is connected to *Cloner*.

3. Select *Cloner* in the Object Manager. In the Attribute Manager, make sure the **Object** button is chosen; the **Object Properties** area is displayed. In this area, set the parameters as follows:

   Count: **33** P . X: **-9** P . Y: **32**
   P . Z: **5** S . X: **97** S . Z: **97**
   Step Rotation . H: **5**

   Figure 11-3 displays *Cloner* in the Perspective viewport. Next, you will create copies of the *Cloner* object.

4. Choose **MoGraph > Cloner** from the main menu; the *Cloner.1* is added to the Object Manager.

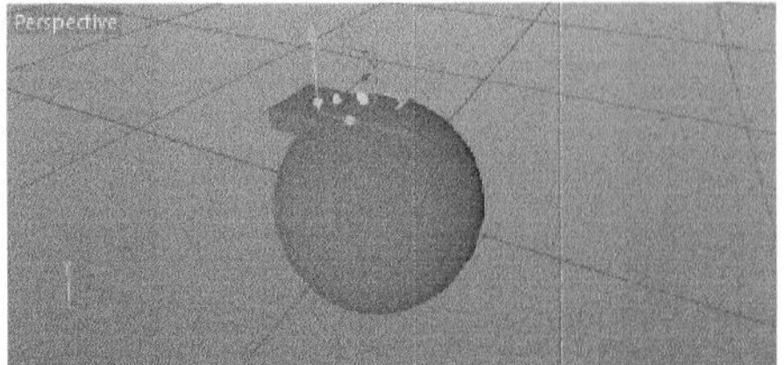

Figure 11-2 *Cube positioned in the Perspective viewport*

Figure 11-3 *Cloner displayed in the Perspective viewport*

5. In the Object Manager, select *Cloner* and then drag it to *Cloner.1*; the *Cloner* is connected to *Cloner.1*. Also, clones of *Cloner* are created in the Perspective viewport.

6. Select *Cloner.1* in the Object Manager. In the Attribute Manager, make sure the **Object** button is chosen; the **Object Properties** area is displayed. In this area, select **Radial** from the **Mode** drop-down list. Next, enter **15** in the **Count** spinner. Figure 11-4 displays *Cloner.1* in the Perspective viewport.

Figure 11-4 *Cloner.1 displayed in the Perspective viewport*

Changing the Background Color of the Scene

To change the background color of the scene to white in the final output, follow the steps given in Tutorial 1 of Chapter 2.

Saving and Rendering the Scene

In this section, you will save and render the model. You can also view the final render of the scene by downloading the file *c11_cinema4d_r20_rndr.zip* from *www.cadsofttech.com*. The path of the file is mentioned at the beginning of the chapter.

1. Choose **File > Save** from the main menu; the **Save File** dialog box is displayed. In this dialog box, browse to the location *\Documents\c4dr20\c11*.

2. Enter **c11tut1** in the **File name** text box and then choose the **Save** button.

3. In the Perspective viewport, set the camera angle using the Viewport Navigation Tools located at the top right of the Perspective viewport. Next, you need to render the scene.

For rendering, refer to Tutorial 1 of Chapter 2. The final output of the model is shown in Figure 11-1.

Tutorial 2

In this tutorial, you will create disco light effect shown in Figure 11-5 using the MoGraph toolset. **(Expected time: 30 min)**

Figure 11-5 *The disco light effect at frame 60*

The following steps are required to complete this tutorial:

a. Open the file.
b. Create clones.
c. Add effectors to the scene.
d. Set render attributes.
e. Save and render the scene.

Opening the File

In this section, you will open the file.

1. Choose **File > Open** from the main menu; the **Open File** dialog box is displayed.

2. In the **Open File** dialog box, browse to *\Documents\c4dr20\c11\c11_tut2_start* and then choose the **Open** button; the *c11_tut2_start.c4d* file is opened, as shown in Figure 11-6.

Creating Clones

In this section, you will create a light and then create its clone using the **Cloner** object.

1. Choose **Create > Light** from the main menu; a cascading menu is displayed. Next, choose **Light** from it; a light is created in the Perspective viewport and *Light* is added to the Object Manager.

2. Choose **MoGraph > Cloner** from the main menu; the *Cloner* object is added to the Object Manager.

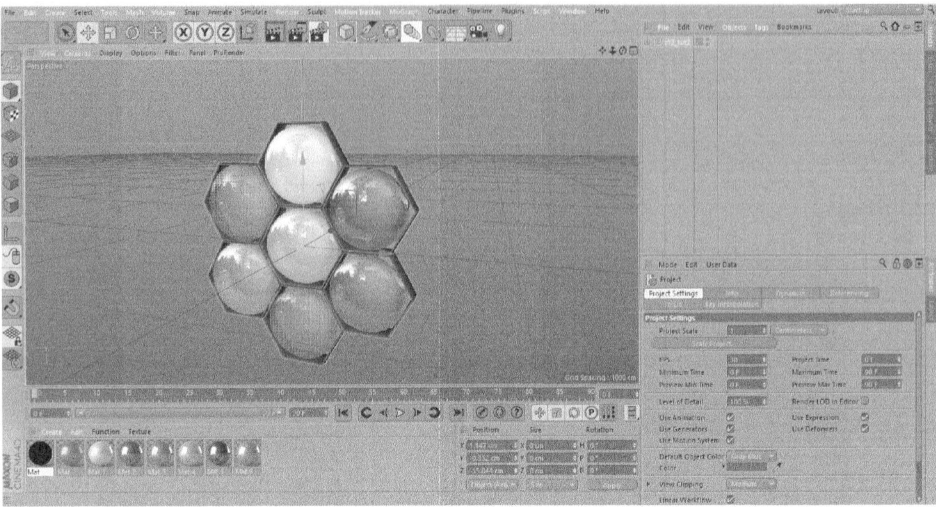

Figure 11-6 The c11_tut2_start.c4d file

3. Make sure *Cloner* is selected in the Object Manager. In the Attribute Manager, make sure the **Object** button is chosen; the **Object Properties** area is displayed. In this area, select **Radial** from the **Mode** drop-down list, as shown in Figure 11-7.

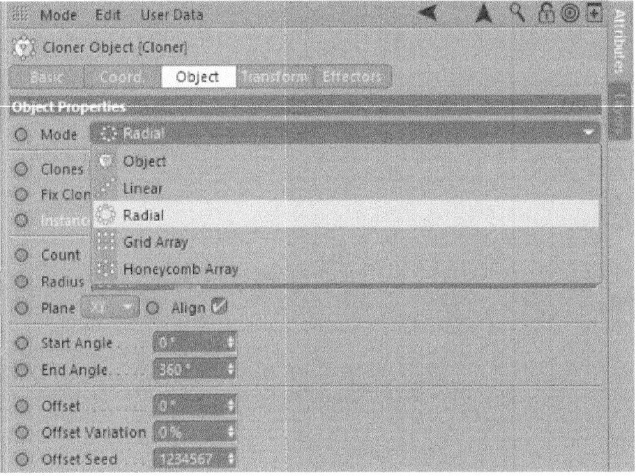

*Figure 11-7 Selecting **Radial** from the **Mode** drop-down list*

The **Radial** mode in the **Mode** drop-down list is used to create clones arranged in a circular shape around the center of cloner.

4. In the Object Manager, select *Light* and drag it to *Cloner*; the *Light* is connected to *Cloner*.

5. Select *Cloner* in the Object Manager. In the **Object Properties** area, select **Random** from the **Clones** drop-down list, as shown in Figure 11-8. Next, set the parameters as follows:

Count: **6** Radius: **482** Start Angle: **364**
End Angle: **-2**

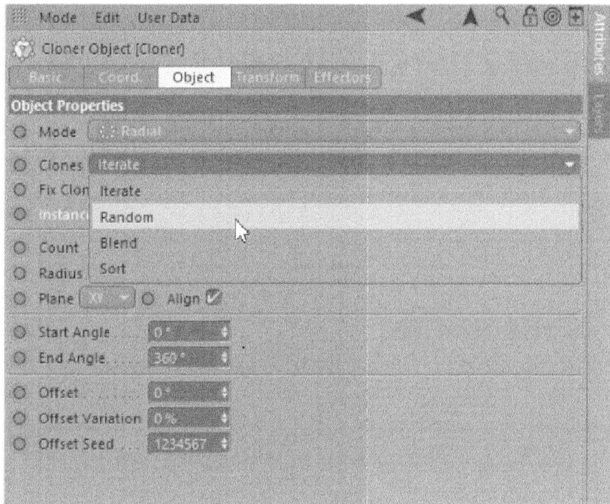

Figure 11-8 *Selecting **Random** from the **Clones** drop-down list*

The **Random** option is used to arrange the clones in a random manner. The **Count** spinner is used to define the number of clones to be arranged. The **Radius** spinner is used to define the radius of the cloner.

6. Make sure the *Cloner* object is selected in the Object Manager. In the Attribute Manager, choose the **Coord** button; the **Coordinates** area is displayed. In this area, set the parameters as follows:

P . X: **-7.772**	P . Y: **4.852**	P . Z: **-198.5**
S . X: **0.9**	S . Y: **0.86**	R . B: **-4**

Figure 11-9 displays clones of *Light* in the Perspective viewport.

Figure 11-9 *The clones of Light displayed in the Perspective viewport*

Next, you will set the properties of *Light*.

7. Select the *Light* object in the Object Manager. In the Attribute Manager, choose the **General** button; the **General** area is displayed. In this area, select **Shadow Maps (Soft)** from the **Shadow** drop-down list. Next, select **Visible** from the **Visible Light** drop-down list.

8. In the Attribute Manager, choose the **Details** button; the **Details** area is displayed. In this area, select **Inverse Square (Physically Accurate)** from the **Falloff** drop-down list and enter **177.258** in the **Radius/Decay** spinner.

9. In the Attribute Manager, choose the **Visibility** button; the **Visibility** area is displayed. In this area, set the parameters as follows:

   Inner Distance: **175.352** Outer Distance: **177.258** Sample Distance: **23.825**

Adding Effectors to the Scene

In this section, you will add effectors in the scene to control the behavior of the lights in the scene.

1. Select *Cloner* in the Object Manager. Next, choose **MoGraph > Effector** from the main menu; a cascading menu is displayed, as shown in Figure 11-10. Choose the **Random** option from it; *Random* is added to the Object Manager.

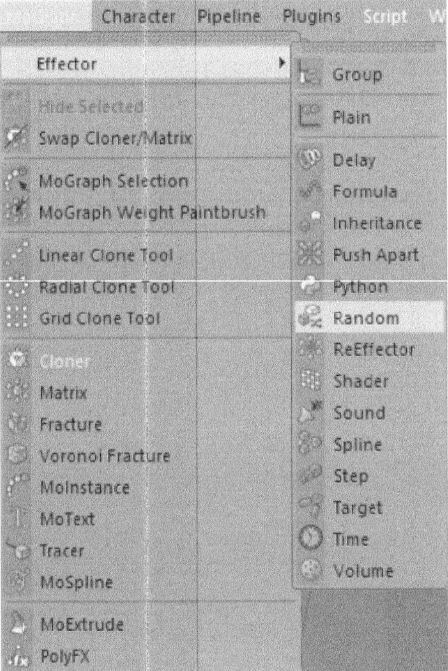

Figure 11-10 *Choosing* ***Random*** *from the cascading menu*

The **Random** effector is used to randomize the value of the clones. It is used to modify the position, rotation, size, color, and weight of the clones.

Note

When you add the ***Random*** *effector to the Object Manager, it is also added to the* ***Effectors*** *area of the* ***Cloner*** *object. To verify this, select the* ***Cloner*** *in the Object Manager and then choose the* ***Effectors*** *button; the* ***Effectors*** *area is displayed. In this area, you will notice that the* ***Random*** *effector is added.*

2. Make sure **Random** is selected in the Object Manager. In the Attribute Manager, choose the **Parameter** button; the **Parameter** area is displayed. In this area, expand the **Transform** area if it is not already expanded and make sure the **Position** check box is selected. Also, select the **Rotation** check box in the **Transform** area.

   The **Position** check box is used to define whether the **Random** effector will affect the position of the cloners. The **Rotation** check box is used to define whether the **Random** effector will affect the rotation of cloners.

3. In the **Color** area, select **Custom Color** from the **Color Mode** drop-down list, as shown in Figure 11-11.

   The **Custom Color** option in the **Color Mode** drop-down list is used to set the color of clones manually.

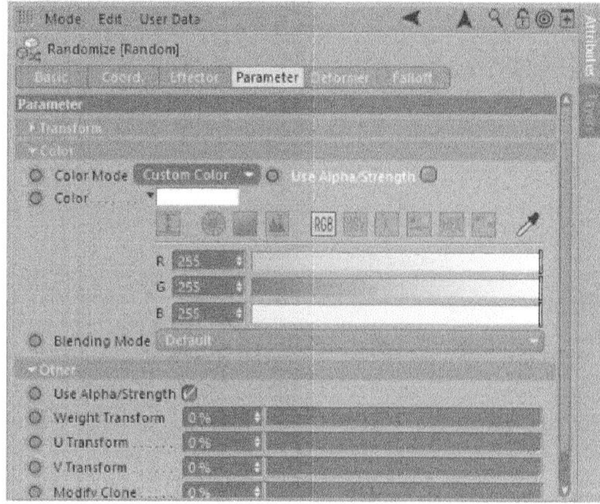

*Figure 11-11 The **Custom Color** option from the **Color Mode** drop-down list*

4. In the **Color** area, choose the **RGB** button and then enter **170** in the **G** spinner and **20** in the **B** spinner; the color of the **Random** effector changes in the Perspective viewport.

   Next, you will add the **Formula** effector to the scene. The **Formula** effector is used to create complex formulae.

5. Select *Cloner* in the Object Manager. Next, choose **MoGraph > Effector** from the main menu; a cascading menu is displayed. Choose **Formula** from it; *Formula* is added to the Object Manager.

6. Make sure *Formula* is selected in the Object Manager. In the Attribute Manager, make sure the **Parameter** button is chosen; the **Parameter** area is displayed. In the **Parameter** area, expand **Transform** if not already expanded and then clear the **Position** and **Scale** check boxes.

7. Expand the **Color** area, if not already expanded and select the **Effector Color** option from the **Color Mode** drop-down list. Next, select the **Add** option from the **Blending Mode** drop-down list, as shown in Figure 11-12.

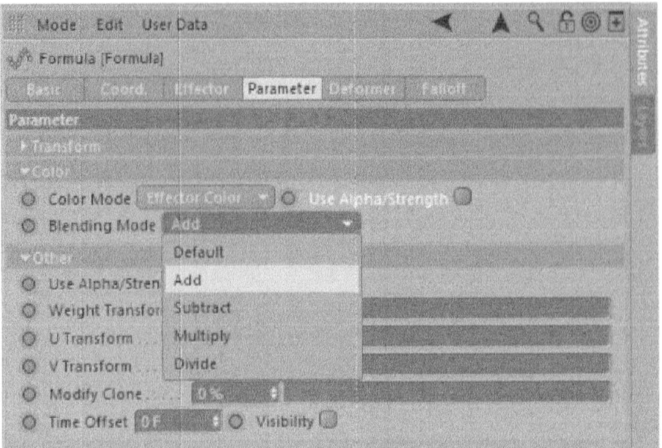

*Figure 11-12 Selecting the **Add** option from the **Blending Mode** drop-down list*

The options in the **Blending Mode** drop-down list are used to specify different modes for blending the colors of the effectors with the cloners. The **Add** option is used to add the colors of the cloner with the color of the effector.

8. Choose the **Play Forwards** button; the animation begins in the Perspective viewport.

Setting Render Attributes

In this section, you will set the global illumination, ambient occlusion, and glow attributes.

1. Choose the **Edit Render Settings** tool in the Command Palette; the **Render Settings** window is displayed. In this window, choose the **Effect** button; a flyout is displayed. From this flyout, choose **Global Illumination**; the **Global Illumination** area is displayed.

2. Choose the **Effect** button again; a flyout is displayed. From this flyout, choose **Ambient Occlusion**.

3. Choose the **Effect** button again; a flyout is displayed. From this flyout, choose **Glow**; the **Glow** area is displayed. In this area, select the **Use** check box. Next, enter **10** in the **Size** spinner and **13** in the **Intensity** spinner. Next, close the **Render Settings** window.

   After entering these values, press CTRL+R; the rendered output of the current frame is displayed in the Perspective viewport, as shown in Figure 11-13.

Saving and Rendering the Scene

In this section, you will save and render the animation. You can also view the final rendered sequence by downloading the file *c11_cinema4d_r20_rndr.zip* from *www.cadsofttech.com*. The path of the file is mentioned at the beginning of the chapter.

1. Choose the **Edit Render Settings** tool from the Command Palette; the **Render Settings** window is displayed. In this window, select the **Output** option; the **Output** area is displayed. In this area, enter **90** in the **To** spinner.

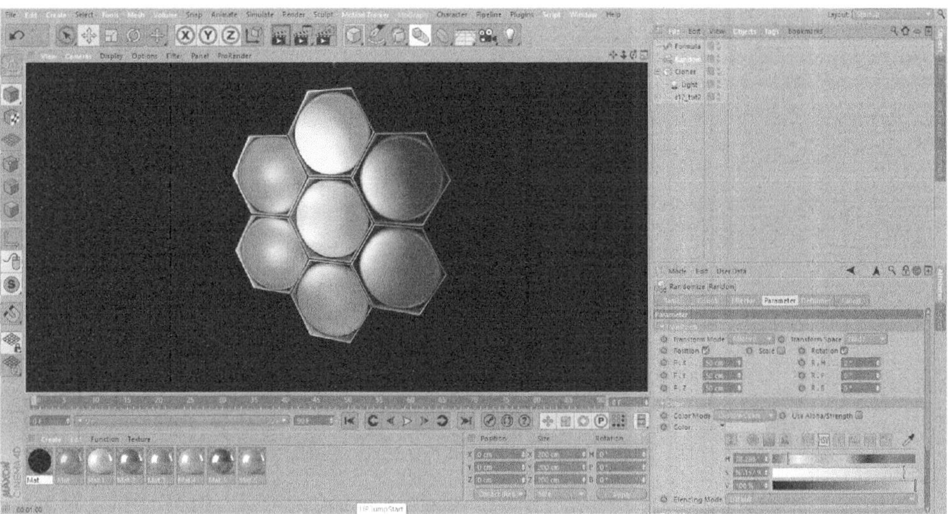

Figure 11-13 The rendered view at the current frame

2. Select the **Save** option from the list displayed at the left side in the **Render Settings** window; the **Regular Image** area is displayed. In this area, make sure that the **Save** check box is selected. Next, choose the browse button located next to the **File** text box; the **Save File** dialog box is displayed.

3. In the **Save File** dialog box, browse to *\Documents\c4dr19\c11* and enter **c11tut2** in the **File name** text box. Next, choose the **Save** button.

4. Select the **QuickTime Movie** option from the **Format** drop-down list. Next, close the **Render Settings** window.

5. Choose the **Render to Picture Viewer** tool from the Command Palette; the **Picture Viewer** window is displayed. Also, the rendering begins and final output is automatically saved at the specified location.

EXERCISE

The rendered output of the model used in the exercise can be accessed by downloading the *c11_cinema4d_r20_exr.zip* file from *www.cadsofttech.com*. The path of the file is as follows: *Textbooks > Animation and Visual Effects > MAXON CINEMA 4D > MAXON CINEMA 4D R20 Studio for Novices*

Exercise 1

Create an abstract model, shown in Figure 11-14 by using the MoGraph toolset.

(Expected time: 15 min)

Figure 11-14 *The abstract model*

Chapter 12

Working with XPresso

Learning Objectives

After completing this chapter, you will be able to:

- *Work with the XPresso Editor*
- *Create and connect nodes*
- *Modify settings of nodes*

INTRODUCTION

XPresso is a node based system in MAXON CINEMA 4D that is used to build automated object interactions. These nodes are created and linked in the **XPresso Editor** by drawing lines from one port of a node to another port of the other node. These lines are also referred to as wires. In this chapter, you will learn to use the **XPresso Editor**.

TUTORIAL

All the files used in the tutorials can be downloaded from the CADSoft website (*www.cadsofttech.com*). These files are compressed in zip file format and are required to be extracted before using them in the tutorials. The path of the files is as follows: *Textbooks > Animation and Visual Effects > MAXON CINEMA 4D > MAXON CINEMA 4D R20 Studio for Novices*

Next, you need to browse to *\Documents\c4dR20* and create a new folder in it with the name *c12*. Next, extract the contents of the zip file in this folder.

Tutorial 1

In this tutorial, you will control the lights of a traffic signal using the **XPresso Editor**, refer to Figure 12-1. **(Expected time: 45 min)**

Figure 12-1 *The traffic signal with the red light on*

The following steps are required to complete this tutorial:

a. Open the file.
b. Create an expression.
c. Connect the nodes.
d. Animate the traffic lights.
e. Save and render the scene.

Opening the File

In this section, you will open the file.

1. Choose **File > Open** from the main menu; the **Open File** dialog box is displayed.

2. In the **Open File** dialog box, browse to *\Documents\c4dr20\c12\c12_tut1_start* and then choose the **Open** button; the *c12_tut1_start* file is opened, as shown in Figure 12-2.

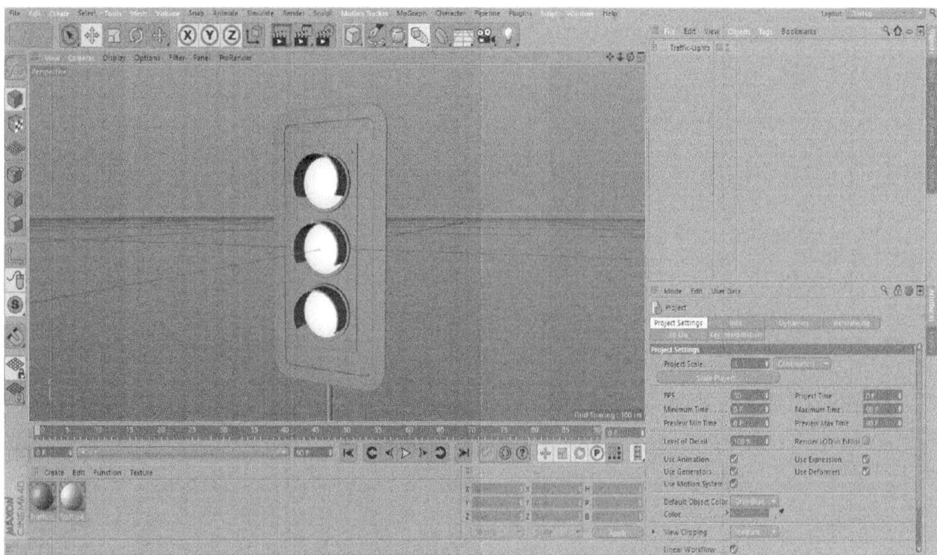

***Figure 12-2** The c12_tut1_start.c4d file*

Creating an Expression

In this section, you will create an expression in the **XPresso Editor**. Next, you will create custom parameters using the **Add User Data** option.

1. Select *Traffic-Lights* in the Object Manager. Choose **User Data > Add User Data** from the Attribute Manager menu, as shown in Figure 12-3; the **Manage User Data** dialog box is displayed, as shown in Figure 12-4.

   The options in the **Manage User Data** dialog box are used to add custom parameters to the attributes of the selected objects. It can be added to every object whose parameters are displayed in the Attribute Manager.

2. In the **Manage User Data** dialog box, make sure that **Data** is selected in the **User Data (Default)** node in the left pane of the dialog box and the **Properties** button is chosen in the right pane. In the **Properties** area, enter **Red** in the **Name** text box and select **Float Slider** from the **Interface** drop-down list, as shown in Figure 12-5. Next, choose the **OK** button in the **Manage User Data** dialog box; the **Red** spinner along with the slider is added to the **User Data** area in the Attribute Manager, as shown in Figure 12-6.

The **Float Slider** option in the **Interface** drop-down list is used to add a slider and a spinner so that you can enter a value for specifying the user data parameter. It is the most commonly used user data parameter.

Next, you will add the Yellow spinner.

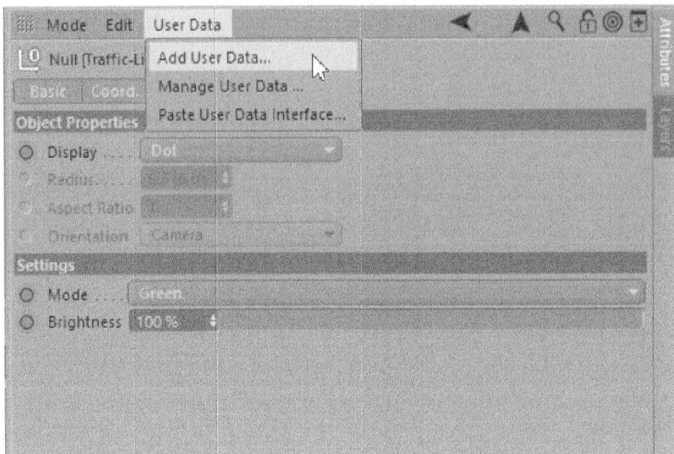

*Figure 12-3 Choosing **Add User Data** from the menu in the Attribute Manager*

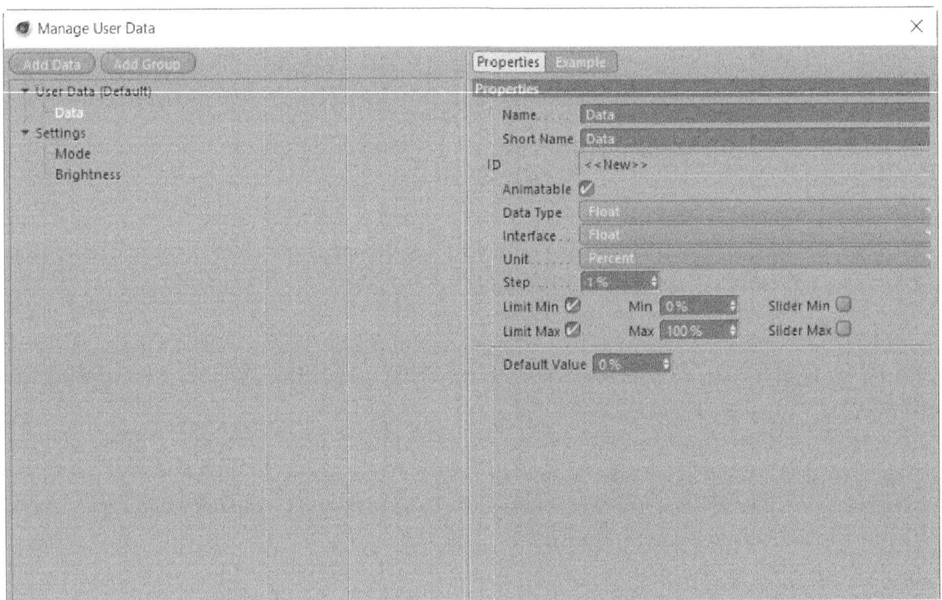

*Figure 12-4 The **Manage User Data** dialog box*

3. Make sure that *Traffic-Lights* is selected in the Object Manager. Choose **User Data > Add User Data** from the menu in the Attribute Manager, refer to Figure 12-3; the **Manage User Data** dialog box is displayed, refer to Figure 12-4.

4. In the **Manage User Data** dialog box, make sure that the **Properties** button is chosen. In the **Properties** area, enter **Yellow** in the **Name** text box and select **Float Slider** from the **Interface** drop-down list, refer to Figure 12-5. Next, choose the **OK** button in the **Manage**

User Data dialog box; the **Yellow** spinner is added to the **User Data** area in the Attribute Manager, as shown in Figure 12-7.

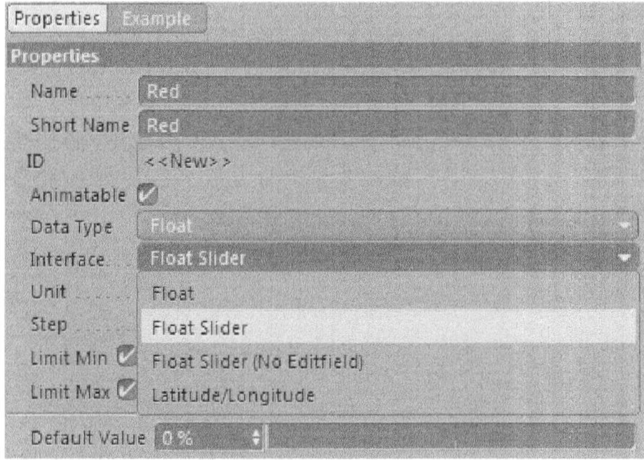

*Figure 12-5 Selecting **Float Slider** from the **Interface** drop-down list*

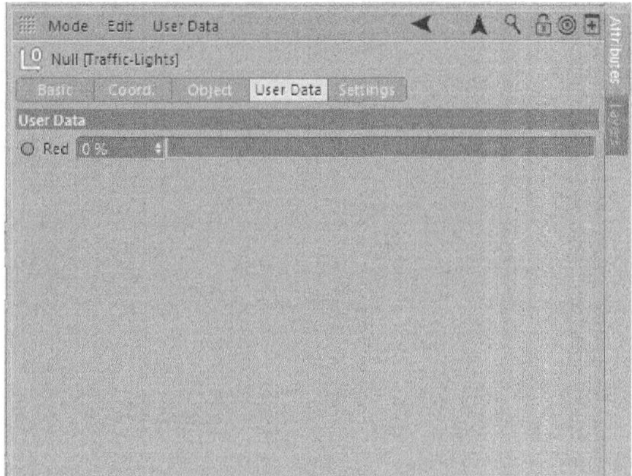

*Figure 12-6 The **Red** spinner added to the **User Data** area in the Attribute Manager*

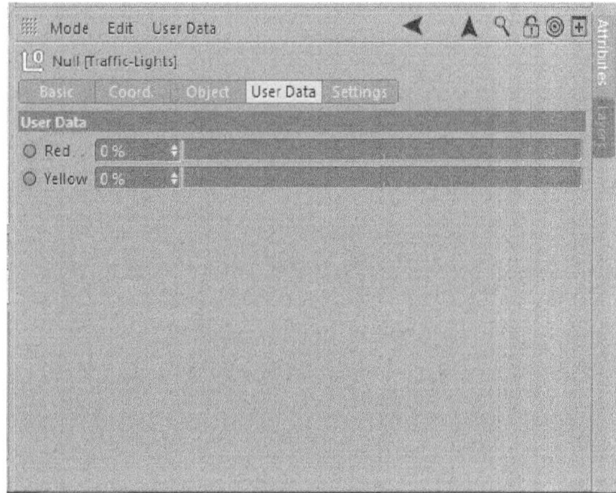

*Figure 12-7 The **Yellow** spinner added to the **User Data** area in the Attribute Manager*

Next, you will create the **Green** spinner.

5. Make sure that *Traffic-Lights* is selected in the Object Manager. Choose **User Data > Add User Data** from the menu in the Attribute Manager, refer to Figure 12-3; the **Manage User Data** dialog box is displayed, refer to Figure 12-4.

6. In the **Manage User Data** dialog box, make sure the **Properties** button is chosen. In the **Properties** area, enter **Green** in the **Name** text box and select **Float Slider** from the **Interface** drop-down list, refer to Figure 12-5. Next, choose the **OK** button in the **Manage User Data** dialog box; the **Green** spinner is added to the **User Data** area in the Attribute Manager, as shown in Figure 12-8.

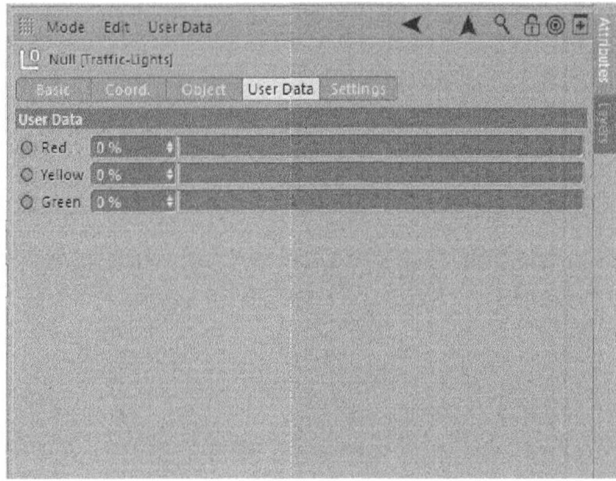

***Figure 12-8** The **Green** spinner added to the **User Data** area in the Attribute Manager*

7. In the Object Manager, right-click on *Traffic-Lights*; a shortcut menu is displayed. From the shortcut menu, choose **CINEMA 4D Tags > XPresso**, as shown in Figure 12-9; the **XPresso Expression** tag is added to *Traffic-Lights* in the Object Manager and the **XPresso Editor** is displayed, as shown in Figure 12-10.

8. In the **XPresso Editor**, right-click in the empty space in the **XGroup** area; a shortcut menu is displayed. From the shortcut menu, choose **New Node > XPresso > General > Object**, as shown in Figure 12-11; the **Traffic-Lights** node is added to the **XPresso Editor**.

Note

*The name of the object selected in the Object Manager is assigned to the added **Object** node.*

Tip

*If you have accidently closed the **XPresso Editor**, you can reopen it by double-clicking on the **XPresso** tag in the Object Manager. The **Object** node is used to represent a CINEMA 4D object, tag, or material.*

Next, you will add the **Red** output port to the **Traffic-Lights** node.

9. In the **XPresso Editor**, click on the output port (red square) of the **Traffic-Lights** node; a flyout is displayed. Choose **User Data > Red** from the flyout, as shown in Figure 12-12; the **Red** output port is added to the **Traffic-Lights** node.

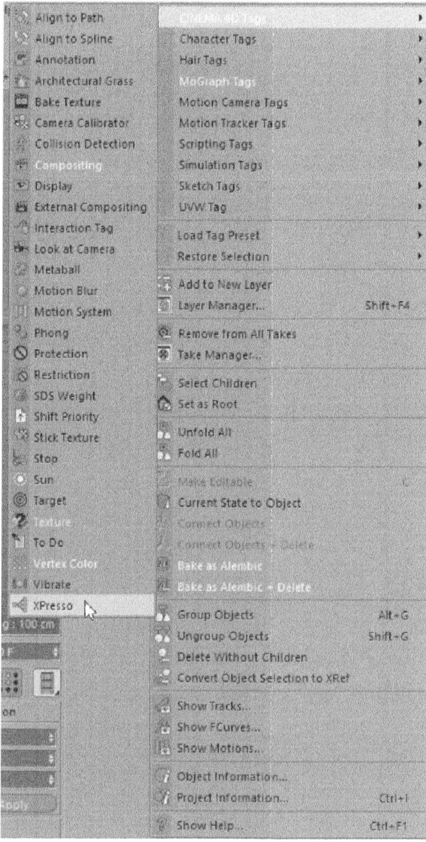

Figure 12-9 *Choosing* ***XPresso*** *from the shortcut menu*

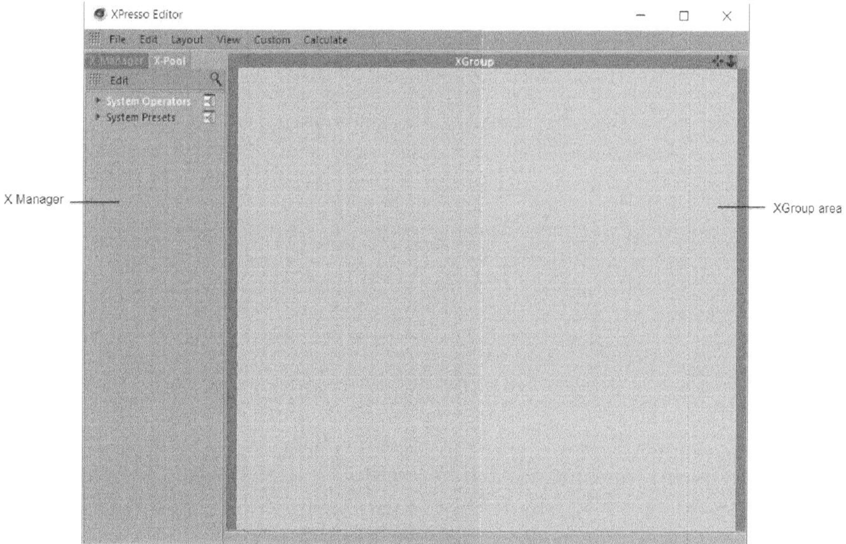

Figure 12-10 *The* ***XPresso Editor***

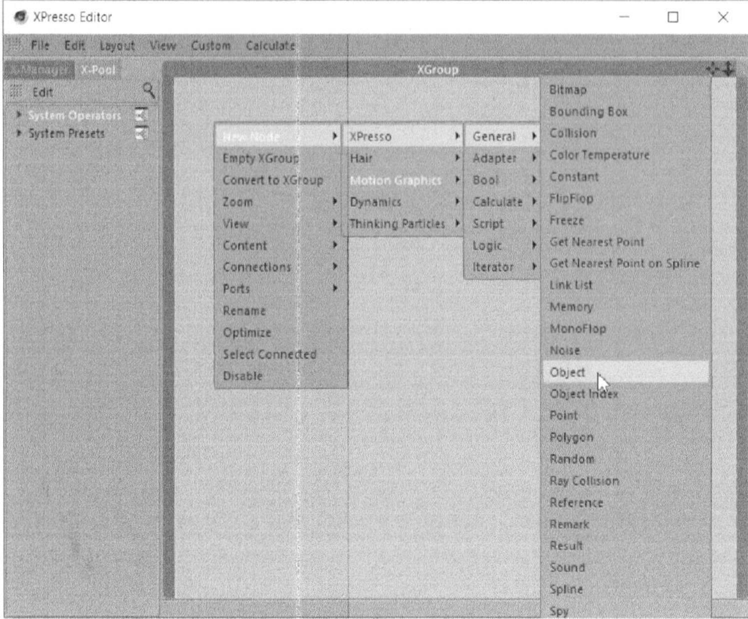

Figure 12-11 *Choosing* ***Object*** *from the shortcut menu*

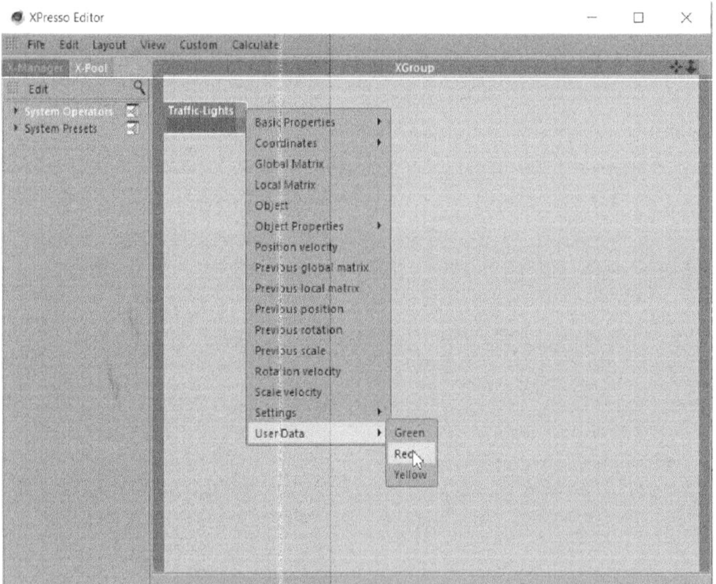

Figure 12-12 *Choosing* ***Red*** *from the flyout in the* ***XPresso Editor***

10. Click on the output port (red square); a flyout is displayed. Choose **User Data > Yellow** from the flyout, refer to Figure 12-12; the **Yellow** output port is added to the **Traffic-Lights** node, refer to Figure 12-13.

If the ports are not properly visible on the **Traffic-Lights** node, press and hold CTRL and then double-click on the node's title bar.

11. Similarly, add the **Green** output port to the **Traffic-Lights** node. Figure 12-13 displays the **Red**, **Yellow**, and **Green** output ports in the **Traffic-Lights** node.

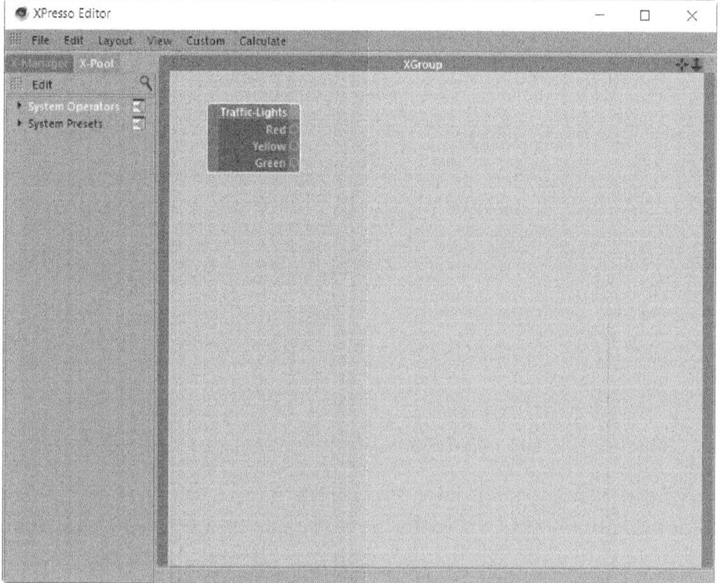

***Figure 12-13** The **Red**, **Yellow**, and **Green** output ports added to the **Traffic-Lights** node*

Next, you will add the **Compare** node to the **XPresso Editor**.

12. In the **XPresso Editor**, right-click in the **XGroup** area; a shortcut menu is displayed. From the shortcut menu, choose **New Node > XPresso > Logic > Compare**, as shown in Figure 12-14; the **Compare** node is added to the **XPresso Editor**.

13. In the **XPresso Editor**, make sure that the **Compare** node is selected. In the Attribute Manager, choose the **Basic** button; the **Basic Properties** area is displayed. In this area, enter **Compare 1** in the **Name** text box; the **Compare** node is renamed as **Compare 1** in the **XPresso Editor**.

The **Compare** node is used to compare two or more values to get a result.

14. Repeat step 12 to add two more **Compare** nodes to the **XPresso Editor**. Next, rename these nodes as **Compare 2** and **Compare 3** respectively, as done in the previous step.

Tip
You can also create the copies of a node by first pressing CTRL+C and then CTRL+V.

Next, you will add the **Condition** node to the **XPresso Editor**.

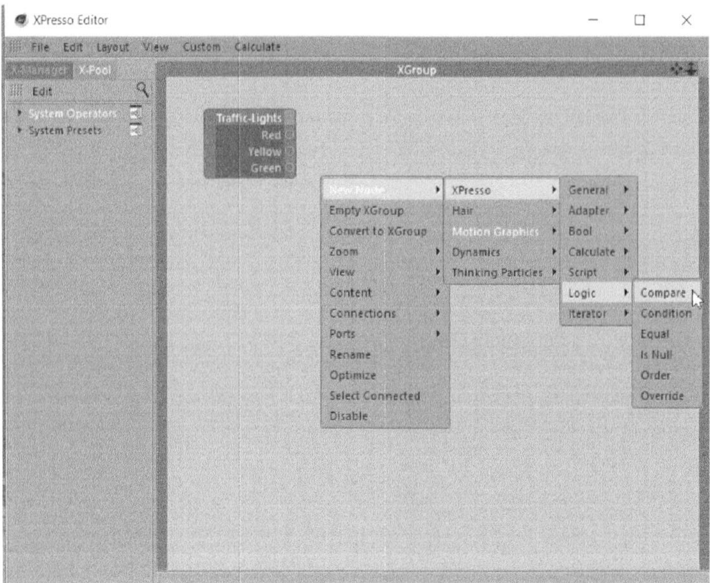

*Figure 12-14 Choosing the **Compare** option from the shortcut menu in the **XPresso Editor***

15. In the **XPresso Editor**, right-click in the **XGroup** area; a shortcut menu is displayed. From the shortcut menu, choose **New Node > XPresso > Logic > Condition**, as shown in Figure 12-15; the **Condition** node is added to the **XPresso Editor**.

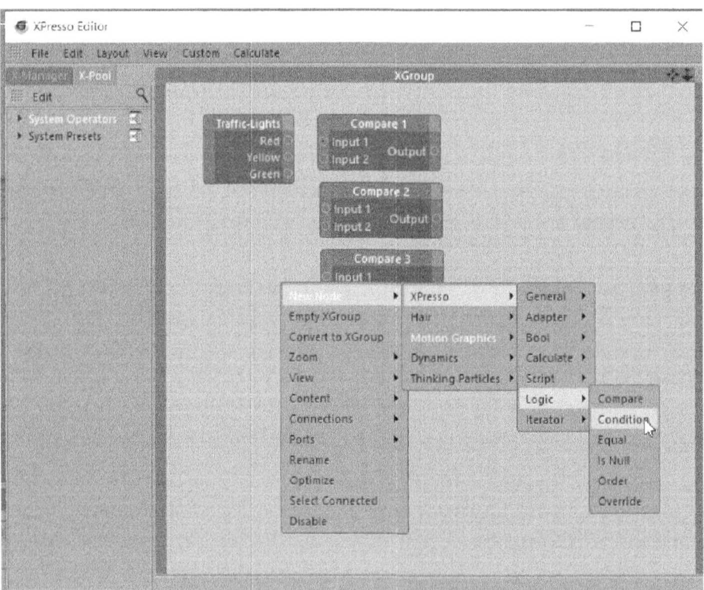

*Figure 12-15 Choosing the **Condition** option from the shortcut menu in the **XPresso Editor***

The **Condition** node acts like a switch which has two or more states.

16. Select the **Condition** node in the **XGroup** area, if not already selected. In the Attribute Manager, make sure the **Basic** button is chosen; the **Basic Properties** area is displayed. In this area, enter **Condition 1** in the **Name** text box; the **Condition** node is renamed as **Condition 1** in the **XPresso Editor**.

17. In the **XPresso Editor**, select the **Condition 1** node in the **XGroup** area. In the Attribute Manager, choose the **Node** button; the **Node Properties** area is displayed. In this area, select the **Color** option from the **Data Type** drop-down list, as shown in Figure 12-16.

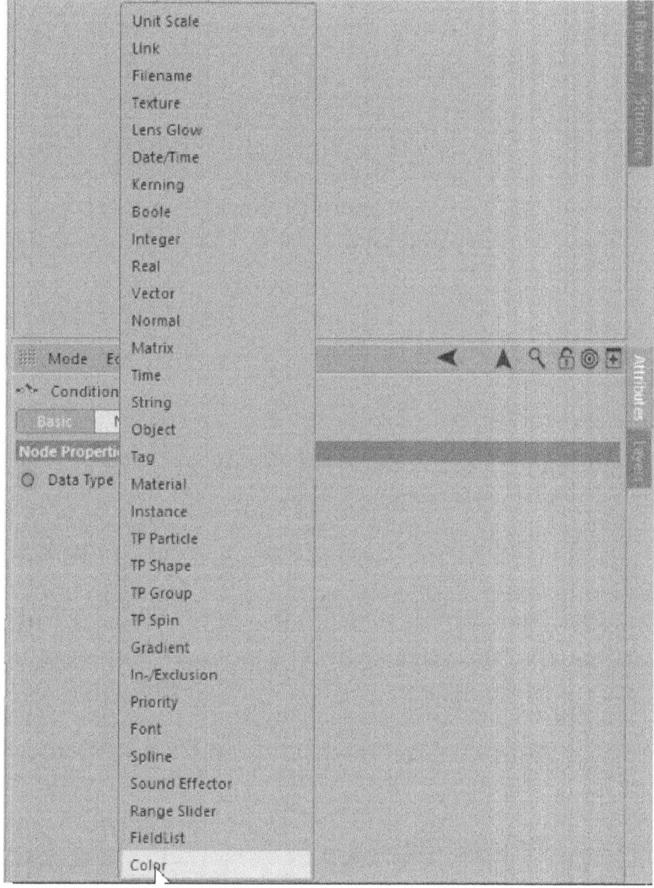

*Figure 12-16 Selecting **Color** from the **Data Type** drop-down list in the **Node Properties** area*

The options in the **Data Type** drop-down list are used to change the data type of the output node in the **XPresso Editor**.

18. In the Attribute Manager, choose the **Parameter** button; the **Parameter** area is displayed. In this area, click on the black color swatch next to the **Input [2]** attribute; the **Color Picker** dialog box is displayed. In the **Color Picker** dialog box, choose the **RGB** button and then

enter **255** in the **R** spinner; the red color is displayed in the color swatch and the black color swatch is replaced by red color.

19. In the **XPresso Editor**, right-click in the empty space of the **XGroup** area; a shortcut menu is displayed. From the shortcut menu, choose **New Node > XPresso > Logic > Condition**, refer to Figure 12-15; the **Condition** node is added to the **XGroup** area.

20. In the Attribute Manager, choose the **Basic** button; the **Basic Properties** area is displayed. In this area, enter **Condition 2** in the **Name** text box; the **Condition** node is renamed as **Condition 2**.

21. In the Attribute Manager, choose the **Node** button; the **Node Properties** area is displayed. In this area, select the **Color** option from the **Data Type** drop-down list, refer to Figure 12-16.

22. In the Attribute Manager, choose the **Parameter** button; the **Parameter** area is displayed. In this area, click on the black color swatch next to the **Input [2]** option; the **Color Picker** dialog box is displayed. In the **Color Picker** dialog box, choose the **RGB** button and then set the parameters as follows:

    R: **255** G: **255**

    The black color in the color swatch is replaced by yellow color.

23. Create a third **Condition** node in the **XPresso Editor** and rename it as **Condition 3** in the Attribute Manager, as done earlier.

24. Choose the **Parameter** button in the Attribute Manager; the **Parameter** area is displayed. In this area, click on the black color swatch next to the **Input [2]** option; the **Color Picker** dialog box is displayed. In the **Color Picker** dialog box, choose the **RGB** button and then enter **255** in the **G** spinner. Next, choose the **OK** button; the black color swatch is replaced by green color.

    Next, you will add the **Red-Glass**, **Yellow-Glass**, and **Green-Glass** nodes to the **XPresso Editor** window.

25. In the Object Manager, expand *Traffic-Lights*. Next, expand *Red-Light*, *Yellow-Light*, and *Green-Light* and then select *Red-Glass*. Next, select both *Yellow-Glass* and *Green-Glass* using the CTRL key. Now, press and hold the left mouse button and drag the cursor to the **XPresso Editor**; the **Red-Glass**, **Yellow-Glass**, and **Green-Glass** nodes are added to the **XPresso Editor**, as shown in Figure 12-17.

Connecting the Nodes

In this section, you will connect the nodes in the **XPresso Editor**.

1. In the **XGroup** area of the **XPresso Editor**, press and hold the left mouse button on the **Red** output port of the **Traffic-Lights** node and drag the cursor to the **Input 1** input port of the **Compare 1** node; a connection is established between the **Compare 1** and **Traffic-Lights** nodes, as shown in Figure 12-18.

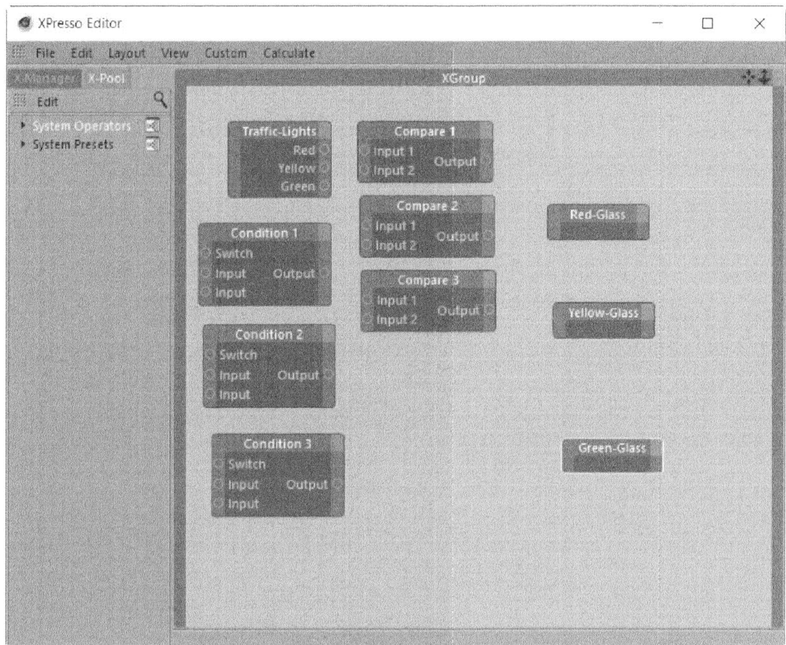

Figure 12-17** The **Red-Glass**, **Yellow-Glass**, and **Green-Glass** nodes added in the **XPresso Editor

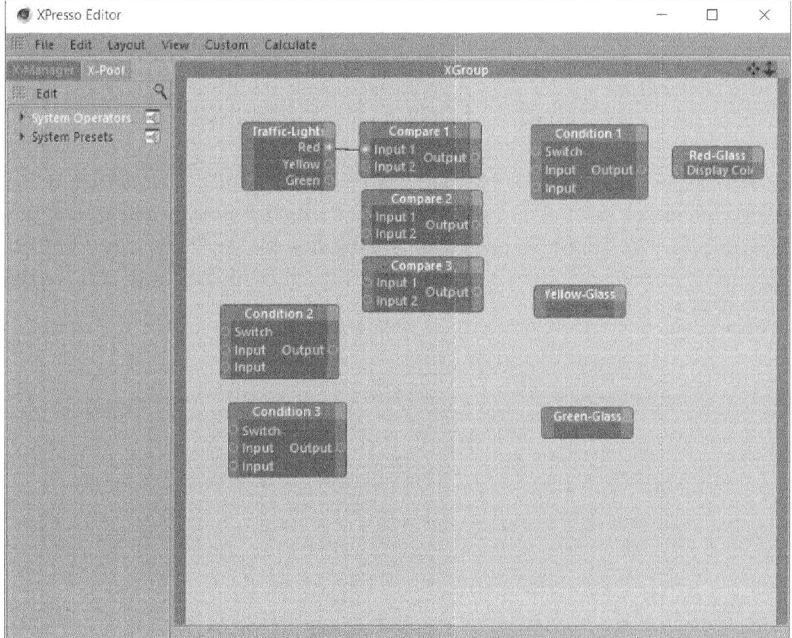

***Figure 12-18** Connection established between the **Red** output port of the **Traffic-Lights** and **Compare 1** nodes*

2. In the **XGroup** area, click on the **Output** output port of the **Compare 1** node and drag the cursor to the **Switch** input port of the **Condition 1** node; a connection is established between **Compare 1** and **Condition 1** nodes, as shown in Figure 12-19.

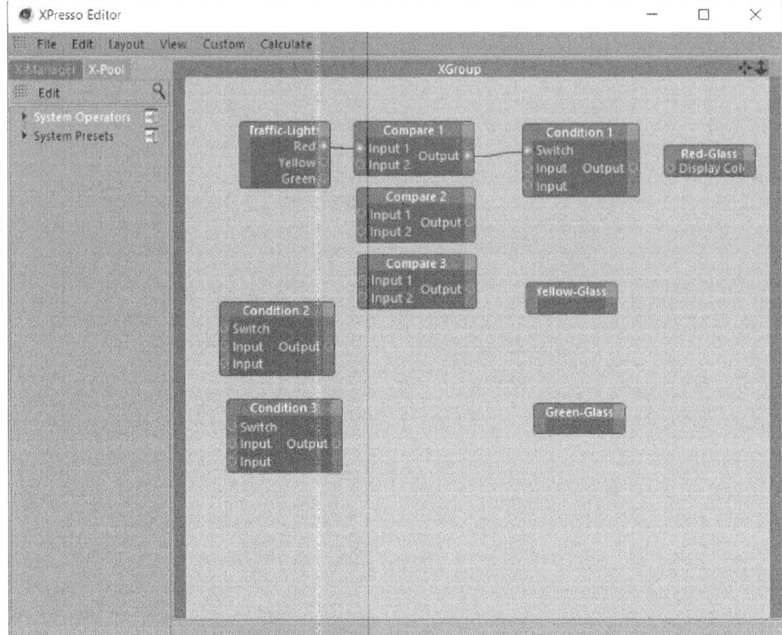

***Figure 12-19** Connection established between the **Compare 1** and **Condition 1** nodes*

Next, you will connect the **Condition 1** node with the **Red-Glass** node.

3. In the **XGroup** area, click on the **Output** output port of the **Condition 1** node and drag the cursor to the input port (blue square) of the **Red-Glass** node; a flyout is displayed. From this flyout, choose **Basic Properties > Display Color > Display Color**, as shown in Figure 12-20; a connection is established between the **Condition 1** and **Red-Glass** nodes. Minimize the **XPresso Editor**.

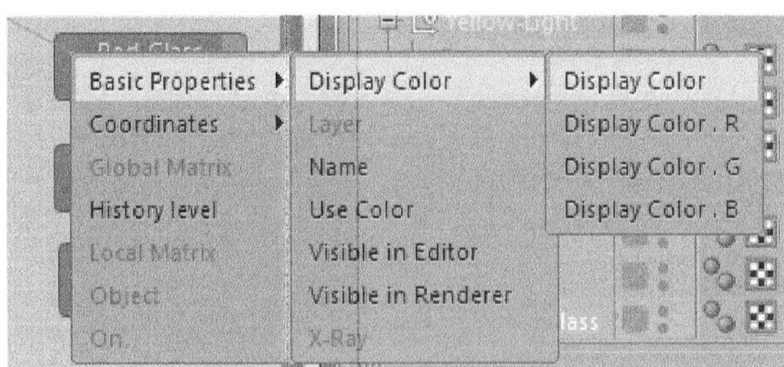

Figure 12-20** Choosing **Display Color** from the flyout in the **XPresso Editor

4. Select *Traffic-Lights* in the Object Manager. In the Attribute Manager, choose the **User Data** button; the **User Data** area is displayed. In this area, specify any value greater than 0 for the **Red** spinner; the red light is activated in the Perspective viewport, as shown in Figure 12-21. To deactivate the red color, enter **0** in the **Red** spinner.

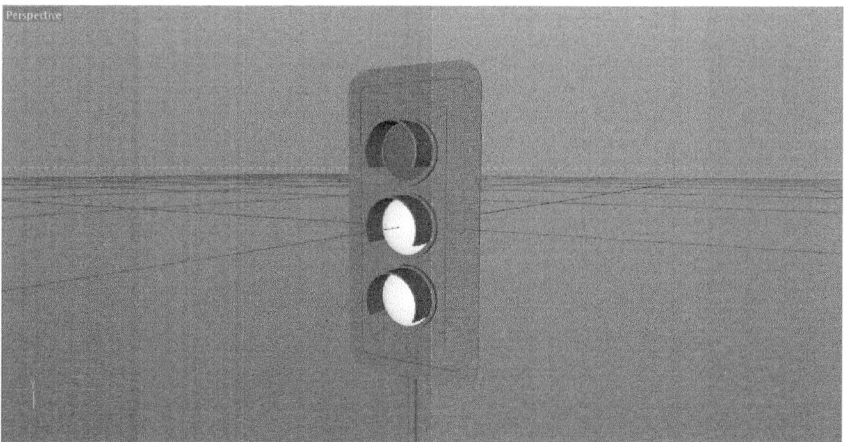

Figure 12-21 *The red light activated in the Perspective viewport*

The **Red** port of the **Traffic-Lights** node feeds data to the **Input 1** port of the **Compare 1** node. By default, the **Red** port passes down the value 0 to the **Input 1** node. Note that by default the **Input 2** option is set to 0 in the attributes of the **Compare 1** node in the **Parameter** area of the Attribute Manager. In the **Node Properties** area of the Attribute Manager, the **Function** option is set to **==** (equality operator). The **Condition 1** node will compare the value passed down by the **Red** port of the **Traffic-Lights** node and the value specified for the **Input 2** option in the **Parameter** area of the **Compare 1** node. The **Compare 1** node will output true (value 1) if the two values are same otherwise it will output false (value 0). When the value of output by the Red port is equal to the value specified for the Input 2 option, the **Compare 1** node will pass down a value of 1 down the tree.

The **Output** port of the **Compare 1** node is connected to the **Switch** port of the **Condition 1** node. Two states (colors) have been specified for the **Condition 1** node. The red color is specified for the **Input [2]** option and black color is specified for the **Input [3]** option in the **Parameter** area of the **Compare 1** node. The **Switch** attribute controls the state the **Condition** node will output. If the value 0 is specified for the **Switch** attribute, the **Condition 1** node will output the first state (red color). Likewise, if the value 1 is specified for the **Switch** attribute, the **Condition 1** node will output the second state (black color). When you specify a value greater than 0 for the **Red** attribute, the **Compare 1** node outputs a value 0 for the **Switch** port and the **Condition 1** node outputs the first state (red color).

Next, you will activate the yellow light of the signal.

5. Maximize the **XPresso Editor**. In the **XPresso Editor**, click on the **Yellow** output port of the **Traffic-Lights** node and drag the cursor to the **Input 1** input port of the **Compare 2** node; a connection is established between the **Compare 2** and **Traffic-Lights** nodes, as shown in Figure 12-22.

6. In the **XPresso Editor**, click on the **Output** output port of the **Compare 2** node and drag the cursor to the **Switch** input port of the **Condition 2** node; a connection is established between the **Compare 2** and **Condition 2** nodes, as shown in Figure 12-23.

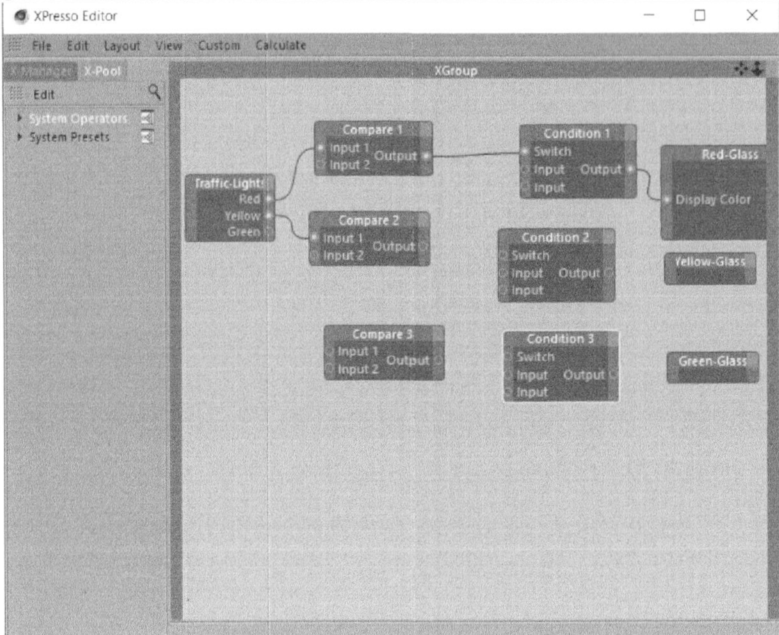

*Figure 12-22 Connection established between the **Yellow** output port of the **Traffic -Lights** and **Compare 2** nodes*

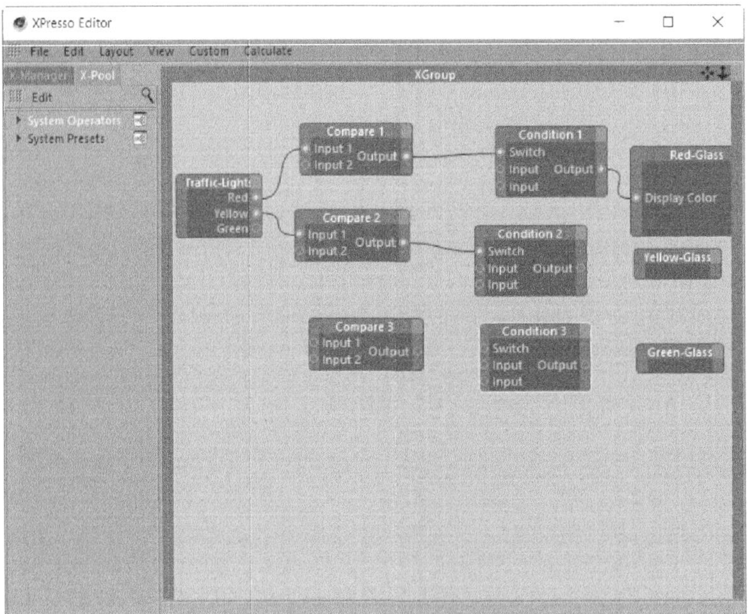

*Figure 12-23 Connection established between the **Compare 2** and **Condition 2** nodes*

7. In the **XGroup** area, click on the **Output** output port of the **Condition 2** node and drag the cursor to the input port (blue square) of the **Yellow-Glass** node; a flyout is displayed. From this flyout, choose **Basic Properties > Display Color > Display Color**, as shown in

Figure 12-24; a connection is established between the **Condition 2** and **Yellow-Glass** nodes. Minimize the **XPresso Editor**.

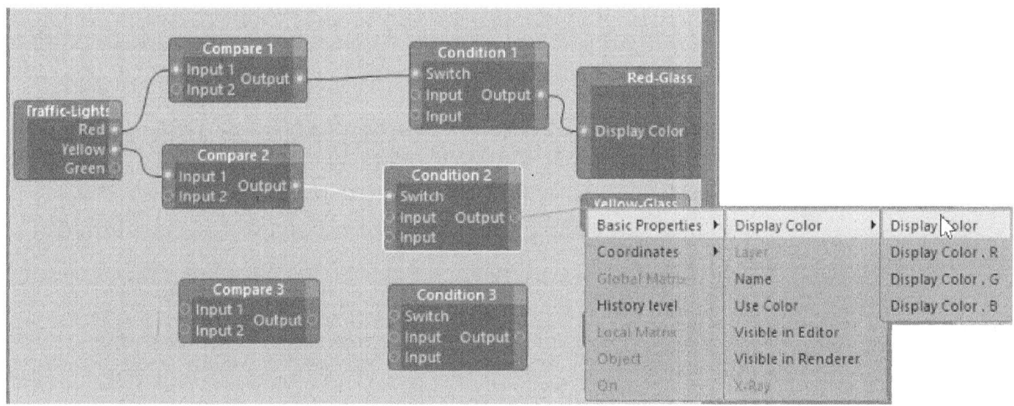

Figure 12-24 *Choosing* ***Display Color*** *from the flyout in the* ***XPresso Editor***

8. Select *Traffic-Lights* in the Object Manager. In the Attribute Manager, make sure the **User Data** button is chosen; the **User Data** area is displayed. In this area, specify any value greater than 0 for the **Yellow** spinner; the yellow light is activated in the Perspective viewport, as shown in Figure 12-25. To deactivate the yellow color, enter **0** in the **Yellow** spinner.

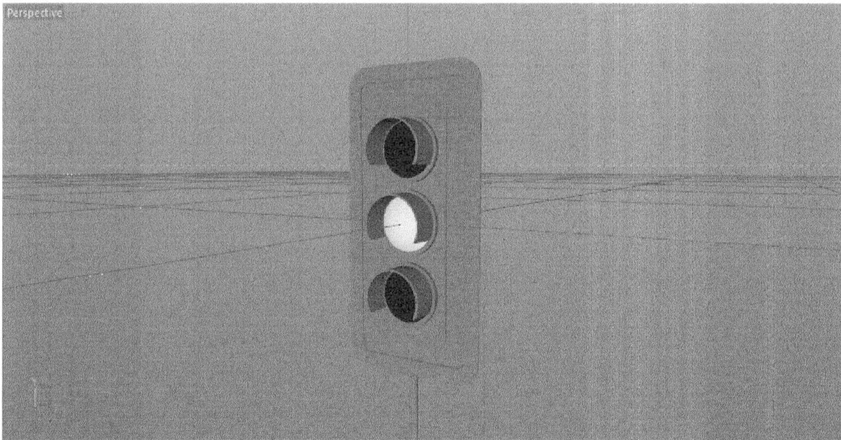

Figure 12-25 *The yellow light activated in the Perspective viewport*

Next, you will activate the green light of the traffic signal.

9. Maximize the **XPresso Editor**. In the **XGroup** area, click on the **Green** output port of the **Traffic-Lights** node and drag the cursor to the **Input 1** input port of the **Compare 3** node; a connection is established between the **Compare 3** and **Traffic-Lights** nodes.

10. In the **XGroup** area, click on the **Output** output port of the **Compare 3** node and drag the cursor to the **Switch** input port of the **Condition 3** node; a connection is established between the **Compare 3** and **Condition 3** nodes.

11. In the **XGroup** area, click on the **Output** output port of the **Condition 3** node and drag the cursor to the input port (blue square) of the **Green-Glass** node; a flyout is displayed. From this flyout, choose **Basic Properties > Display Color > Display Color**; a connection is established between the **Condition 3** and **Green-Glass** nodes. Next, close the **XPresso Editor**.

12. Select *Traffic-Lights* in the Object Manager. In the Attribute Manager, make sure the **User Data** button is chosen; the **User Data** area is displayed. In this area, specify any value greater than 0 for the **Green** spinner; the green light is activated in the Perspective viewport, as shown in Figure 12-26. To deactivate the green color, enter **0** in the **Green** spinner.

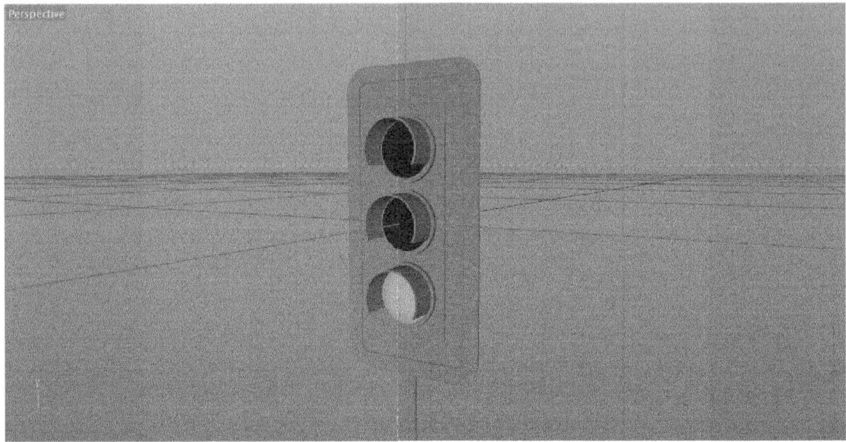

Figure 12-26 *The green light activated in the Perspective viewport*

Animating the Traffic Lights

In this section, you will animate the traffic lights using keyframes.

1. Make sure that the timeslider is set to frame 0. Select *Traffic-Lights* in the Object Manager.

2. In the Attribute Manager, make sure the **User Data** button is chosen and the **User Data** area is displayed.

3. In the **User Data** area, enter **1** in the **Red** spinner. Next, press and hold the CTRL key and then click on the name of the **Red** spinner to select it. Similarly, add the **Yellow** and **Green** spinners to the selection; the color of the labels changes.

4. Right-click on the selected labels in the **User Data** area; a shortcut menu is displayed. From this menu, choose **Animation > Add Keyframe**, refer to Figure 12-27; a keyframe is added at frame 0.

5. Move the timeslider to frame 25 and add a keyframe by repeating the process mentioned in step 4.

6. Move the timeslider to frame 26 and then enter **0** and **1** in the **Red** and **Yellow** spinners, respectively, in the **User Data** area of the Attribute Manager. Next, add a keyframe.

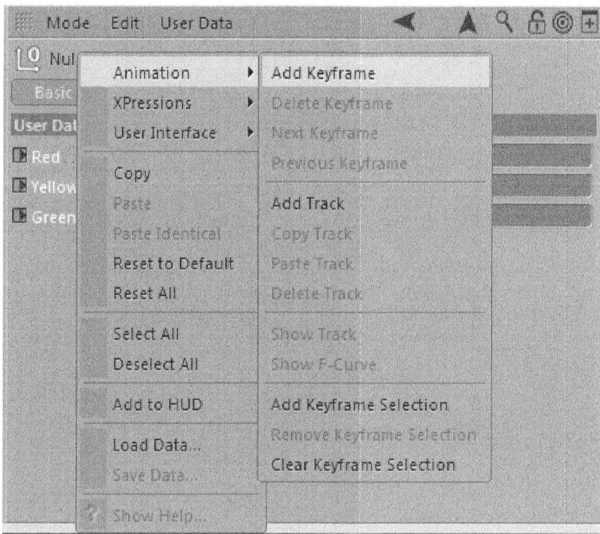

Figure 12-27 *The shortcut menu displayed on right-clicking in the* ***User Data*** *area*

7. Move the timeslider to frame 50 and add a keyframe by repeating the process mentioned in step 4.

8. Move the timeslider to frame 51 and then enter **0** and **1** in the **Yellow** and **Green** spinners, respectively, in the **User Data** area of the Attribute Manager. Next, add a keyframe.

9. Choose the **Play Forwards** button from the Animation toolbar to preview the animation.

Saving and Rendering the Scene

After completing the tutorial, you will save the file using the steps given next.

1. Choose **File > Save As** from the main menu; the **Save File** dialog box is displayed. In this dialog box, browse to the location *\Documents\c4dr20\c12*.

2. Enter **c12tut1** in the **File name** text box and then choose the **Save** button.

3. For rendering, refer to Tutorial 1 of Chapter 8.

EXERCISE

The rendered output of the model used in the exercise can be accessed by downloading the *c12_cinema4d_r20_exr.zip* file from *www.cadsofttech.com*. The path of the file is as follows: *Textbooks > Animation and Visual Effects > MAXON CINEMA 4D > MAXON CINEMA 4D R20 Studio for Novices*

Exercise 1

Using the **User data** parameters and the **XPresso Editor**, animate the logo shown in Figure 12-28. **(Expected time: 35 min)**

Figure 12-28 The logo at frame 49

Index

Other Titles of Interest- BPB/TICKOO SERIES

Publication by BPB/TICKOO SERIES

The following is the list of some of the publications by BPB/TICKOO series:

CINEMA 4D Textbooks

- MAXON CINEMA 4D R20 Studio Workbook
- MAXON CINEMA 4D R19 Studio: A Tutorial Approach, 6th Edition
- MAXON CINEMA 4D R18 Studio: A Tutorial Approach, 5th Edition

3ds Max Textbooks

- Autodesk 3ds Max 2019: A Comprehensive Guide, 19th Edition
- Autodesk 3ds Max 2018: A Comprehensive Guide, 18th Edition

Autodesk Maya Textbooks

- Autodesk Maya 2019 for 3D Artists
- Autodesk Maya 2019 Workbook
- Autodesk Maya 2018: A Comprehensive Guide, 10th Edition

ZBrush Textbooks

- Pixologic ZBrush 2018 for Digital Artists
- Pixologic ZBrush 4R8: A Comprehensive Guide, 4th Edition

Computer Programming Textbooks

- Introducing PHP/MySQL
- Introduction to C++ Programming, 2nd Edition
- Learning Oracle 12c: A PL/SQL Approach, 2nd Edition
- Introduction to Java Programming, 2nd Edition

AutoCAD Textbooks

- AutoCAD 2020 for Engineers and Designers - Basic and Intermediate
- AutoCAD 2020 Workbook
- AutoCAD 2019: A Problem-Solving Approach, Basic and Intermediate, 25th Edition

Autodesk Inventor Textbooks

- Autodesk Inventor Professional 2020 for Engineers and Designers
- Inventor 2020 Workbook
- Autodesk Inventor Professional 2019 for Designers, 19th Edition

AutoCAD MEP Textbooks

- AutoCAD MEP 2020 for Engineers and Designers
- AutoCAD MEP 2018 for Designers, 4th Edition

AutoCAD Plant 3D Textbook
- AutoCAD Plant 3D 2018 for Designers, 4th Edition

NX Textbooks
- Siemens NX 2019 for Engineers and Designers
- Siemens NX 2019 Workbook
- Siemens NX 12.0 for Designers, 11th Edition

NX Mold Textbook
- Mold Design Using NX 11.0: A Tutorial Approach

AutoCAD LT Textbooks
- AutoCAD LT 2020 for Engineers and Designers
- AutoCAD LT 2017 for Designers, 12th Edition

Solid Edge Textbooks
- Solid Edge 2019 for Engineers and Designers
- Solid Edge ST 10 for Designers, 15th Edition

SolidWorks Textbooks
- SOLIDWORKS 2019 for Engineers and Designers
- SOLIDWORKS 2018 for Designers, 16th Edition

SolidWorks Simulation Textbooks
- SOLIDWORKS Simulation 2018: A Tutorial Approach
- SOLIDWORKS Simulation 2016: A Tutorial Approach

Creo Parametric Textbooks
- Creo Parametric 6.0 for Engineers and Designers
- Creo Parametric 6.0 Workbook
- Creo Parametric 5.0 for Designers, 5th Edition

CATIA Textbook
- CATIA V5-6R2018 for Engineers and Designers

AutoCAD Electrical Textbooks
- AutoCAD Electrical 2019 for Engineers and Designers
- AutoCAD Electrical 2018 for Electrical Control Designers, 9th Edition

Autodesk Revit Architecture Textbooks
- Exploring Autodesk Revit 2020 for Architects and Building Designers
- Revit Architecture 2020 Workbook
- Exploring Autodesk Revit 2019 for Architecture, 15th Edition

Autodesk Revit Structure Textbooks

- Exploring Autodesk Revit 2019 for Structure, 9th Edition
- Exploring Autodesk Revit 2018 for Structure, 8th Edition

Autodesk Revit MEP Textbooks

- Exploring Autodesk Revit 2019 for MEP, 6th Edition
- Exploring Autodesk Revit 2018 for MEP, 5th Edition

RISA-3D Textbook

- Exploring RISA-3D 14.0

Bentley STAAD.Pro Textbooks

- Exploring Bentley STAAD.Pro (CONNECT Edition), 3rd Edition
- Exploring Bentley STAAD.Pro V8i (SELECT series 6)

AutoCAD Civil 3D Textbooks

- Exploring AutoCAD Civil 3D 2019 for Engineers and Designers
- Exploring AutoCAD Civil 3D 2018, 8th Edition

AutoCAD Map 3D Textbooks

- Exploring AutoCAD Map 3D 2018, 8th Edition
- Exploring AutoCAD Map 3D 2017, 7th Edition

Autodesk Navisworks Textbooks

- Exploring Autodesk Navisworks 2019 for BIM
- Exploring Autodesk Navisworks 2017, 4th Edition

Oracle Primavera Textbooks

- Exploring Oracle Primavera P6 Professional 18 for Planners and Engineers
- Exploring Oracle Primavera P6 R8.4

AutoCAD Raster Design Textbook

- Exploring AutoCAD Raster Design 2017

CAD/CAM/CIM/ANIMATION/CIVIL BOOKS

by Prof. Sham Tickoo (Purdue University, USA and Autodesk Authorised Author)

Pixologic ZBrush 4R8
A Comprehensive Guide
ISBN: 9789387284128
Price: 899 /-

Pixologic ZBrush 2018
for **Digital Artists**
ISBN: 9789388511193
Price: 899 /-

AutoCAD 2018
A Problem Solving Approach
ISBN: 9789386551634
Price: 1299 /-

Advanced AutoCAD 2018
A Problem Solving Approach
ISBN: 9789386551603
Price: 899 /-

AutoCAD 2019
A Problem Solving Approach
ISBN: 9789388176286
Price: 1499 /-

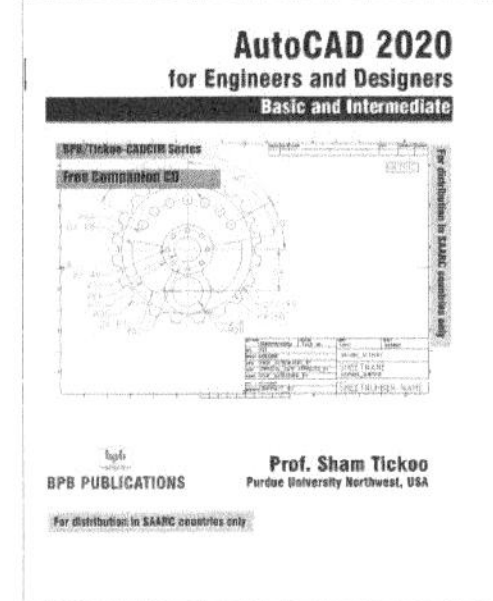

AutoCAD 2020
for **Engineers and Designers**
ISBN: 9789389423099
Price: 1499 /-

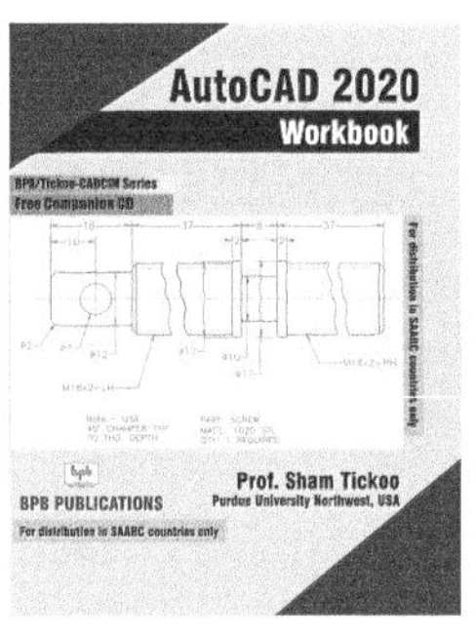

Autocad 2020
Workbook
ISBN: 9789389423044
Price: 360/-

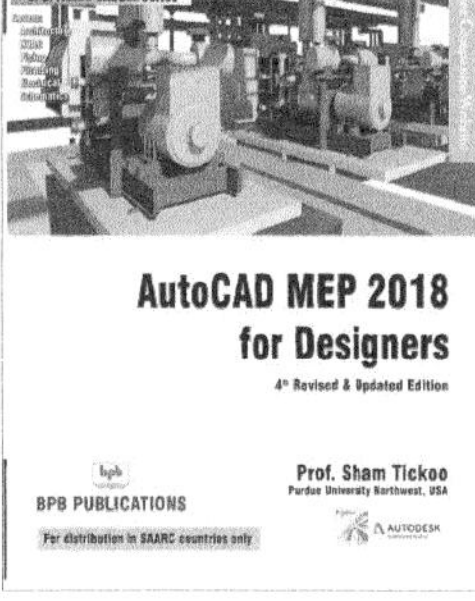

AutoCAD MEP 2018
for **Designers**
ISBN: 9789386551610
Price: 749 /-

AutoCAD MEP 2020
for **Engineers and Designers**
ISBN: 9789389423150
Price: 899 /-

AutoCAD Plant 3D 2018
for **Designers**
ISBN: 9789386551719
Price: 799 /-

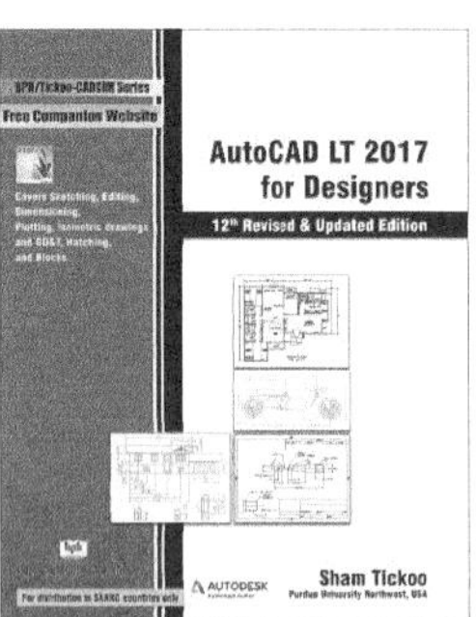

AutoCAD LT 2017
for **Designers**
ISBN: 9789386551252
Price: 1299 /-

AutoCAD LT 2020
for **Engineers and Designers**
ISBN: 9789389423143
Price: 1399 /-

CAD/CAM/CIM/ANIMATION/CIVIL BOOKS

by Prof. Sham Tickoo (Purdue University, USA and Autodesk Authorised Author)

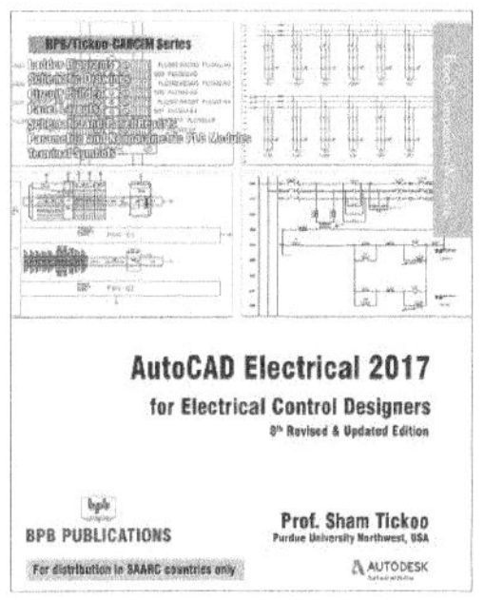

AutoCAD Electrical 2017
for **Electrical Control Designers**
ISBN: 9789386551238
Price: 1099 /-

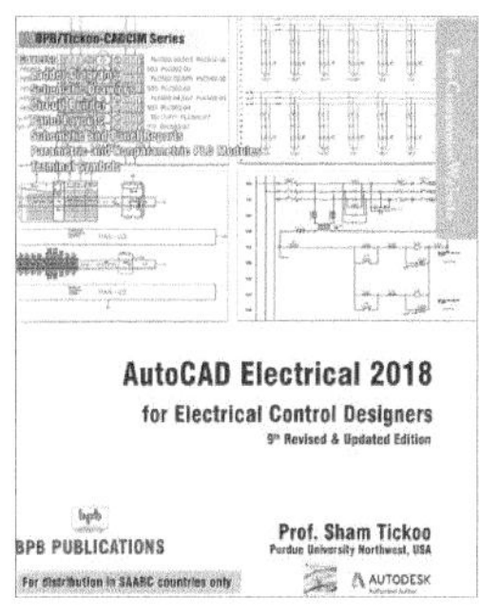

AutoCAD Electrical 2018
for **Electrical Control Designers**
ISBN: 9789386551627
Price: 1099 /-

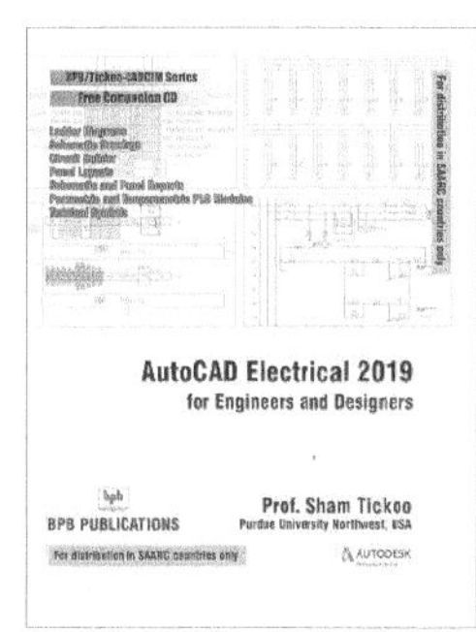

AutoCAD Electrical 2019
for **Engineers and Designers**
ISBN: 9789388511179
Price: 1299 /-

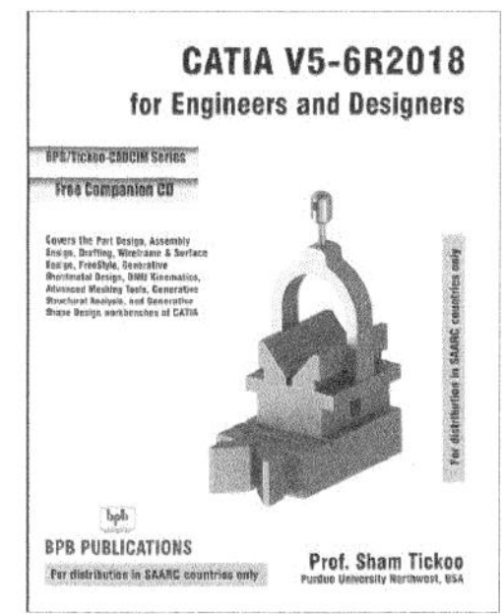

CATIA V5-6R2018
for **Engineers and Designers**
ISBN: 9789388511308
Price: 1399 /-

CATIA V5-6R2016
for **Designers**
ISBN: 9789386551191
Price: 1099 /-

CATIA V5-6R2017
for **Designers**
ISBN: 9789387284043
Price: 1099 /-

MAXON CINEMA 4D
R18 StudioA Tutorial Approach
ISBN: 9789386551115
Price: 799 /-

MAXON CINEMA 4D
R19 StudioA Tutorial Approach
ISBN: 9789387284050
Price: 799 /-

Maxon Cinema 4D R19 Studio
for **Digital Artists**
ISBN: 9789389423174
Price: 799 /-

Maxon Cinema 4D R20 Studio
Workbook
ISBN: 9789389423082
Price: 360/-

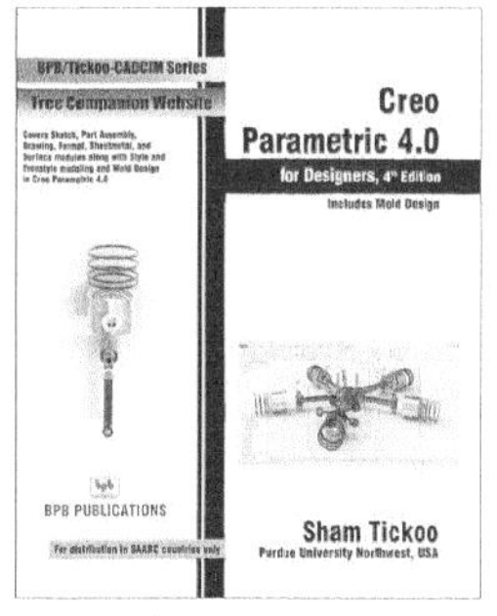

Creo Parametric 4.0
for **Designers**
ISBN: 9789386551658
Price: 1099 /-

Creo Parametric 5.0
for **Designers**
ISBN: 9789388176309
Price: 1299 /-

CAD/CAM/CIM/ANIMATION/CIVIL BOOKS

by Prof. Sham Tickoo (Purdue University, USA and Autodesk Authorised Author)

Creo Parametric 6.0
for **Engineer and Designer**
ISBN: 9789389423136
Price: 1299 /-

Creo Parametric 6.0
Workbook
ISBN: 9789389423075
Price: 360/-

NX Nastran 9.0
for **Designers**
ISBN: 9789386551221
Price: 899 /-

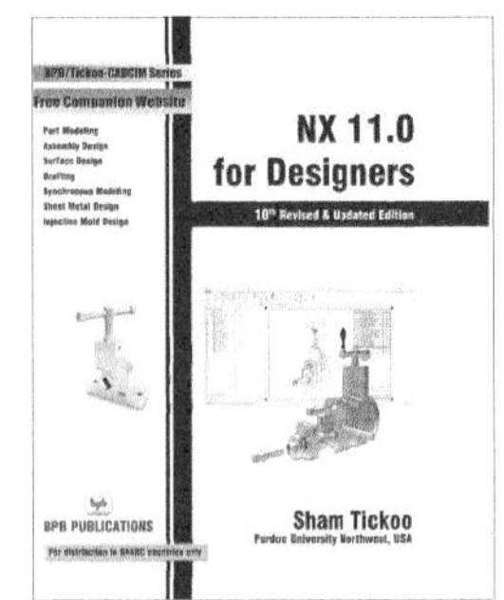

NX 11.0
for **Designers**
ISBN: 9789386551245
Price: 1099 /-

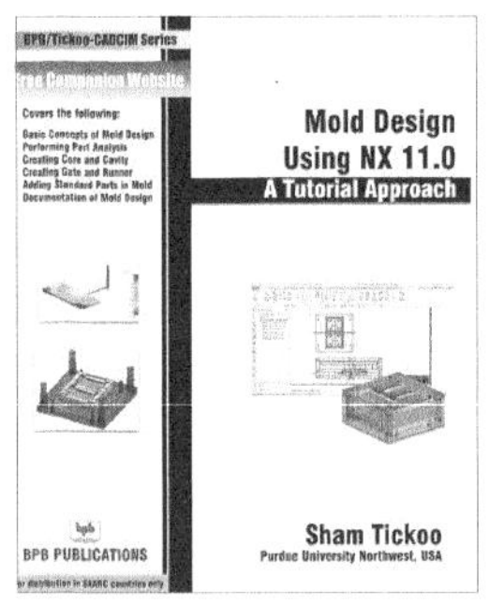

Mold Design Using NX 11.0
A Tutorial Approach
ISBN: 9789387284067
Price: 599 /-

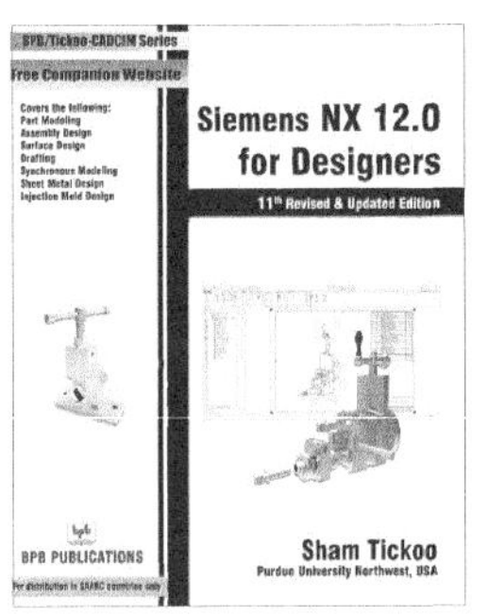

Siemens NX 12.0
for **Designers**
ISBN: 9789387284074
Price: 1099 /-

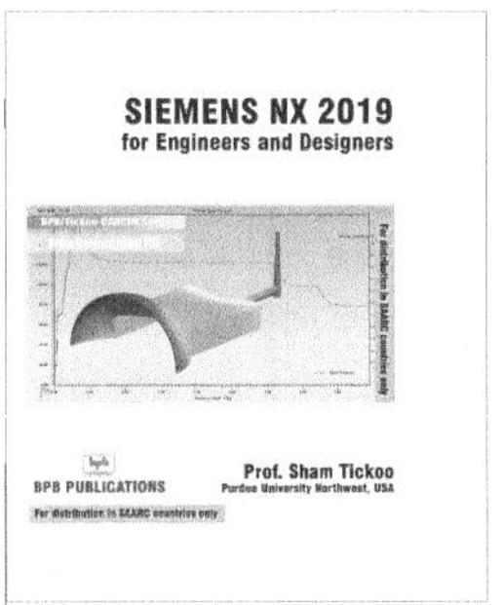

Siemens NX 2019
for **Engineers and Designers**
ISBN: 9789389423112
Price: 1299 /-

Siemens NX 2019
Workbook
ISBN: 9789389423051
Price: 360/-

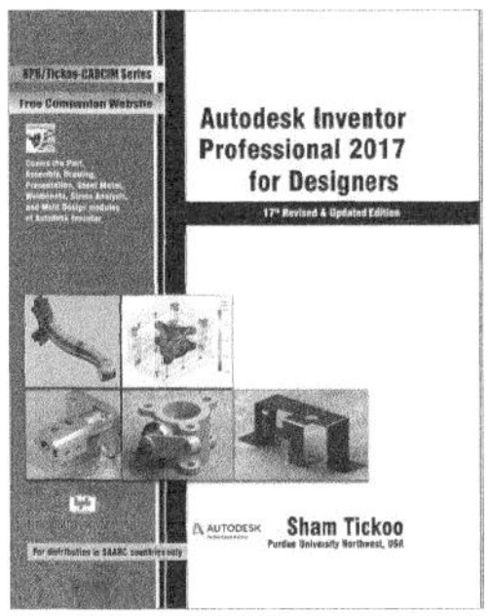

Autodesk Inventor
Professional 2017
for **Designers**
ISBN: 9789386551269
Price: 1299 /-

Autodesk Inventor
Professional 2018
for **Designers**
ISBN: 9789386551641
Price: 1199 /-

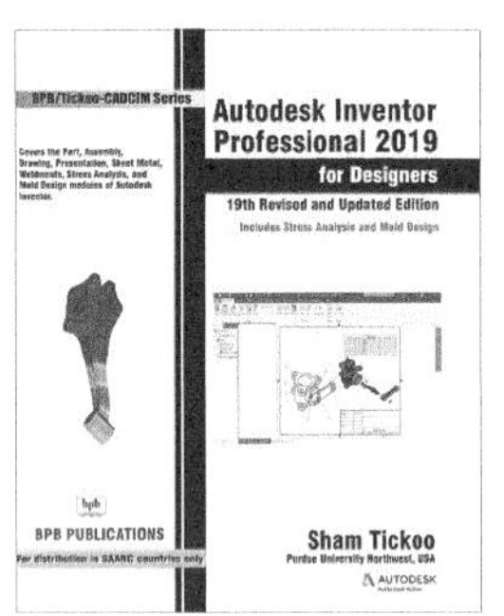

Autodesk Inventor
Professional 2019
for **Designers**
ISBN: 9789388176293
Price: 1299 /-

Autodesk Inventor
Professional 2020
for **Engineers and Designers**
ISBN: 9789389423105
Price: 1299 /-

CAD/CAM/CIM/ANIMATION/CIVIL BOOKS

by Prof. Sham Tickoo (Purdue University, USA and Autodesk Authorised Author)

Inventor 2020 Workbook
ISBN: 9789389423020
Price: 360/-

Autodesk Fusion 360
A Tutorial Approach
ISBN: 9789387284418
Price: 599 /-

Solid Edge ST9
for **Designers**
ISBN: 9789386551207
Price: 1099 /-

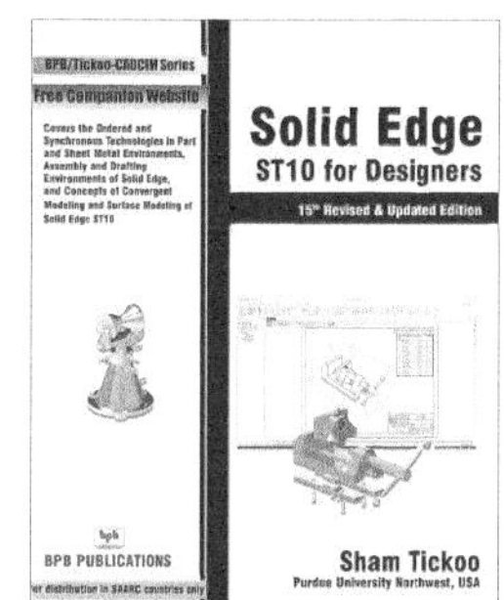

Solid Edge ST10
for **Designers**
ISBN: 9789387284104
Price: 1099 /-

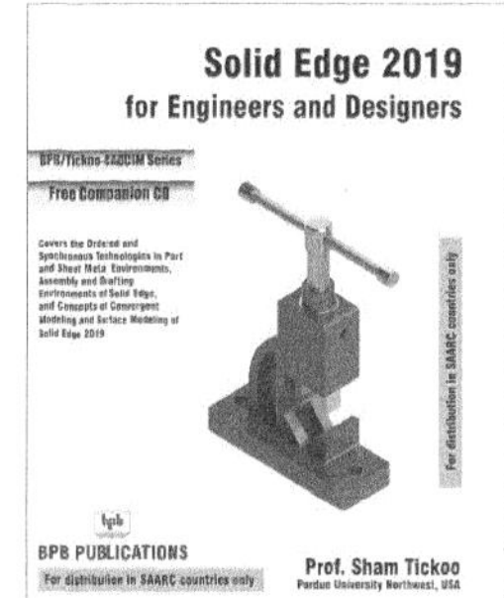

Solid Edge 2019
for **Engineers and Designers**
ISBN: 9789388511230
Price: 1099 /-

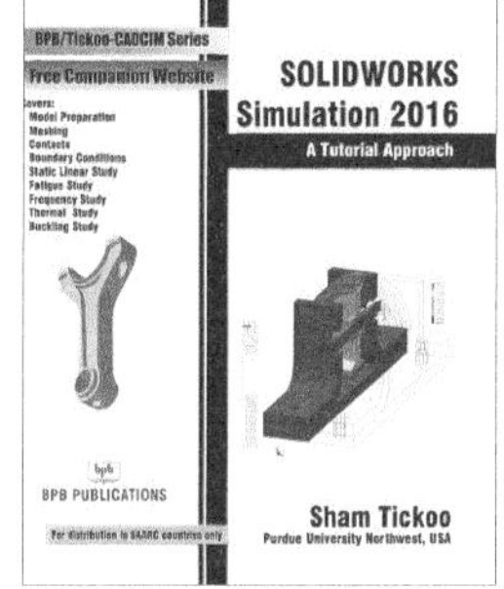

SOLIDWORKS Simulation 2016
A Tutorial Approach
ISBN: 9789386551757
Price: 499 /-

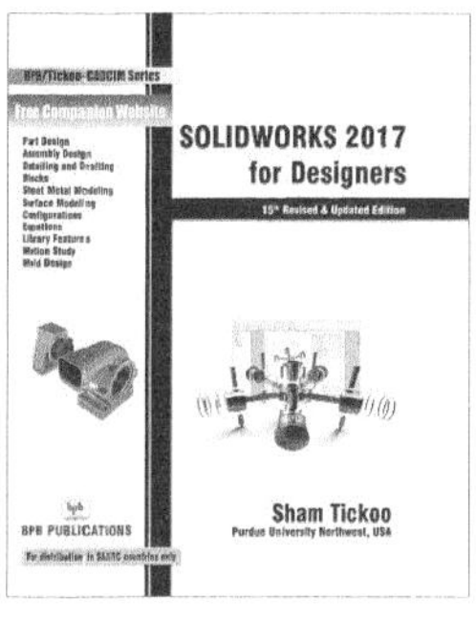

SOLIDWORKS 2017
for **Designers**
ISBN: 9789386551214
Price: 1299 /-

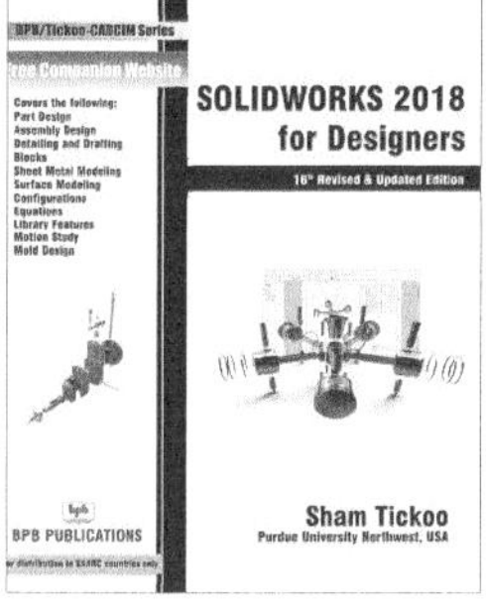

SOLIDWORKS 2018
for **Designers**
ISBN: 9789387284098
Price: 1299 /-

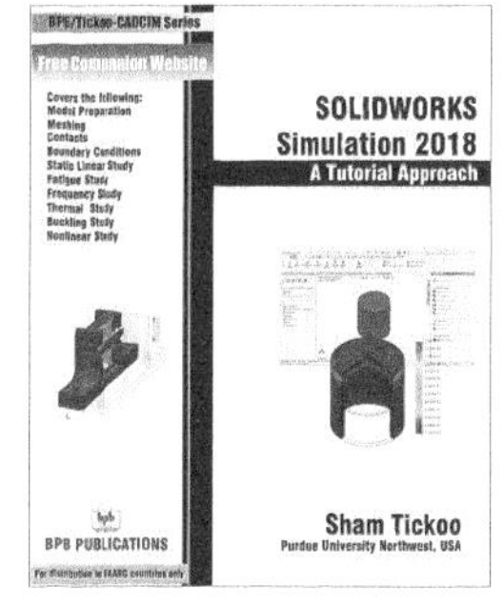

SOLIDWORKS Simulation 2018
A Tutorial Approach
ISBN: 9789387284111
Price: 599 /-

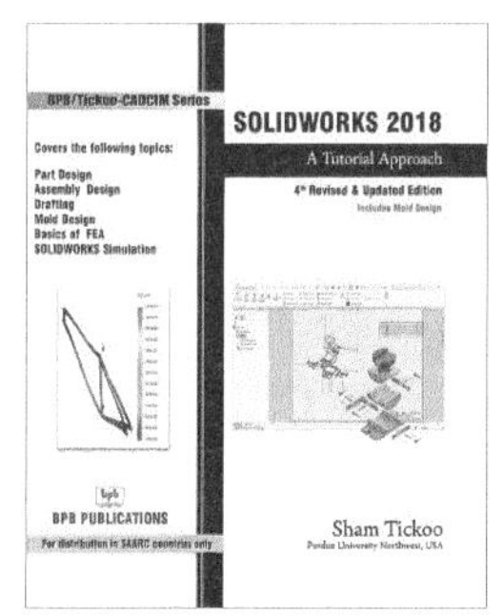

SOLIDWORKS 2018
A Tutorial Approach
ISBN: 9789388176316
Price: 799 /-

Learning Solidworks 2018
A project based Approach
ISBN: 9789388176323
Price: 699 /-

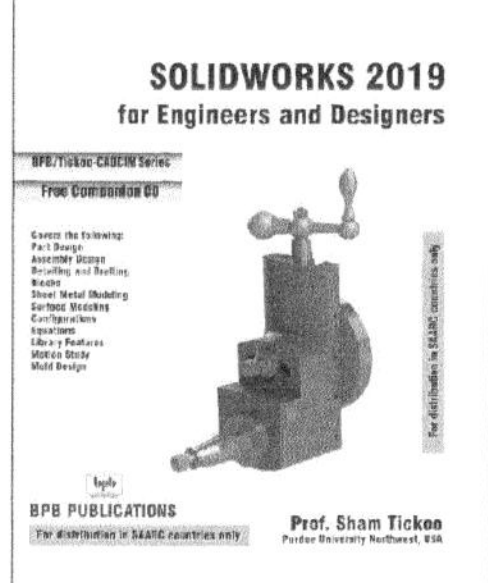

SolidWorks 2019 for
Engineers and Designers
ISBN 9789388511223
Price: 1599 /-

CAD/CAM/CIM/ANIMATION/CIVIL BOOKS

by Prof. Sham Tickoo (Purdue University, USA and Autodesk Authorised Author)

Exploring AutoCAD
CIVIL 3D 2017
ISBN: 9789386551023
Price: 999 /-

Exploring AutoCAD
CIVIL 3D 2018
ISBN: 9789387284135
Price: 1099 /-

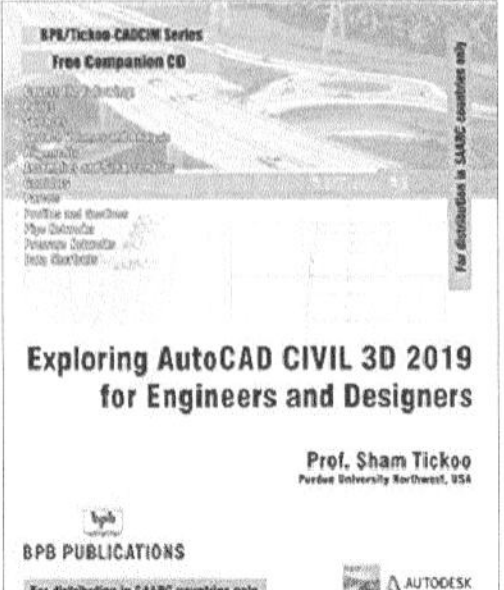

Exploring AutoCAD
CIVIL 3D 2019
for Engineers and Designers
ISBN: 9789388511216
Price: 1199 /-

Exploring AutoCAD
Map 3D 2017
ISBN: 9789386551030
Price: 499 /-

Exploring AutoCAD
Map 3D 2018
ISBN: 9789386551665
Price: 799 /-

Exploring Autodesk
Navisworks 2017
ISBN: 9789386551047
Price: 699 /-

Exploring Autodesk
Navisworks 2019 for **BIM**
ISBN: 9789388511278
Price: 899 /-

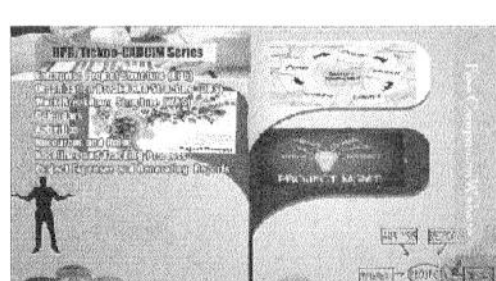
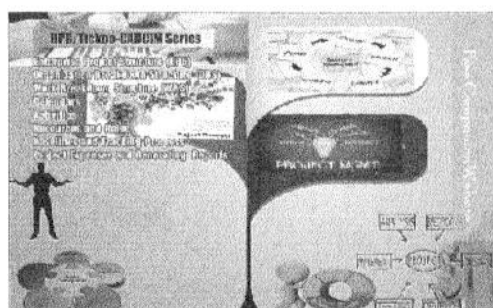

Exploring
Oracle Primavera P6 R8.4
ISBN: 9789386551054
Price: 699 /-

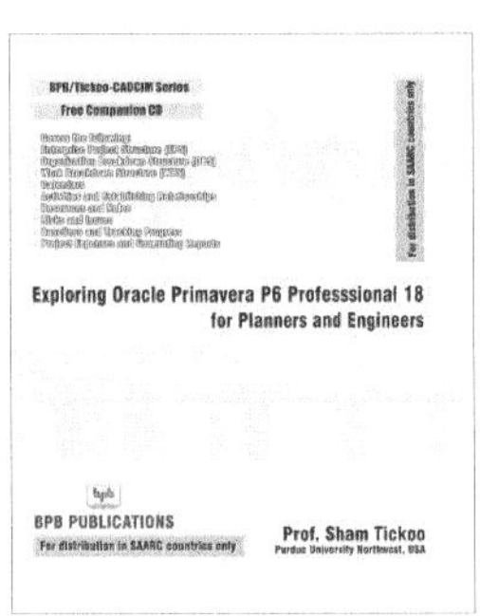

Exploring Oracle
Primavera P6 Professional 18
for **Planners and Engineers**
ISBN: 9789388511292
Price: 699 /-

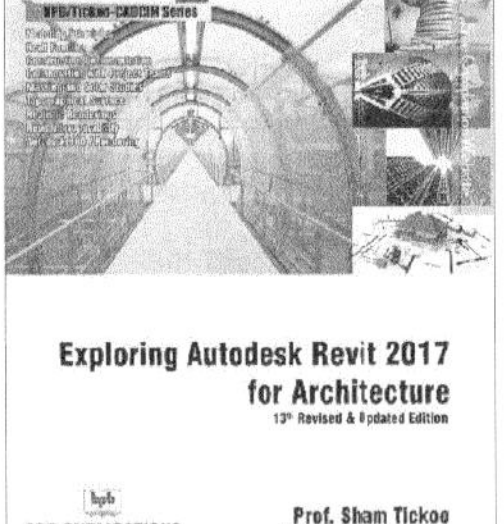

Exploring Autodesk
Revit 2017 for **Architecture**
ISBN: 9789386551061
Price: 999 /-

Exploring Autodesk
Revit 2017 for **MEP**
ISBN: 9789386551078
Price: 799 /-

Exploring Autodesk
Revit 2017 for **Structure**
ISBN: 9788183335065
Price: 899 /-

CAD/CAM/CIM/ANIMATION/CIVIL BOOKS

by Prof. Sham Tickoo (Purdue University, USA and Autodesk Authorised Author)

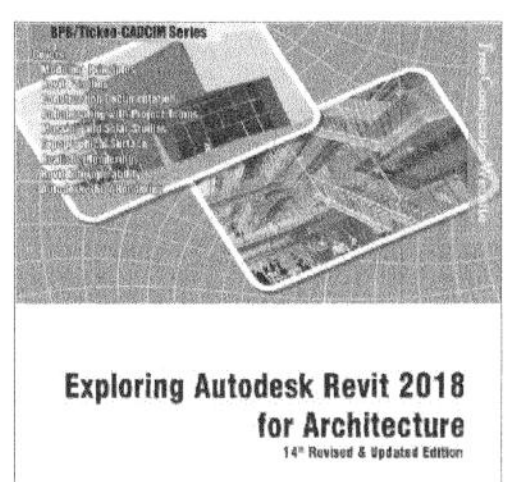

Exploring Autodesk Revit 2018 for **Architecture**
ISBN: 9789386551726
Price: 999 /-

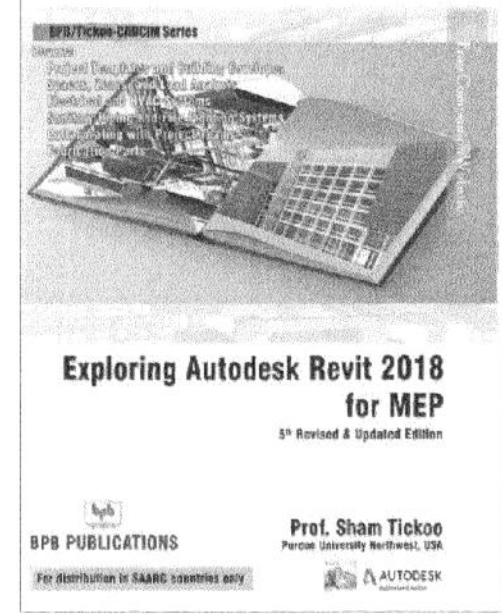

Exploring Autodesk Revit 2018 for **MEP**
ISBN: 9789386551733
Price: 799 /-

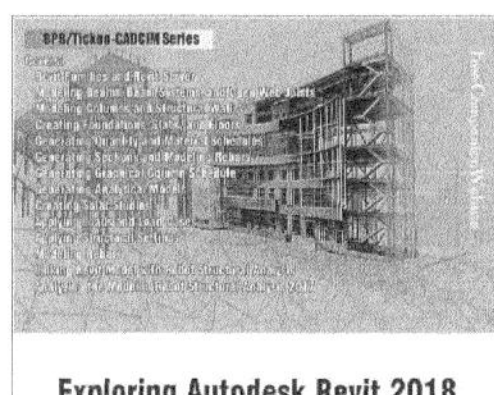

Exploring Autodesk Revit 2018 for **Structure**
ISBN: 9789386551740
Price: 799 /-

Exploring Autodesk Revit 2019 for **Architecture**
ISBN: 9789388176330
Price: 1199 /-

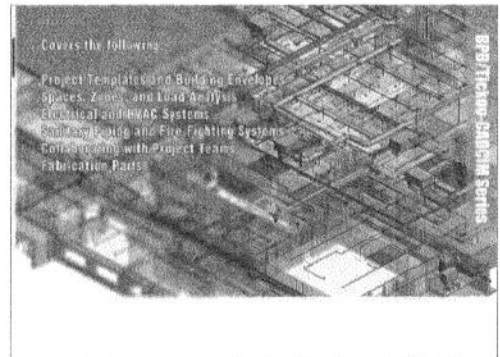

Exploring Autodesk Revit 2019 for **MEP**
ISBN: 9789388176354
Price: 899 /-

Exploring Autodesk Revit 2019 for **Structure**
ISBN: 9789388176347
Price: 899 /-

Revit Architecture 2020 Workbook
ISBN: 9789389423037
Price: 360/-

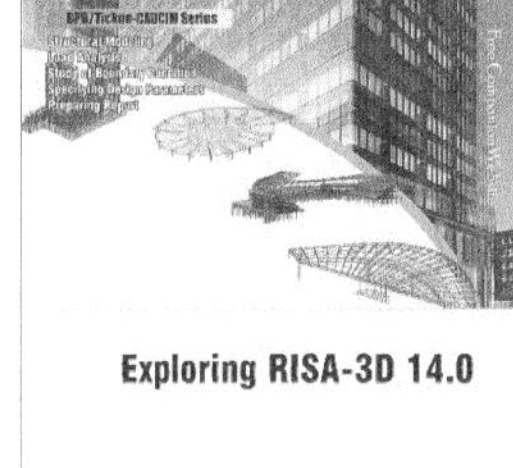

Exploring RISA-3D 14.0
ISBN: 9789386551085
Price: 499 /-

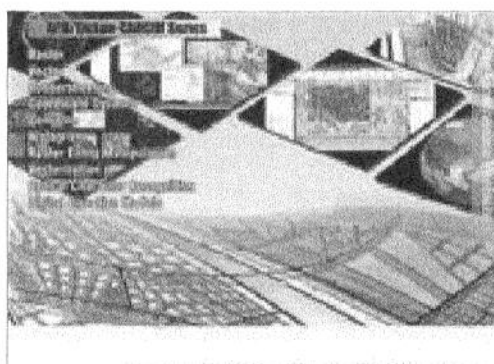

Exploring AutoCAD Raster Design 2017
ISBN: 9789386551092
Price: 499 /-

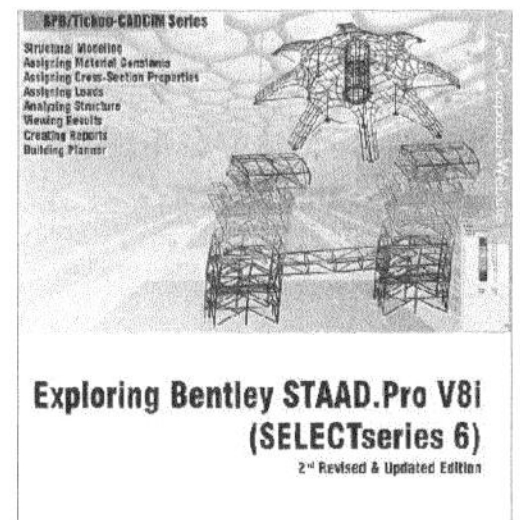

Exploring Bentley STAAD.Pro V8i (SELECTseries 6)
ISBN: 9789386551108
Price: 599 /-

Exploring Bentley STAAD.Pro (CONNECT Edition)
ISBN: 9789387284142
Price: 499 /-

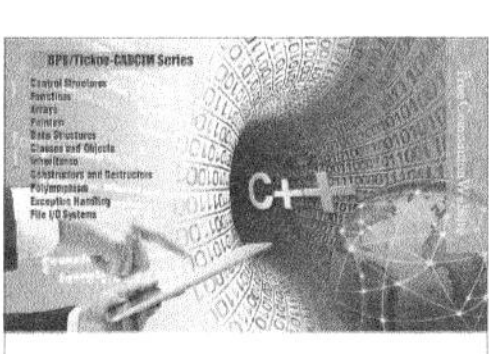

Introduction to C++ Programming
ISBN: 9789386551160
Price: 699 /-